RAF
in action 1939 - 1945

RAF

in action 1939 - 1945

Roy Conyers Nesbit

Public Record Office

Credits

Public Record Office
Richmond
Surrey
TW9 4DU

© Crown Copyright 2000

ISBN 1 873162 82 0

A catalogue card for this book is available from the British Library

Designed by Paul Johnson

Printed by Bath Press Ltd, Glasgow

By the same author

Woe to the Unwary
Torpedo Airmen
The Strike Wings
Target: Hitler's Oil
      (with Ronald C. Cooke)
Arctic Airmen
      (with Ernest Schofield)
Failed to Return
An Illustrated History of the RAF
RAF Records in the PRO
      (with Simon Fowler, Peter Elliott and Christina Goulter)
The Armed Rovers
The RAF in Camera 1903–1939
Eyes of the RAF
The RAF in Camera 1939–1945
The RAF in Camera 1945–1995
RAF Coastal Command in Action 1939–1945
RAF: An Illustrated History from 1918
Britain's Rebel Air Force
      (with Dudley Cowderoy and Andrew Thomas)
The Flight of Rudolf Hess
      (with Georges Van Acker)

Acknowledgements

I should like to express my gratitude to all those staff members of the Public Record Office who have given so much help with the preparation of this book. They are Hugh Alexander, Brian Carter, Oliver Hoare, Anne Kilminster, Sheila Knight, Aidan Lawes, Angela Mullen, Paul Sinnott and Chris Staerck. A special mention should go to Paul Johnson, who not only researched most of the images but undertook the whole of the book design.

I also thank the proofreader, Alan Thatcher, for his careful work. Welcome help with research came from Ron Bramley and Fred Stead of the Air Gunners' Association; Dr Gianandrea Bussi in Italy; Rick Chapman in Germany; Warrant Officer Jack Eggleston, RAF (Ret'd); Roger Hayward; Flight Lieutenant A.H. Hilliard, RAFVR; Roger Leney and Glyn Loosmore of the wartime Special Operations Executive; Clive Richards of the Air Historical Branch (RAF); Richard S. Robinson; Mike Seymour; Halvor Sperbund in Norway; Georges Van Acker in Belgium; and Gerrit J. Zwanenburg in The Netherlands.

Thanks are also due to two prominent aviation artists who so kindly provided their superb paintings for the book. They are Mark Postlethwaite and Charles Thompson.

Lastly, my gratitude goes to my old friend Squadron Leader Dudley Cowderoy RAFVR, who checked through all the narrative and captions with me, and to his wife Jane who tolerated the lengthy research sessions in their home.

Contents

Acknowledgements   4

Foreword   6

Introduction   8

PART ONE: NORTH-WEST EUROPE
AND THE ATLANTIC   10

1   'Sitzkrieg'   12
2   The Storm Bursts   18
3   A British Victory   24
4   The Dark Days   30
5   Daylight Bombing   34
6   German Capital Ships   40
7   Combined Operation   46
8   The Bruneval Raid   50
9   Bombing Policy   56
10 Fighter Sweeps   62
11 Disaster at Dieppe   68
12 Atlantic Lifeline   74
13 Thousand Bombers   80
14 Strike Wings   86
15 Dambusting   92
16 Firestorm   98
17 Allied Expeditionary Air Force   104
18 Coup de Main   110
19 British Bridgehead   116
20 The Ninth in Action   122
21 Breakout   128
22 Hitler's Secret Weapons   134
23 One-Way Ticket   140
24 End of the Kriegsmarine   146
25 The Roads to Germany   152
26 End of the Third Reich   158

PART TWO: AFRICA
AND SOUTHERN EUROPE   164

27 Triumph and Disaster   166
28 Seesaw Battles   172
29 Desert Victory   178
30 The End in Africa   184
31 From Sicily to Rome   190
32 RAF Middle East   198
33 The End in Italy   206

PART THREE: INDIA
AND SOUTH-EAST ASIA   214

34 Japanese Victories   216
35 Against Odds in Burma   222
36 A New Form of Warfare   228
37 The Rise of the Phoenix   234
38 Advances into Burma   240
39 The Defeat of Japan   246

Aircraft Index   254

Picture Captions   255

Foreword

This major new hardback published by the Public Record Office is a pictorial history of the Royal Air Force in the Second World War, backed by a concise narrative. This is a subject which attracts a large number of our regular readers as well as former members of the service or their relatives.

We have known for many years that our archives contain numerous photographs of the Royal Air Force. Many are remarkable, and some are probably unique as they were taken in action and under fire over enemy territory. Very few of these photographs were recorded or listed before they were released to the Public Record Office, but are scattered in hundreds of documents. Thus a book such as this, which contains over 450 representative photographs, has been very difficult to research and write.

The work of compiling the book has been carried out by Roy Conyers Nesbit, an experienced writer who served in the Royal Air Force throughout the Second World War, on stations at home, in Africa, India and the Far East. He has included photographs taken by the United States Army Air Force where these operated under joint control with the Royal Air Force in the various theatres of war, as well as some taken by the Commonwealth squadrons and those squadrons formed with aircrews from our European allies. The book also includes war artists' paintings, but as these do not cover all major episodes, paintings by modern artists have been added.

This research has enabled our Image Library to build up a wide selection of photographic negatives of the Royal Air Force's activities in the Second World War, including some which do not appear in the book. We hope to extend this collection in future years and thus improve the service provided to the public.

Sarah Tyacke

Sarah Tyacke, CB
Keeper of Public Records

Introduction

Certain documents at the Public Record Office contain original photographs taken by the RAF during the Second World War. These documents have been available to researchers for many years under the '30 year rule' for their release, but until recently very few of the photographs within them have been copied or catalogued. Following researches over the past few years, the Public Record Office is now able to bring a representative selection to the notice of the public.

Some of the action photographs are clear but others are less well defined. Many were taken from a moving aircraft while under fire and during evasive action. Thus conditions were not ideal, but some of the results are extremely rare and of historical interest. It should also be noted that light anti-aircraft fire in the form of machine-gun bullets or cannon fire did not show on photographs taken in daylight, but tracer and searchlights can be seen in night photographs. Exploding shells of heavier calibre can appear in both day and night photographs.

An attempt has been made to include photographs of all major episodes during the war in all theatres, but some have not been found. For example, there are none of the campaign in Norway in 1940, the defence of the RAF Habbaniya in Iraq during 1941, the Japanese invasions of Malaya and Sumatra in 1941–1942, or the operations of RAF armoured cars in the Western Desert. It seems probable that none survived, at least in these official records. However, time has not permitted a complete examination of the thousands of documents in the AIR, AVIA and DEFE class lists, and it is possible that some will come to light in the future.

Although the title of this book refers solely to the RAF, it must be stressed that this force included squadrons formed with personnel from Australia, Canada, New Zealand, India, the Rhodesias, France, Belgium, Greece, the Netherlands, Poland, Yugoslavia and Czechoslovakia, each with their own distinctive badges and characteristics. Squadrons of the South African Air Force also came under the operational control of the RAF in the Mediterranean theatre. It may seem strange to include photographs taken by the USAAF, but the US Ninth and Twelfth Air Forces were under joint control with the RAF in the Mediterranean theatre, the re-formed US Ninth Air Force was part of the Allied Air Force Expeditionary Force for the invasion of Normandy, and the US Tenth Air Force combined with the RAF to form Air Command, South East Asia. This book would seriously lack balance if it did not include a selection of photographs taken by these essential allies.

The collection at the Public Record Office Image Library also includes some paintings and drawings by war artists in the period 1939–1945. It is possible to be critical of their technical inaccuracies, but the pictures are representative of the wartime years. Of course, these war artists seldom had access to aircraft at the time and were using their imaginations from newspaper reports and a few permitted photographs, in order to boost public morale.

As these war artists did not cover every episode, two modern artists have contributed some of their paintings. Charles J. Thompson, GAvA, ASAA, GMA, EAA, became an air enthusiast while still a schoolboy and completed his national service in the RAF in 1955–1956. After many years of styling automobiles, he began painting in oils in 1979 and won several awards in London Exhibitions. He was elected an Artist Fellow of the American Society of Aviation Artists in 1988, then a Master Artist of the Experimental Aircraft Association at Oshkosh in 1992, and served as Chairman of the Guild of Aviation Artists in London from 1977 to 1999. He is always searching for new ways of 'capturing' light, and prefers painting on a commission basis to catering for the mass market. Mark Postlethwaite, GAvA, is an artist who has been painting in oils on canvas since he was a teenager. He is another aviation enthusiast with a detailed knowledge of aircraft, and likes painting after discussions with RAF air-crew members. Although the Second World War is one of his specialisms, he also has contacts with the present-day RAF squadrons and has taken the opportunity to fly in jets such as Harrier, Hawk and Tucano.

Roy Conyers Nesbit

Copies of the photographs in this book may be obtained from:
Public Record Office Image Library
Kew
Surrey TW9 4DU
United Kingdom

Telephone: 0181 392 5225
Fax: 0181 392 5266
e-mail: image-library@pro.gov.uk

Prices are obtainable on request. Document reference numbers are recorded for each photograph in the book but as these documents often include several photographs it is advisable to give page numbers and descriptions.

PART ONE: NORTH-WEST EUROPE AND THE ATLANTIC

1 'Sitzkrieg'

Immediately before the outbreak of the Second World War, the home-based RAF consisted of fifty-five bomber squadrons, thirty-five fighter squadrons, eighteen squadrons in Coastal Command, and seven army co-operation squadrons. These were equipped with 1,466 operational aircraft, of which about 1,000 were fairly modern, but the remainder needed replacement. There were twenty-two more squadrons overseas, in the Middle East, Palestine, Iraq, Aden, the Mediterranean, India and the Far East. Personnel numbered just under 200,000, including the part-time enthusiasts in the RAF Volunteer Reserve and the Auxiliary Air Force.

The day after Germany invaded Poland on 1 September 1939, ten Fairey Battle squadrons of Bomber Command flew to France to form the RAF's Advanced Air Striking Force (AASF). When Britain declared war on Germany on 3 September, the British Expeditionary Force which sailed to France to form the left flank of the defences was supported

Above: The motor transport section of 4 (Army Co-operation) Squadron leaving Odiham in Hampshire on 17 September 1939, bound for France as part of the British Expeditionary Force's Air Component. This ground party reached Mons-en-Chaussée a week later and the squadron's Lysanders followed on 2 October, flying via Shoreham-on-Sea and Le Tréport.
AIR 27/51

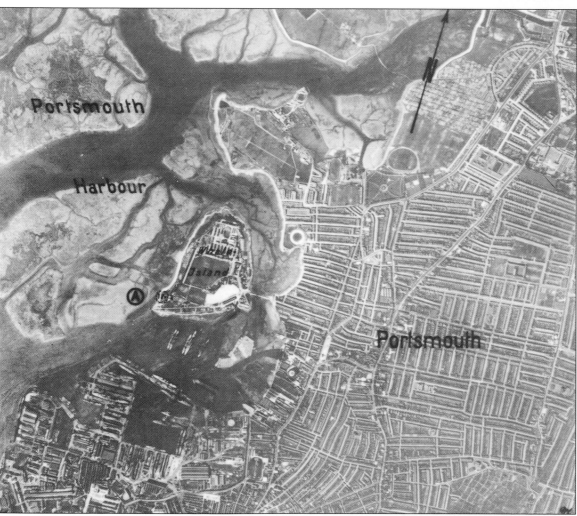

Left: Heinkel He111-VA registration D-AHAO *Dresden* and Heinkel He111C-03 registration D-AXAV *Köln*, which formed part of Germany's national airline *Deutsche Lufthansa*, were assigned in late 1937 to *Kommando Rowehl*. This was a Luftwaffe unit commanded by *Oberstleutnant* Theodor Rowehl which came under the direct orders of Hermann Goering. The two aircraft were engaged ostensibly on route-proving but in fact made clandestine sorties over British, French and Soviet territory. This example of their air photography was taken over the important naval base of Portsmouth on 12 April 1939.
AIR 34/734

Left: Two Hudsons of 220 Squadron, flown from Thornaby in Yorkshire by Sergeant Kenneth E. Scotney and Flight Lieutenant Harold W.A. Sheahen, attacked this Dornier Do18D flying boat over the North Sea on 10 November 1939. The radio code was K6+DL, the works number 0804, and it was on the strength of *3/Küstenfliegergruppe 406*. The flying boat landed in the sea but later turned over and sank. *Oberleutnant zur See* Lütjens was killed but the remaining crew members were picked up by Dutch vessels. AIR 28/828

Below: Westland Lysanders in the early months of the war. Five squadrons went to France in September 1939 as part of the Air Component of the British Expeditionary Force. Their functions were artillery spotting, reconnaissance, taking oblique photographs and dropping supplies. CN 11/6

by its 'Air Component' – five squadrons of Bristol Blenheims, five of Westland Lysanders and four of Hawker Hurricanes. Two squadrons of Gloster Gladiators followed in November. These two RAF formations were much inferior in numbers to the Luftwaffe, but most military authorities in Britain and France anticipated a long war of attrition in which their countries would be able to build their air strength with reasonable rapidity.

During the seven months which followed the opening of the conflict, the expression 'Phoney War' was increasingly used to describe inactivity on the Franco-German frontier. The opposing armies stood and glowered at each other from a distance while the air forces trained and serviced their aircraft but seldom made any contact with each other apart from reconnaissance sorties. The German word 'Blitzkrieg' had not entered the vocabulary of the Western Powers, but later the American word 'Sitzkrieg' tended to replace 'Phoney War' to describe the sense of unreality of those early months.

Meanwhile the home-based RAF was not certainly not inactive, even though it was not very effective. Bomber Command despatched its first aircraft on 3 September, hunting for German warships in the North Sea, without result. On the following day, twenty-nine Bristol Blenheims and Vickers Wellingtons were despatched to attack warships, but they caused little damage and seven were shot down. At this time, the War Cabinet enforced an absolute ban on any raids which might cause civilian casualties (partly for fear of retaliation) – but warships were legitimate targets.

Above: Bristol Blenheim Is of the Air Component, British Expeditionary Force, taking off on a reconnaissance sortie from a French airfield. No 53 Squadron flew to France in September 1939 and was followed by 59 Squadron in the following month. Their main role was taking vertical photographs of enemy positions.

CN 11/6

Right: Aircrews of Fairey Battles trudging through the snow to their aircraft in France during the winter of 1939/40. Ten of these Battle squadrons flew to France on 2 September 1939 to form the RAF's Advanced Air Striking Force.

CN 11/6

Armstrong Whitworth Whitleys had begun 'Nickel' raids at night over Germany, carrying no bombs but dropping millions of leaflets which exhorted German people to abandon the war. Some of the aircraft of the AASF joined in this activity. This continued for months with no visible results apart from demonstrating that the RAF could penetrate German air space, while the loss rate was relatively high at about five per cent on average.

Another daylight raid, carried out on 2 September by eleven Handley Page Hampdens against warships in the Heligoland area, met with disaster. No hits were scored and five Hampdens were shot down. Further operations of this type continued fairly regularly but met with no results except losses of aircraft. It became apparent that daylight raids by Bomber Command were completely unprofitable. Power-operated turrets, which were intended to provide strong protection against fighter attack when flying in close formation, proved far less effective than had been hoped. By the end of the year, daylight attacks were abandoned almost entirely

Above: This photograph of a Fairey Battle of 226 Squadron, Advanced Air Striking Force, was one of the earliest of the war. It was taken on 20 September 1939, twelve miles south-south-west of Saarbrücken, when the squadron was based at Reims-Champagne.

AIR 34/235

Left: Sorties over enemy territory during the 'Phoney War' were mostly confined to leaflet-dropping and reconnaissance. This photograph of Glaadt, west of Coblenz, was taken at 15.30 hours on 25 September 1939 by Sub-Lt Gavoille of the French Air Force. It shows the railway station on the centre right and an ammunition dump at Junkerath a little above it.

AIR 35/352

and Bomber Command committed itself to night operations, in spite of the difficulties of navigating over enemy territory with inadequate aids.

Coastal Command operated at full stretch from the beginning of the war, but its aircraft were inadequate. Avro Ansons numbered 135 within the Command's total strength of 183 aircraft. These were highly reliable machines but lacked sufficient range or bomb-carrying capacity. However, they carried out reconnaissance over part of the North Sea and provided escort for convoys near the shores of Britain. Short Sunderland flying boats, although in insufficient numbers, were effective machines for long-range work. Lockheed Hudsons began to replace Ansons and were sometimes in combat with enemy aircraft over the North Sea. It was a Hudson which scored the RAF's first combat victory of the war, when a crew of 224 Squadron shot down a Dornier Do18 flying boat near Jutland on 8 October 1939.

There were, however, some encouraging aspects to the condition of the inadequate RAF. Two modern fighters, the Hawker Hurricane and the Supermarine Spitfire, were among the most advanced in the world, while other machines and equipment were being designed and produced. The pilots and aircrews in all commands were highly trained in flying the aircraft and using the equipment available, although operational training to meet modern operational conditions was woefully inadequate. Some of those who survived the Blitzkrieg and the Battle of Britain which

Above: Pilots of 87 Squadron scrambling to their Hurricane Is at an airfield in France. Together with 1, 73 and 85 Squadrons, they flew to France in September 1939 to form the fighter element of the Air Component, British Expeditionary Force.

CN 11/6

Below: On 30 November 1939 ten Battles of 218 Squadron, part of the Advanced Air Striking Force in France, took off to make dummy attacks against their own airfield of Auberive-sur-Suippes. Three were allocated an anti-aircraft battery about a mile east of the airfield, as shown in this photograph taken with a Leica Contax camera by Sergeant Wynne, the air observer in Battle serial K9355 flown by Pilot Officer W.H. Shaw.

AIR 27/1354

Right: Battle K9355 peeling away from the dummy attack, which was made with shallow dives to low level, followed by another Battle of 218 Squadron.

AIR 27/1354

Below: RAF ground crews with parts of a Dornier reconnaissance aircraft shot down in France.

CN 11/6

followed became commanders of squadrons, stations and wings in a rapidly expanding air force. A great recruitment drive was in progress, to be followed by the far-seeing and successful Empire Air Training Scheme. Scientists in British Intelligence were beginning to achieve unparallelled success in decrypting enemy signals. A new reconnaissance force, known originally as the Heston Flight and then No 2 Camouflage Unit, became the Photographic Development Unit in January 1940. With unarmed Spitfires, and later with Mosquitos, this would grow into separate squadrons which provided the high command with photographic intelligence of unique importance. The RAF was not asleep in those early months, nor were the other armed services.

2 The Storm Bursts

The invasion of Denmark and Norway by the Wehrmacht, which began on 9 April 1940, came as no surprise to British Intelligence. The British had made preparations to help Finland resist the Russian invasion which began on 30 November 1939, but the problem of establishing a supply route via Norway had proved insuperable. In addition, they had always realized that an interdiction of the supply of high-grade iron ore from Sweden, which passed through Norwegian ports to feed the German war machine, would constitute a serious blow to the enemy. Hitler could not stand by indefinitely against this threat, and the build up of his invasion force was known to the British. The Royal Navy laid mines in Norwegian waters on 8 April, but nothing could be done to help prevent the airborne landings which followed the next day, at the same time as the Wehrmacht rolled almost unopposed into Denmark.

Below: The Order of Battle of the British and French Air Forces in France on the eve of the opening of the Wehrmacht's Blitzkrieg in the west. The map was drawn by the RAF's Air Historical Branch. AIR 41/22

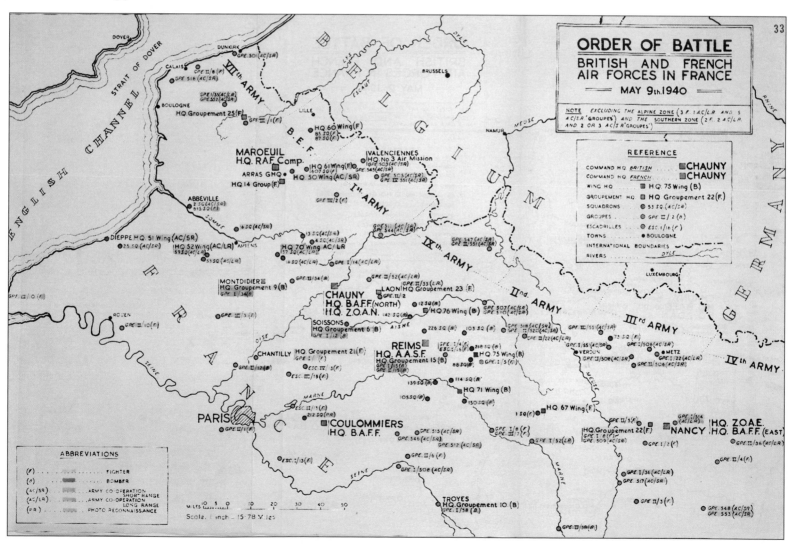

The German assault on Norway began on 9 April 1940, from both land and sea. Units of the Kriegsmarine entered Norwegian territorial waters under cover of darkness at Oslofjord, Arendal, Egersund, Kristiansand, Trondheim and Narvik. Under operation *Weserübung*, nearly 600 fighter or bomber aircraft of the Luftwaffe were available for the invasion, together with over 600 transport aircraft carrying airborne soldiers. This painting shows Heinkel He111H-3 aircraft of *Kampfgruppe 100*, part of X. *Fliegerkorps*, making low-level bombing attacks on Oscarsborg Fortress in Oslofjord, about 30 km south of Oslo. Three *Staffeln* (squadrons) of the same unit, transferred from Lüneburg to Nordholz, also bombed Oslo-Kjeller airfield, flak batteries on Holmenkjollen and coastal batteries on islands in Oslofjord.

The outcome of this campaign was inevitable. Bomber Command did its best to bomb airfields occupied by the Germans, while the Royal Navy hunted for enemy warships and supply ships. Contingents of an Allied Expeditionary Force which landed at Namsos and the area of Narvik on 14 April, followed by Aandalsnes, fought bravely but they were outnumbered and out-gunned, while air cover could be provided only by carrier-borne aircraft of the Fleet Air Arm.

The RAF was thwarted since no airfields were available, but a squadron of Gladiators from an aircraft carrier landed on a frozen lake on 24 April only to find that the engines could not be started in the extreme cold. Most were destroyed by bombing, and the remainder returned to the UK. The squadron re-equipped and on 24 May landed in Norway once more, on a hastily constructed landing strip north of Narvik. A Hurricane squadron followed two days later, but by then the German Blitzkrieg was crushing the Anglo-French forces and it was decided to withdraw from Norway. On 7 June the surviving aircraft flew to the aircraft carrier HMS *Glorious*, but she was sunk by German battleships. The expedition to Norway ended in disaster. There was, however, one consolation. The Kriegsmarine lost several cruisers, destroyers and torpedo boats, from coastal defences and sea battles. These were more than the service could afford, in view of the later intention to invade Britain.

Below: One of the attacks made by the RAF against the German forces invading Norway took place on 17 April 1940 when twelve Blenheim IVs bombed Stavanger airfield. This photograph of the action was taken from a Blenheim of 107 Squadron based at Wattisham in Suffolk. Two Blenheims were lost in the operation.
AIR 14/3696

Similarly, the British were not surprised when the Wehrmacht attacked in the west on 10 May 1940, outflanking the Maginot Line and entering the Low Countries. Anglo-French armies moved into Belgium to support the forces of that hard-pressed country, anticipating a long war of attrition. But nothing worked according to plan. The Luftwaffe, in almost overwhelming strength, delivered effective attacks on the airfields occupied by the Armée de l'Air, although the RAF's bases in France escaped more lightly. The air forces of the Netherlands and Belgium were soon knocked out. There was a ruthless air attack on Rotterdam which resulted in 1,000 deaths and 20,000 buildings destroyed. The Netherlands was forced to capitulate, to avoid the destruction of all the country's towns and cities.

Meanwhile, the German method of attack confounded the Allied commanders, and the few of middle rank who anticipated the tactics had failed to get their voices heard. The combination of screaming Stuka dive-bombers, Panzer thrusts, mobile artillery and flak guns, coupled with remorseless infantry attacks, punched holes in the Allied

Above: A Junkers Ju52 transport on a beach south of Ijmuiden in the Netherlands, photographed on 31 May 1940 from a Hudson of 220 Squadron flown by Pilot Officer Charles T. Dacombe from Bircham Newton in Suffolk. It was one of twenty-five which landed with airborne soldiers on 10 May 1940 to take Dutch positions in the rear. Only five were able to take off again and Blenheims of Bomber Command destroyed nine of those which remained.
AIR 28/75

Left: A German propaganda photograph of captured RAF men brought down by flak at the airfield of Aalborg in Denmark, standing in front of a Junkers Ju52 which probably took them to a PoW camp. They appear to be Flying Officer F.T. Knight and his crew of five from Wellington IA serial P9218 of 149 Squadron at Mildenhall in Suffolk. These were the only men lost when twelve aircraft raided the airfield on the night of 21–22 April 1940. They were known to have crash-landed and been taken prisoner.
CN 11/9

Above: 'Flying Officer Garland and Sergeant Gray' by unknown war artist

By 11 May 1940, German forces had captured intact bridges over the Albert Canal near Maastricht and were streaming towards Brussels. The Belgians were unable to withstand them. Eight RAF Battles were ordered to attack a German column but all were shot down. By the following day, the Blenheims of the Advanced Air Striking Force in France had been almost wiped out. When the pilots of 12 Squadron, equipped with Battles and based at Amifontaine in France, were asked to volunteer to attack two bridges with six aircraft, every man stepped forward. One Battle was unserviceable but five took off. They were escorted by seven Hurricanes of 1 Squadron, but these were swamped near the targets by Messerschmitt Bf109s. Two Battles in one section damaged their bridge in a dive-bombing attack with 250lb bombs but one was shot down and the other crash-landed back near its base. The three Battles in the other section bombed their bridge from low level but all were shot down. The target was hit and it was estimated that the bombs were dropped by the leader, Flying Officer Donald E. Garland in serial P2204. Garland and his navigator, Sergeant Thomas Gray, were awarded posthumous Victoria Crosses. The gunner in the aircraft, Leading Aircraftman L.R. Reynolds, was also killed.

INF 3/409

Below: Battles attacking a German mechanized column on a road in Belgium on 12 May 1940. The squadron making the attack cannot be identified in the photograph or in Battle squadron records, some of which are missing for this month.

AIR 14/3696

lines and caused disorganized retreats, the Army columns mixed with streams of terrified civilian refugees.

Many of the French aircraft were obsolescent, while their control system was hopelessly inadequate. The RAF in France rose to the occasion, but they were too few in number. Tactical reconnaissance was carried out by the Lysanders escorted by Hurricanes. These Hurricanes scored successes against the Luftwaffe, but they did not have the endurance to support the Battle and Blenheim squadrons which attempted to stem the German advance. The bomber crews acted with astonishing bravery but their aircraft were shot down in droves, mainly by the 20 mm flak guns which protected the German columns and positions around key bridges. There were 135 RAF bombers in France when the

Left: A pontoon bridge over the river Meuse at Dinant in Belgium, alongside the destroyed road bridge nearby. It was photographed on 15 May 1940.

AIR 34/234

Bottom: On 3 June 1940, Squadron Leader Douglas W. Lydall of Coastal Command's 220 Squadron led three Hudsons from Bircham Newton in Suffolk to reconnoitre Dunkirk. One of the photographs brought back showed troops awaiting embarkation.

AIR 28/75

Below: This is the first successful night photograph taken by the RAF on operations. The Royal Aircraft Establishment had made up three or four F8 cameras with photo-electric cells and provided a small quantity of eight-inch photoflashes. On the night of 30/31 May 1940, twenty-eight Wellingtons of Bomber Command took off to attack targets on roads leading to Dunkirk, each carrying about 3,500lb of bombs. The photograph was taken from 4,000 feet over Courtrai in Belgium by a Wellington of 115 Squadron based at Marham in Norfolk.

AIR 14/3696

Blitzkrieg began, but almost half this number were lost in the first three days. Of the remaining aircraft, forty were shot down during the following day. Thus the RAF's Advanced Air Striking Force was almost wiped out. Moreover, the RAF's mobile radar stations near the front line were forced to retreat, adding to the difficulty of the operations.

It was obvious that the airfields in France would soon be overrun. All the surviving Hurricanes flew to England on 19 May, to continue operating from home stations. While these events were taking place, some of the home-based RAF squadrons entered the fray. Hampdens, Whitleys and Wellingtons attacked German lines of communication at night, extending their operations to the Ruhr, but these operations had little effect on the German advances. Fighter Command swept over France and the Low Countries. Spitfires and Hurricanes proved good matches for Messerschmitt Bf109s, especially in manoeuvrability, and more than capable against the twin-engined Messerschmitt Bf110s. Boulton Paul Defiants scored initial successes with their turrets, partly because the German pilots mistook them for Hurricanes, but the Bf109s soon made short work of them by attacking from below or head-on.

On the ground, no amount of heroism or counter-attacks could withstand the onward rush of the Panzer divisions. The British and French equipment was out-dated, in both armour and artillery. The armies made fighting retreats to Dunkirk and some other French ports, from where they hoped to reach England. On 23 May, Herman Goering was unwise enough to tell Hitler that the Luftwaffe alone could destroy these beleaguered forces. But what became described as the 'miracle of Dunkirk' took place, when a

Left: Soldiers of the British Expeditionary Force captured near Merville, south-south-east of Dunkirk. They are still wearing their steel helmets and carrying gas masks. The German soldier standing next to the motorcycle has the badge of a signals operator on his arm.

CN 11/9

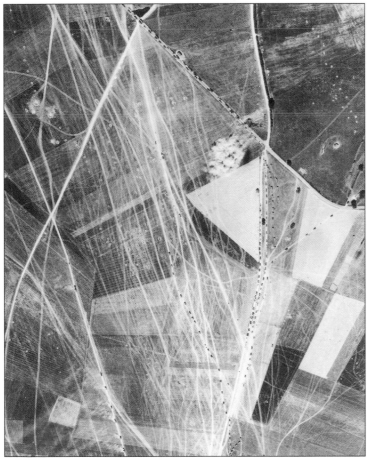

Left: German forces streaming south towards Paris after the evacuation at Dunkirk. This photograph, taken over Montagne Fayel on 7 June 1940, shows a concentration of over 300 vehicles which include motor transport, armoured fighting vehicles, gun limbers and ammunition limbers.

AIR 34/239

flotilla of small privately-owned vessels joined the Royal Navy in a rescue operation. A total of over 335,000 men were brought over the Channel by 4 June, while RAF fighters engaged the Luftwaffe in fierce air battles, some distance from the beaches. The soldiers left almost all their equipment behind.

The Battle for France was almost over but some fighting continued. Italy decided to share in the spoils of war by invading the south of France on 10 June, although the citizens of Turin and Genoa were given unpleasant shocks when Bomber Command began night attacks against their cities. France gave up the unequal struggle by agreeing to an armistice on 22 June, when a major part of the country became German-controlled. The long years of occupation in western Europe and Scandinavia had begun, while the vicious oppression continued in Poland. Britain, backed by her Commonwealth, stood alone against an all-conquering enemy.

3 A British Victory

The RAF lost over 900 aircraft during the Battle for France, half of which were Hurricanes and Spitfires. Many of the fighter losses occurred during the evacuation from Dunkirk, but almost all these air combats took place out of sight of British troops, who believed that the RAF had abandoned them in their hour of need. Nevertheless, there is no doubt that the Commander-in-Chief of Fighter Command, Air Chief Marshal Sir Hugh Dowding, was reluctant to commit all his squadrons to France during the retreat, since he foresaw their vital need over England in the months to come.

It is not generally realized that the Luftwaffe also suffered grievously. Although figures vary, partly since some German records seen to have been destroyed, it is believed that about 1,700 aircraft were destroyed on the Western Front. Losses of personnel included many of the more experienced and senior pilots. German historians record that the Luftwaffe had lost forty per cent of its effective strength during the campaigns in Norway and France. Thus it also needed time to recover, while Hitler continued to hope that the British would recognize the weakness of their military position and come to terms with the Third Reich.

By the time the Battle of Britain is considered to have begun, on 10 July, Dowding was able to deploy fifty squadrons, consisting of about six hundred and fifty serviceable aircraft. Twenty-two squadrons were equipped with Hurricanes, nineteen with Spitfires, seven with Blenheims and two Defiants. Eight more Hurricane squadrons were being formed, and by the end of the month a flight of Gladiators was sent down from the Shetlands and increased to squadron status. About 1,050 fighter pilots were available to man these squadrons, although not all were operationally trained. This number was augmented by about fifty pilots transferred from the Fleet Air Arm.

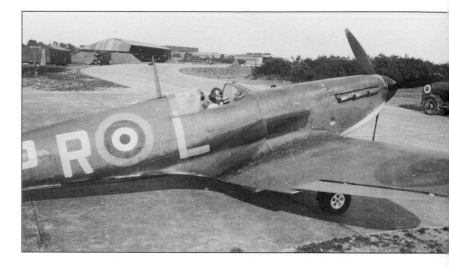

Above: Spitfire I serial R6699 of 609 (West Riding) Squadron at Northolt in Middlesex, with Pilot Officer David M. Crook at the controls. The squadron flew to this station on 1 July 1940 from Warmwell in Dorset preparatory to a reconnaissance over France. This took place the following day, with Crook flying over Rouen and Loos. The pilots saw few enemy aircraft on the ground but they flew through accurate flak, without suffering any damage.
AIR 4/21

Below left: The RAF's Balloon Command, formed in 1938, became a vital part of the defences during the Battle of Britain. They could be close-hauled or bedded down on pickets awaiting any order to be raised.
CN 11/6

During these early weeks, the Luftwaffe concentrated on attacks against British coastal convoys, with limited success. RAF fighter pilots took a grim delight in attacking the Junkers Ju87 dive-bombers, which had been so dreaded in the Blitzkrieg, for these proved vulnerable to their aircraft.

Britain's obstinacy, under the charismatic leadership of Winston Churchill, eventually convinced Hitler that steps must be taken to eliminate the country before he launched his planned attack against Russia. On 30 July 1940 he ordered Goering to start preparing for an 'air battle against England' as a prelude to a seaborne invasion. The RAF squadrons, their airfields and the aircraft industry were to be destroyed. Then ports were to be attacked, apart from those required for German landing operations. The date set for the main attack, named 'Adlertag', was initially set for 5 August.

The main assault was postponed owing to unfavourable weather and finally began on 13 August. By this date the three *Luftflotten* (Air Fleets) in France, the Low Countries, Denmark and Norway mustered 1,350 twin-engined

Left: The Boulton Paul Defiant, which first entered squadron service in December 1939, was fitted with four Browning .303 inch machine-guns in the turret but had no forward-firing armament. Defiant squadrons had initial successes during the Battle of France, when Luftwaffe pilots thought they were Hurricanes, but suffered heavy losses in the Battle of Britain from head-on or belly attacks. They were withdrawn from service in August 1940 and modified as night-fighters with air interception radar, as a stop-gap until Beaufighters appeared.

CN 11/6

Right: 'Flight Lieutenant Nicolson jumping from blazing aircraft' by unknown war artist

The only Victoria Cross of Fighter Command was awarded to Flight Lieutenant James B. Nicolson, who was known as 'Nick' to his RAF friends. Although an experienced pilot who had served in 72 Squadron, Nicolson's first combat took place on 16 August 1940 when he was a flight commander with 249 Squadron, equipped with Hawker Hurricane Is and based at Boscombe Down in Wiltshire. Flying serial P3576, he led three Hurricanes of Red Section on a patrol towards the south, during an attack by the Luftwaffe on Gosport. Three Junkers Ju88s were spotted but these were tackled by a formation of Spitfires over Southampton. Red Section was turning away when it was jumped by Messerschmitt Bf109s.

All three Hurricanes were badly hit. One pilot baled out but was killed when his parachute was torn by ground fire. Another pilot managed to crash-land at Boscombe Down. Nicolson's Hurricane was hit by four 20mm cannon shells. One set the gravity tank on fire, one ripped a trouser leg, another tore his left eyelid, while the fourth wounded his left foot.

With his aircraft on fire, he prepared to bale out but a Messerschmitt Bf110 appeared in front of him. He remained in the cockpit while flames were scorching his left hand, face and legs, continuing to fire at the enemy. He baled out eventually but during the descent was hit in the buttocks by a trigger-happy member of the Home Guard who fired a shotgun at him.

The Victoria Cross was gazetted on 15 November 1940. His wounds were slow to heal, but he returned to active service in February 1941. Wing Commander Nicolson commanded 27 Squadron in the Burma theatre for a year from August 1943, when it was equipped with Beaufighters and Mosquitos, and was awarded the DFC. He was killed in the Bay of Bengal on 2 May 1945 when acting as a supernumerary observer in a Liberator of 355 Squadron on a bombing mission.

INF 3/418

bombers, 406 single-engined dive-bombers, 319 twin-engined fighters and 813 single-engined fighters. However, German Intelligence underestimated the strength of Fighter Command and was seriously wrong in its estimate of the capacity of the British aircraft industry to make good future losses.

Although the RAF squadrons were heavily outnumbered, Fighter Command at Bentley Priory in Middlesex possessed several advantages. Britain's defences included anti-aircraft guns and barrage balloons, under its operational control. There was an excellent radar system around the coasts, in addition to numerous posts dependent on visual sightings by the efficient Observer Corps. A superb interlocking network of communications gave the headquarters almost instantaneous information of approaching enemy formations. Air Intelligence was able to help, with the aid of Enigma decrypts, by accurately assessing the number of German bombers as about 1,250, after gross exaggerations made previously.

On the day before *Adlertag*, dive-bombers attacked radar stations along the south-east coast of England. Some of these stations were put out of action but all save one were repaired rapidly and the system was not seriously impaired. Then followed three and a half weeks of attacks against RAF airfields. These caused considerable damage to buildings and resulted in casualties to personnel, but very few fighters were lost since advance warning usually enabled them to take off before the bomber forces arrived. The emergency services carried out miracles of repair work and improvisation soon after the attacks.

On 15 August, *Luftflotte 5* in Denmark and Norway despatched about 150 aircraft against targets in north-east England. The RAF shot down fifteen and damaged many others, on a day when the other two *Luftflotten* lost sixty aircraft. It was the worst day of all for the Luftwaffe. Both sides exaggerated enemy losses when reporting the air battles, usually as a result of 'double-counting' by pilots or aircrew members who claimed the same aircraft shot down. But the

Below: Disposition in South-East England and the Midlands at the commencement of the Battle of Britain. The map was drawn by the RAF's Air Historical Branch.

AIR 41/16

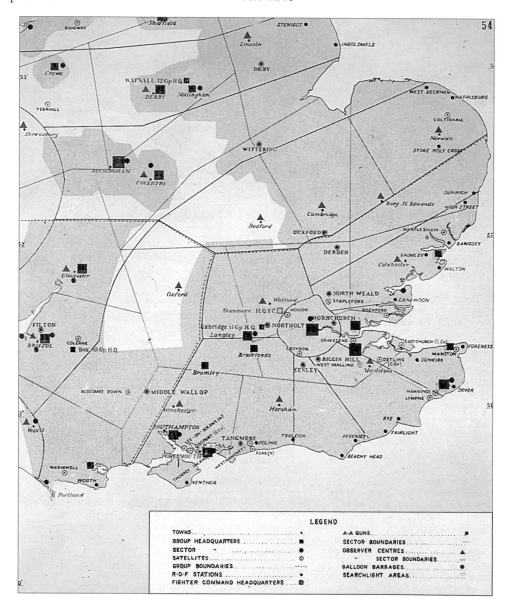

LEGEND

TOWNS........................ •	A-A GUNS........................ •
GROUP HEADQUARTERS........ ■	SECTOR BOUNDARIES............
SECTOR........................ ◉	OBSERVER CENTRES............ ▲
SATELLITES.................... ⊚	" SECTOR BOUNDARIES......
GROUP BOUNDARIES............	BALLOON BARRAGES............ ●
R·D·F STATIONS................	SEARCHLIGHT AREAS............
FIGHTER COMMAND HEADQUARTERS......▣	

Right: 'British fighter aircraft attacking bombers over the sea' by war artist Roy Nockolds

This dramatic painting, completed by the artist in 1942, appears to represent the Battle of Britain. The squadron letters OJ on the Spitfires were in fact those of No 149 Squadron, which was equipped with Wellingtons in 1940, but it is unlikely that the artist would have had access to such information at the time.
INF 3/824

Below: 'British and German fighters over convoy' by war artist Roland Davies
INF 3/1624

RAF was winning overall, while some of its pilots who baled out were unhurt and able to rejoin their squadrons.

The Germans had been assured that they were wiping out Fighter Command, but the same number of aircraft seemed to rise against them each day. Under the forceful authority of the new Minister of Aircraft Production, Lord Beaverbrook, production in factories was diverted to the needs of Fighter Command, while many fighters damaged in combat or accidents were repaired by 'cannibalizing' parts from others which normally would have been 'written off'. New pilots arrived from the training schools, although they were operationally inexperienced.

Bomber Command intensified its attacks against targets in Germany, to Hitler's fury. He ordered the Luftwaffe to shift its attacks to London, and the first major daylight raid against the capital began on 7 September. The bomber offensive at night also began. Although great devastation was caused in the capital, particularly in the

A British Victory

Right: A Messerschmitt Bf109E-1 of *Stab* III./*Jagdgeschwader* 26, one of about forty led by Major Adolf Galland escorting two *Staffeln* of Dornier Do17s on 24 July 1940 to attack a Thames Estuary convoy. It was shot down by a Spitfire I of 65 Squadron based at Hornchurch in Essex, but operating from Manston in Kent, flown by Squadron Leader Henry C. Sawyer, and crash-landed at Northdown near Margate. The pilot, *Oberleutnant* Werner Bartels, the Adjutant of III./*Jagdgeschwader* 26, was wounded when captured.

AIR 40/127

Above: These Dornier Do17s were photographed in the evening of 7 September 1940 over the West Ham district during a heavy daylight raid on London.

AIR 34/734

Right: A German parachute mine fell in Park Lane, Croydon on the night of 28/29 September 1940 and buried itself three feet deep in a footpath without exploding. Volunteers surrounded it with sandbags, sheerlegs were erected and a rope with a steel hawser was attached to the mine. The hawser was passed round a lamppost 720 feet away and then to a winch thirty feet round the corner. During an attempt to lift the mine the following evening the sheerlegs collapsed and the mine exploded. Five houses, including St Anselm's School (shown), were completely demolished, eight partly demolished, and thirty-five damaged. Fortunately the area had been evacuated.

HO 192/336

East End, this move was advantageous to the RAF. It was able to repair shattered buildings on airfields in the south-east, while the change of direction brought the bombers within easier range of fighter airfields in the eastern counties.

The date when the Battle of Britain was won is considered to be 15 September, when fifty-nine German aircraft were shot down in daylight for the loss of twenty-six by Fighter Command. The Luftwaffe could take no more, at least on this scale. Hitler postponed the invasion two days later and his fleet of barges and other light craft in French ports began to disperse. Daylight attacks tailed off while RAF fighters still came up in strength.

In the period from 20 July to 26 October, the RAF lost 1,490 Hurricanes or Spitfires damaged beyond repair on

Above: Some of the fighter pilots who flew in 303 (Polish) Squadron in the Battle of Britain were reviewed by the Polish President, M. Raciewicz. The squadron was formed with Hurricane Is on 2 August 1940 at Northolt in Middlesex from elements of No 1 Warsaw Squadron who had escaped after fighting in Poland and France.

INF 1/244

Below: Arguably Britain's most celebrated aircraft, the Supermarine Spitfire first entered squadron service in August 1938, as the Mark I. This was powered by a Merlin II engine of 990hp and fitted with four .303 inch Browning machine-guns, later increased to eight.

CN 11/6

Right: 'Hampdens attacking canal' by war artist W. Krogman

Bomber Command despatched Handley Page Hampdens on many attacks against the German communication system after the German Blitzkrieg began in the west on 10 May 1940. On the night of 12/13 August, Flight Lieutenant R.A.B. Learoyd dived his badly hit Hampden serial P4403 of 49 Squadron through flak and blinding searchlights to attack an aqueduct forming part of the Dortmund-Ems Canal. He dropped delay-action bombs from 150 feet and then brought his crippled aircraft back to Scampton in Lincolnshire, landing after dawn without injury to the crew. The canal was still blocked ten days later. Learoyd was awarded Bomber Command's first Victoria Cross of the war.

INF 3/1600

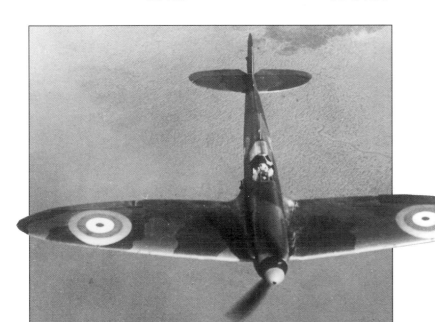

operations, plus 360 more in flying accidents. However, 1,333 new fighters were produced while 723 damaged aircraft were made serviceable. Thus the overall strength of fighters increased, although 537 pilots or other aircrew were killed in the period from 10 July to the end of October, and others wounded. By comparison, the Luftwaffe lost 1,887 aircraft in combat, apart from those seriously damaged, while 2,662 Luftwaffe airmen were killed and many others taken prisoner.

The Battle of Britain was undoubtedly a resounding victory. Equally important, it boosted morale in Britain and convinced the rest of the world, especially America, that the country could withstand all the enemy could throw at it.

It was the 'unsinkable aircraft carrier' from which victory could be attained.

4 The Dark Days

Although the Battle of Britain had been fought and won, the country faced an uncertain future. London and other cities were being battered nightly from the air, while very few of the attackers were being shot down. U-boats were playing havoc with convoys crossing the Atlantic, while airborne radar for their detection had not been produced. Coastal Command was still equipped with many obsolescent aircraft. Bomber Command did not have the strength to deliver heavy blows against the enemy, nor was advanced navigational equipment available for the crews to find their targets on cloudy nights. The country was hard-pressed in trying to supply her possessions in Malta, the Middle East, India and the Far East with military personnel and equipment. Britain had entered a period which Winston Churchill called 'The Dark Days'. She stood alone in Europe against an immensely powerful enemy, although unstinting help was provided by her Commonwealth and people of good will in the USA.

Fighter Command was relatively the strongest in the RAF, since so much production had been diverted to its needs during the Battle of Britain. This had been at the expense of other types of aircraft, for production flows in some factories had been so seriously disrupted that there was a loss of output. But new versions of the Hurricane, fitted with cannons and carrying bombs, and the more powerful Spitfire armed with cannons, enabled fighter squadrons to begin aggressive sweeps over enemy territory from December 1940. These were infrequent and small in scale at first but grew in size, sometimes escorting small forces of light bombers.

In some ways, Coastal Command was the most hard-pressed service in the RAF. Germany's short coastline with

Above: 'Legend – Douglas Bader in action over France in 1941' by Mark Postlethwaite

Wing Commander Douglas Bader, the celebrated fighter pilot who overcame the enormous handicap of flying with two artificial legs, was shot down on 9 August 1941 while leading the Tangmere Wing as part of an escort to Blenheims of 226 Squadron attacking power stations at Gosnay in France, on operation 'Circus 68'. He took off at 10.40 hours from Westhampnett in Sussex, flying Spitfire Va serial W3185 attached to 616 Squadron. He baled out after combat with Messerschmitt Bf109s near Béthune, and became an extremely troublesome PoW to the Germans for the rest of the war.

Left: WAAFs handling a tractor and petrol bowser while refuelling a Hurricane on a fighter airfield.

INF 2/42

Right: 'The Beaufort'
by Charles J. Thompson

A Bristol Beaufort of 217
Squadron, based at St Eval in
Cornwall, unexpectedly comes
across a sinking British tanker
when flying through a sea mist
in the English Channel, in early
1941.

the North Sea had been stretched from the north of Norway to the Franco-Spanish border. U-boats possessed superb ports from which they could operate over the oceans, while Coastal Command did not possess enough aircraft to cope with its vastly increased duties. However, some new aircraft such as the powerful Bristol Beaufighter began to trickle through the factories, to supplement the Bristol Beaufort torpedo-bomber which had entered service in November 1939. Hudsons continued to replace the venerable Ansons. New Sunderlands replaced older flying boats. Whitleys, no longer required by Bomber Command, were transferred. But British aircraft could not cover vast stretches of mid-Atlantic where U-boats were taking their toll, and Consolidated Catalinas were bought in from the USA. Moreover, new equipment such as Air to Surface-Vessel radar was being rapidly developed, while the Government Code and Cypher School at Bletchley Park was beginning to decrypt some of the signals sent by the Kriegsmarine. The outlook became somewhat brighter when the battleship *Bismarck* was spotted by the RAF, and then sunk by the Royal Navy on 27 May 1941.

On 3 September 1940, Winston Churchill had declared that 'The fighters are our salvation but the bombers alone provide the means of victory'. Once released from the need to attack enemy invasion ports and airfields, Bomber Command could resume a strategic offensive at night against the German heartland, supported by an overwhelming desire of the public to retaliate when British cities were being ruthlessly bombed. Of course, Berlin was a prime target, in spite of the distance. It had been raided by as many as 122 aircraft on 24/25 September 1940, and there was no longer any compunction about causing civilian casualties. There was a lull in these strategic operations, owing to difficult flying conditions over such distances during the long night, but they began again in mid-February 1941. Hannover, Bremen, cities in the Ruhr, Wilhelmshaven and Cologne were among the targets, and the first of the new four-engined bombers, the Short Stirling, was coming into service. Nevertheless, the raids were on a small scale compared with the later stages of the campaign.

Meanwhile, London and other cities continued to endure the Blitz, which had begun in earnest on 7

Left: 'Sergeant J. Hannah fighting fire' by unknown war artist

Sergeant J. Hannah of 83 Squadron was the youngest recipient of the Victoria Cross awarded to the RAF. He was only eighteen when his squadron sent fifteen Handley Page Hampden Is from Scampton in Lincolnshire to bomb invasion barges at Antwerp on 15 September 1940. His duty was that of a WOp/AG in serial P1355 flown by a Canadian in the RAF, Pilot Officer C.A. Connor, which took off at 22.30 hours.

The aircraft was hit by flak over the target while the bombs were being released. This pierced both petrol tanks and also set the rear of the narrow fuselage on fire. Connor remained at the controls to give his crew a chance to bale out. The rear gunner, Sergeant George James, went through a hole in the floor. The navigator, Sergeant D.A.E. Hayhurst, worked his way out of the nose but was unable to open the buckled midships door and also baled out, thinking both WOp/AGs had left. Meanwhile, with ammunition exploding around him and fumes almost suffocating him, Hannah did not bale out but began to tackle the flames with two extinguishers. Then he beat them with his hands and threw exploding ammunition pans out of the aircraft. He managed to put out the fire eventually, but was badly burnt in the process.

Connor flew the damaged Hampden back to Scampton, where Hannah was rushed to hospital. His Victoria Cross was gazetted on 1 October 1940, while Connor was awarded a DFC and Hayhurst (by then a PoW) a DFM. Hannah never recovered fully from his injuries and was discharged from the RAF on 10 December 1941, with a disability pension. He died from tuberculosis on 7 June 1947.

INF 3/419

September 1940. The Luftwaffe had the advantage of short range and the ease of picking out the Thames from the air. Its bomber crews took the precaution of flying above the effective range of the anti-aircraft batteries and searchlights which defended the capital and other major cities. They were also able to use a system known as *Knickebein* (crooked leg), whereby they flew along one radio beam until it crossed another, giving a point when the bombs should be released. Fortunately British scientists were soon able to identify the method and take countermeasures by jamming the radio waves or even 'bending' the beams. Another German navigation aid consisted of medium wave direction-finding, which enabled wireless operators in the aircraft to obtain position lines. This was thwarted by Post Office engineers who distorted the signals.

Left: Thirty Blenheims of Bomber Command were despatched on 16 April 1941 on coastal patrols. An aircraft of 82 Squadron, based at Bodney in Norfolk, bombed a power station at Leiden in the Netherlands and took this photograph during a second run over the target. Ten other Blenheims bombed various targets and all returned safely.

AIR 34/741

Right: The British merchant tanker *San Conrado* of 7,982 tons, photographed by the RAF on 1 April 1941 when 13 miles south-west of Smalls lighthouse off Pembrokeshire. She was on fire and sinking, with burning oil on the water, as a result of an enemy bombing attack.

AIR 34/770

But these nightly bombing raids caused enormous devastation and at first the RAF did not possess heavily-armed night-fighters or the airborne equipment to locate enemy bombers, while the radar system which picked up bombers approaching British shores was not directed inland. Once again, British ingenuity was at hand. The first airborne interception radar had been fitted in Blenheims in November 1939 but its range was extremely limited and the aircraft was too slow to catch the intruder. Single-engined fighters were not equipped with the system, nor were the pilots adept at night flying in these circumstances, for an additional and specially trained crew member was required.

However, British scientists were making significant advances. A more advanced set was tested in August 1940, at the time when the fast and powerful Beaufighter was coming into service. It took some months before the new device could be fitted and the crews trained, and meanwhile the German bombers used a specialized pathfinder force, *Kampgeschwader 100*, to mark targets further inland for the main bomber force. Coventry and Birmingham received the full weight of the Luftwaffe's bombs. Liverpool, Bristol, Manchester, Sheffield, Portsmouth, Cardiff, Southampton and Plymouth soon followed.

It was not until March 1941 that most of the RAF's night-fighter squadrons were trained on the new Beaufighter with the latest airborne interception sets and an effective ground control system was established. During that month, the 'kills' of enemy aircraft suddenly rose to twenty-two, compared with an average of only three in the previous two months. In April they more than doubled to forty-eight, and then continued at a high rate in the early part of May. But then something strange happened, for the enemy's night

Above: On 19 September 1940, the RAF's 71 Squadron was reformed at Church Fenton in Yorkshire as the first 'Eagle' squadron with volunteer pilots from the USA, some of whom had fought in other RAF squadrons during the Battle of Britain. It worked up on Brewster Buffalo Is, but Hurricane Is arrived in November. The squadron became operational on 5 February 1941 while at Kirton-in-Lindsey in Lincolnshire, as shown here.
INF 1/244

Below: The Spitfire II, with the more powerful Merlin XII engine of 1,150 hp, entered service in August 1940. It was employed from the end of the year on sweeps over enemy territory, known as 'Rhubarbs'. The IIA was armed with eight .303 inch machine-guns while the IIB was armed with four of these guns and two 20mm cannons. This Spitfire IIA was on the strength of 72 Squadron, which was equipped with these machines from April 1941.
INF 2/42

attacks died away. The public did not understand the cause, but British Intelligence had known about the prospect for months. The bombers were being withdrawn for the forthcoming German invasion of Russia. This duly began on 22 June 1941, and the war suddenly took on a new dimension.

5 Daylight Bombing

The initial advance of the Wehrmacht into Russia made so much progress that the collapse of the huge Communist country seemed imminent. There was little that Britain could do to help her new ally, except supply her with armaments and attempt to draw some of the Luftwaffe's units back to the west.

The RAF was at the forefront of these endeavours. One method was to encourage patriots in the occupied territories to take action against their oppressors. The Special Operations Executive (SOE) had been formed in July 1940 to sabotage military installations, resulting in the creation of a special RAF flight to supply arms for secret organizations in France, Belgium and the Netherlands. This flight employed Lysanders on night operations, using their short take-off and landing capabilities to carry supplies and small teams of organizers and wireless operators. Although the resulting operations proved thorns in the flesh of the Germans later

Above: On 16 July 1941, thirty-six Blenheim IVs from 18, 21, 105, 139 and 226 Squadrons made a low-level attack against the docks at Rotterdam. Flak was intense and four aircraft were shot down. No ships were sunk but many were damaged, while damage was also caused to dock installations.

AIR 37/47

Left: A 'Circus' operation against Comines Power Station in north-east France took place in the early morning on 28 June 1941, when twenty-four Blenheim IVs from 18, 21, 139 and 226 Squadrons were supported by fourteen squadrons of Spitfires and five of Hurricanes. Two Blenheims had to turn back but the others dropped eleven tons of bombs which caused considerable damage to the turbine rooms and killed six employees. All the Blenheims returned safely but two Spitfires and one Hurricane were lost in combat.

AIR 37/47

Below: The view from the dorsal turret of a Blenheim IV leaving Rotterdam on 16 July 1941, past the 'ring and bead' sight of the twin .303 inch machine-guns.

AIR 37/47

Above: 'Low level attack on power station' by war artist Jobson

Blenheims on the daylight raid of 12 August 1941, when the power stations at Knapsack and Quadrath, near Cologne, were bombed.

INF 3/833

Above: A major attempt to draw German fighters back from the Russian front was made on 12 August 1941, when fifty-four Blenheim IVs were despatched in daylight to raid power stations, one at Knapsack and the other at Fortuna in Cologne. Fighter Command was able to escort the light bombers for only part of the way and carried out diversions elsewhere. This Blenheim of 114 Squadron was photographed en route to Knapsack.

AIR 37/47

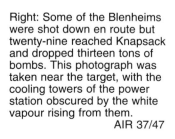

Right: Some of the Blenheims were shot down en route but twenty-nine reached Knapsack and dropped thirteen tons of bombs. This photograph was taken near the target, with the cooling towers of the power station obscured by the white vapour rising from them.

AIR 37/47

in the war, the efforts were on only a small scale in 1941.

Apart from the continuation of night bombing, an intensification of the RAF's daylight attacks which had begun earlier in the year took place. These were known as 'Rhubarbs' when carried out solely as fighter sweeps, with the purpose of challenging enemy aircraft to combat. When a large fighter force known as a 'Beehive' escorted a few light bombers, the operations were called 'Circuses'. These attacks usually took place over northern France and sometimes Belgium, with the objects of destroying enemy aircraft on the ground or in the air, bombing airfield buildings or railway networks, and generally forcing the enemy to keep strong defensive forces in the west.

But the RAF fighters had only a limited range, since they had not been fitted with drop-tanks, and they could not escort light bombers on raids deeper into enemy territory. Thus the light bombers were left to their own devices when attacking targets in Germany or sometimes the Netherlands. Where such attacks were directed against German coastal shipping, they were known as 'Roadsteads'. These anti-shipping operations augmented those made by the Beauforts and Hudsons of Coastal Command, and frequently resulted in heavy losses for minor gains.

Above: A Blenheim leaving Knapsack at low level, with flak bursts in the sky. In all, ten of the original fifty-four Blenheims were shot down by flak or fighters. Several diversionary attacks were made by Bomber Command, losing two more Blenheims. Fighter Command flew 175 sorties, claiming ten German fighters destroyed but losing six Spitfires.

AIR 37/47

Right: Seventeen Blenheims reached the two Fortuna power stations at Quadrath in Cologne and dropped six and a half tons of bombs. This photograph of Fortuna II was taken by an aircraft of the second wave to attack. It shows a direct hit in the centre, on one of the towers in the conveyor plant.

AIR 16/514

Daylight Bombing

During the six weeks after the German invasion of Russia, about 8,000 sorties were made by RAF fighters and about 375 by bombers. It was claimed that 322 enemy aircraft were destroyed in these operations, but a post-war examination of German records indicated that the true figure was only 81. The equivalent figure for RAF losses was

Left: On 21 September 1941, twelve Blenheim IVs from 18 and 139 Squadrons, with twelve squadrons of Spitfires and two of Hurricanes, took part in a 'Circus' operation against the power station and chemical works at Gosnay, about three miles south-west of Béthune in France. The attack was very successful, with direct hits on both targets. All the bombers returned but the fighters were engaged in a major air battle, claiming twenty Messerschmitt Bf109s and one unidentified aircraft destroyed for the loss of eleven Spitfires and one Hurricane.

AIR 37/47

Above: Twelve Blenheim IVs from 107 and 114 Squadron, escorted by three squadrons of Spitfires, attacked the Iron and Steel works at Ijmuiden in the Netherlands on 21 August 1941. Bomb bursts were seen on the rolling mill warehouse and a cooling tower, and another close to the blast furnace. All the Blenheims returned but two Spitfires failed to return.

AIR 37/47

Right: At 10.56 hours on 2 September 1941, three Blenheim IVs of 139 Squadron, escorted by two squadrons of Spitfires and one of Hurricanes, attacked a convoy about four miles west of Zeebrugge in Belgium. The Blenheims bombed a 4,000 ton merchant vessel while the Hurricanes shot up the escort vessels. The Spitfire pilots reported that they destroyed two Messerschmitt Bf109s. One Blenheim was shot down by flak. This photograph shows smoke pouring from a hit aft of the funnel of the merchant vessel, while there are two splashes from near misses on the port side.

AIR 16/514

Above: Six Blenheim IVs were despatched with fourteen squadrons of Spitfires to attack the power station at Sylkens, east of Ostend in Belgium, on 3 October 1941. The bombs overshot but hit warehouses and the dock area. All bombers returned but some of the Spitfires were in combat with Messerschmitt Bf109s, claiming one destroyed for the loss of three of their own number.

AIR 37/744

123. However, it seems that the operations did force the Luftwaffe to withdraw some fighter pilots from the east although the German units were able to make good their losses with ease. The RAF reduced the scale of these sweeps in August 1941, but they continued until the invasion of Normandy took place.

On 7 December 1941, the Japanese attacked Pearl Harbour and the USA was at war. Hitler was unwise enough to declare war on the USA and the extension of the conflict which followed justified the title of the Second World War.

6 German Capital Ships

After the fall of France in June 1940, the chief naval station of the country, Brest in Brittany, became a prime target for both Bomber and Coastal Commands. This port harboured U-boats and warships which threatened Britain's very existence. Sinkings of merchant ships in the Atlantic during late 1940 and early 1941 became so serious that Winston Churchill wondered if Britain could prevail the war.

The huge battleships *Scharnhorst* and *Gneisenau* arrived at Brest on 22 March 1941 for refitting, having sunk or captured 115,622 tons of shipping since leaving Germany on 23 January. The presence of these warships was reported by wireless to the British Admiralty two days later by a member of the French Resistance, Lieutenant de Vaisseau Jean Phillipon. Confirmation came from a sortie made by a Spitfire of the RAF's No 1 Photographic Reconnaissance Unit. The RAF intensified its bombing of the port and also dropped magnetic mines in its approaches whenever the weather permitted.

Above: '*Gneisenau* attacked by Flying Officer K. Campbell' by unknown war artist
INF 3/424

Left: The effect of the defences at Brest is exaggerated by this time exposure taken by an F24 camera with the aid of a flash bomb dropped by Wellington IC of 115 Squadron from Marham in Norfolk on the night of 4/5 May 1941 over the Porte de Commerce. Nevertheless, the combination of coloured tracer, heavy flak and searchlights at Brest produced a dazzling and fearsome effect when bombing at medium level. The photo-interpreters were able to identify: 1) A flak battery; 2) Tracer; 3) Fogging of the negative by searchlights. Bomber Command despatched 97 aircraft on that night. All returned safely but there were no hits on the battleships.
AIR 14/3696

Above: The daylight attack of 18 December 1941, showing two Halifaxes over the target.
AIR 34/239

Left: This enlarged photograph of Brest was taken on 18 December 1941. It shows (1) *Scharnhorst* (2) *Gneisenau* (3) an incomplete dry dock (4) camouflage being extended to cover burnt-out oil tanks. Both battleships are partially covered with white camouflage, evidently incomplete.

AIR 34/743

Churchill ordered that the Royal Navy and the RAF should make every effort to destroy the warships, regardless of risks and sacrifices. By this time, Brest was believed to be the most heavily defended place in occupied Europe. The raids on the port damaged the docks but did not score hits on the battleships. However, on the night of 4/5 April a 500lb semi-armour piercing bomb fell into the shallow water in Dry Dock No 8, where *Gneisenau* was berthed – but failed to explode. Divers went down and reported that it was alongside her hull. Preparations were made to move the battleship out of the dock, which was then flooded. On the same night, another bomb fell on the Continental Hotel, killing several of the German Naval Staff who were billetted there. At noon on 5 April the battleship was towed carefully out of the dock into the outer harbour, the Rade Abri, and moored 400 yards south of the dock. She was photographed two hours later by a Spitfire of No 1 Photographic Reconnaissance Unit. Coastal Command was ordered to attack.

Right: *Gneisenau* at Kiel on 2 March 1942, after the crippling attack by Bomber Command on the night 26/27 February 1942. Much of the deck plating has been removed from the bows.

AIR 34/239

Left: 'Attack by Wellingtons of 149 Squadron on *Scharnhorst* and *Gneisenau*' by Mark Postlethwaite

Wellington IC serial R1593, flown by Squadron Leader Reginald Sawrey-Cookson, was one of eight from 149 Squadron which attacked on the night of 30/31 March 1941, taking off from Mildenhall in Suffolk at 19.33 hours. Cookson was so determined to hit the targets that he made 10–12 runs over Brest before dropping his bombs in two sticks. Bursts were seen on the north side of the dock. In spite of intense flak, all the 109 aircraft which bombed on that night – Wellingtons, Blenheims, Hampdens and Manchesters – returned safely. The battleships were not hit but the docks were badly damaged.

Six Beaufort Is of 22 Squadron prepared to take off from St Eval in Cornwall in the early hours of 6 April 1941, three carrying Mark XII torpedoes and three carrying land mines. The weather was atrocious and two of the latter became bogged in mud. One aircraft, serial N1016 flown by Flying Officer Kenneth Campbell, found the target. He made a solo attack at 05.16 hours in murky twilight. The defences did not see the Beaufort until the torpedo was dropped, but intense flak opened up when it banked away. The aircraft crashed into the harbour. The Germans raised it and gave the four men a military funeral. A posthumous award of the Victoria Cross was gazetted to Kenneth Campbell on 13 March 1942.

On the night of 10/11 April 1941, the same battleship was hit by four bombs dropped by Bomber Command, killing fifty sailors and injuring ninety others. One Wellington was lost from the fifty-three despatched. Then, on 1 June 1941, the heavy cruiser *Prinz Eugen* also arrived at Brest, having parted company from the battleship *Bismarck* before the latter was sunk by the Royal Navy on 27 May. The cruiser was badly damaged on the night of 1/2 July 1941 during a raid by fifty-two Wellingtons of Bomber Command. A bomb exploded inside her hull, killing sixty-one sailors, wounding thirty-two, and putting her out of action for three months. Two Wellingtons were lost.

The bombing attacks continued but *Scharnhorst* was refitted and on 23 July 1941 sailed south to La Pallice for testing

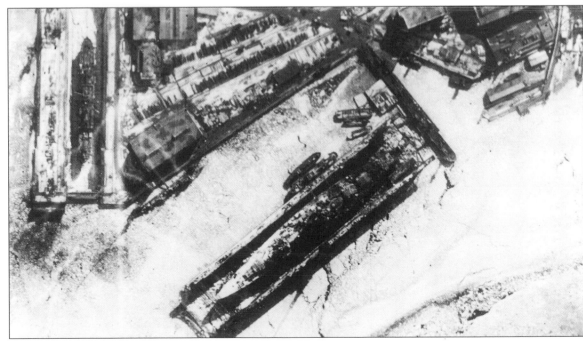

and gunnery practice. A tanker was left in her place, but the battleship was identified by reconnaissance aircraft in her new port. During the following day, Bomber Command went to both ports. A hundred aircraft raided Brest while fifteen Halifaxes went to La Pallice. Flak and German fighters shot down twelve of the force sent to Brest while other fighters destroyed five of the Halifaxes sent to La Pallice and damaged all the others. But *Scharnhorst* was hit by five bombs, three of which passed right through her. She limped back to Brest, requiring four months for repairs.

Bomber Command was diverted to the German heartland for the next five months and made only occasional attacks on Brest. However, 121 aircraft were despatched to the port on the night of 17/18 December 1941. No hits were scored on the warships and one bomber was lost. These were followed by a daylight attack by forty-seven bombers during the following morning. Six aircraft were shot down but *Gneisenau* was damaged once more.

By February 1942, Hitler had become tired of the inactivity of these capital ships in the French port. He believed they were of more use in helping to repel a potential attack

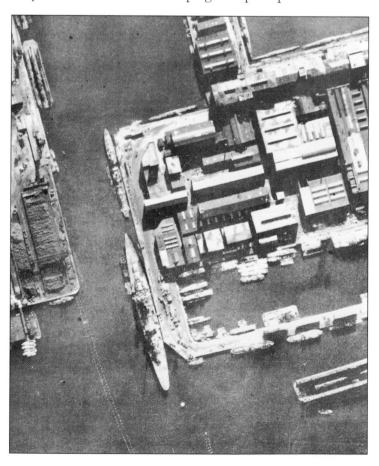

Left: The heavy cruiser *Prinz Eugen* on 14 October 1942, lying at the entrance to the inner dockyard basin of Kiel. Her stern has been repaired after the hit by a torpedo fired by a Royal Navy submarine off Trondheim on 23 February 1942. Booms protect the entrance to the basin.

AIR 34/234

Above: *Gneisenau* (centre) in floating dock at Gdynia on 5 October 1942, with her forepart dismantled and her entire armament removed. The arrow in the lower part of the photograph indicates the aircraft carrier *Graf Zeppelin*, heavily camouflaged. This warship was never completed.

AIR 34/234

Left: *Scharnhorst* (centre) on 5 October 1942, berthed alongside the French Wharf at Gdynia. Photo-interpreters picked out two new flak positions forward of the main control tower. The liner *Potsdam* is berthed behind her, both protected by a double line boom. After two unsuccessful forays when she was identified by British surveillance, *Scharnhorst* left Gdynia in early March 1943 and reached Altenfjord in Norway.

AIR 34/234

by the allies on Norway. On the foggy night of 11 February 1942, *Scharnhorst*, *Gneisenau* and *Prinz Eugen* slipped out of Brest and dashed up the English Channel. They were escorted by a flotilla of destroyers, torpedo boats and E-boats, with relays of German fighters forming an umbrella overhead. Although British Intelligence was aware of such an eventuality, there was a combination of accidents and the armada was not detected until near Le Touquet. Coastal batteries scored no hits. The Fleet Air Arm despatched six Swordfish but all were shot down. Royal Navy destroyers were unable to penetrate the enemy screen. Bomber Command despatched 242 aircraft but fifteen were lost for no results. Coastal Command despatched fifty-two bombers, mostly torpedo-carrying, with no successes and at the loss of two aircraft.

The only damage sustained by the capital ships was when *Scharnhorst* struck two of the RAF's magnetic mines and *Gneisenau* hit another, but both were able to continue their journeys to Germany. Britain was humiliated while Hitler was jubilant, but this success availed him little. The cruiser *Prinz Eugen* was torpedoed off Trondheim on 23 February 1942 by a British submarine and remained unserviceable for the rest of the war. A bombing attack on Kiel during the night of 26/27 February 1942 resulted in the crippling of *Gneisenau* and the deaths of 116 sailors. Her guns were transferred to coastal defences and her hull was eventually sunk as a blockship in Gdynia. The Royal Navy sank *Scharnhorst* off the North Cape of Norway on 26 December 1943.

7 Combined Operation

In the early morning of 27 December 1941, British forces launched their first combined operation against territory in occupied Europe. A cruiser and four destroyers escorted two assault ships carrying Commandos to Vaagsö, an island off the Norwegian coast north of Bergen. Bomber Command provided the air strike force. Ten Hampden Is of 50 Squadron from Skellingthorpe in Lincolnshire took part, taking off from Wick in Caithness. At 08.58 hours, three of these bombed a German gun position on nearby Maaloy Island, to protect a landing party, while seven others laid a smoke screen to cover a landing party on South Vaagsö. Two of the latter Hampdens were shot down by ground defences. Long-range fighter protection was provided ini-

Right: 'Attack on Herdla' by Mark Postlethwaite

Below: This photograph shows small clouds of bomb impacts on Herdla airfield and a Messerschmitt Bf109 (top left) taking off. In the exhaust smoke behind the Bf109 is an Arado Ar96B training monoplane used at Herdla for communications, while on the runway across the photograph (below the Bf109) is a Focke-Wulf Fw58 utility aircraft.
AIR 14/3696

tially by four Blenheim IVFs of Coastal Command's 254 Squadron from Wick, but one of these was shot down by a German fighter and another badly damaged. As a diversion, six Blenheim IVs of Bomber Command's 110 Squadron took off at 08.50 hours from Lossiemouth in Morayshire. These attacked a convoy in the Stavanger area, but four were shot down.

To provide another diversion, thirteen Blenheim IVs of 114 Squadron based at West Raynham in Norfolk took off from Lossiemouth in Morayshire. Led by Wing Commander John F.G. Jenkins, they made an attack at 12.02 hours on the fighter airfield of Herdla, 80 miles to the south of Vaagsö. This was a base for the Messerschmitt Bf109s of 3./*Jagdgeschwader* 77 and 1. (Z)/*Jagdgeschwader* 77. Two of these fighters had just been rearmed after helping to repel the attack on Vaagsö, while others had been sent off to protect the convoy.

Each Blenheim carried four 250lb general-purpose bombs with 11 second delay action, plus some 25lb incendiaries. They swept over the airfield at Herdla at 250 feet, aiming at the timber runways, while the air gunners in the turrets opened fire on enemy gun emplacements. As the bombs exploded, one Messerschmitt was seen to turn over and roll into a crater. Heavy flak was inaccurate but light flak came much closer. Two Blenheims collided, possibly because one had been hit by this light flak, and both crashed into Lake Instetjörna close to Herdla, killing all crew members. The other Blenheims returned safely. Later reconnaissance photographs showed at least twenty craters in and around the runways, with one workshop vehicle shot up. The Germans recorded two ground crew killed and three wounded.

Below: The delay-action bombs exploding on Herdla airfield, with splashes from flak in the water.

AIR 34/745

The Commando landings at Vaagsö went well. Further fighter cover was provided by four successive sorties of Coastal Command's Beaufighter ICs, totalling fourteen aircraft, operating from Sumburgh in the Shetlands. These drove off and destroyed or damaged German aircraft, but one Beaufighter of 236 Squadron was lost. Royal Navy warships sank five merchant ships, two trawlers and a tug, totalling about 16,000 tons. The landing parties destroyed industrial plants and defence installations, captured German troops and 'Quislings' (Norwegian traitors), and brought back Norwegian patriots to join the armed forces. They suffered only light casualties before withdrawing in good order to Scapa Flow. The Germans buried twenty-five of their own dead. The British considered that the operation had been very successful, although ten RAF aircraft had been lost. It was the forerunner of many combined operations on occupied Europe.

8 The Bruneval Raid

It was known from photo-reconnaissance as early as 22 February 1941 that the Germans had set up radar stations named *Freya* along the coasts of occupied Europe. It was also believed that smaller paraboloidal equipment known as *Würzburg* had been installed, from interceptions which could be heard on wavelengths of about 53 centimetres. There was further evidence of this from a sortie made on 2 August 1941 by a Spitfire flown by Flight Lieutenant P.H. Watts of No 1 Photographic Reconnaissance Unit at Benson in Oxfordshire. A photograph showed a tiny dot beside a former sanatorium on the headland of Cap d'Antifer, near the village of Bruneval twelve miles from Le Havre.

Closer photographs from low level were required and on 5 December 1941 another sortie was made by Flight Lieutenant A.E. 'Tony' Hill in Spitfire VD serial R7044, resulting in some excellent obliques. British scientists, including those of the Telecommunications Research Establishment at Swanage in Dorset, needed to confirm the identity of the apparatus and to discover German techniques on wavelengths of about 50 cms as well as any of their anti-jamming measures. A landing party was required to capture the receiver, transmitter and presentation gear, and perhaps bring back some prisoners.

This plan was given on 1 January 1942 to Lord Louis Mountbatten, Commodore Combined Operations. He worked with Major-General F.A.M. 'Boy' Browning, who commanded all airborne forces. The Naval Force Commander was Commander F.N. Cook, the Military Force Commander was Major J.D. Frost of the Cameronians, while the RAF Commander was Group Captain Sir Nigel Norman. The Supreme Commander was Admiral Sir William James, and the enterprise was code-named operation 'Biting'.

The RAF's No 51 Squadron at Dishforth in Yorkshire, equipped with Armstrong Whitworth Whitley Vs and commanded by Wing Commander P.C. Pickard, was taken off normal operations for training preparatory to the operation. In 1 February 1942 a radar technician in the RAF, Flight Sergeant Charles W.F. Cox, was summoned to the Air

Above: 'Casing the Joint' by Charles J. Thompson

Flight Lieutenant A.E. 'Tony' Hill of No 1 Photographic Reconnaissance Unit making a low-level sortie in Spitfire PR IV serial R7044 over the *Würzburg* radar installation at Bruneval on 5 December 1941.

Right: A low-level oblique of the cliffs near the village of Bruneval, taken on 2 August 1941 from Spitfire I serial N3117 of No 1 Photographic Reconnaissance Unit, flown by Flight Lieutenant P.H. Watts from RAF Benson in Oxfordshire. Photo-interpreters picked out a tiny speck, as arrowed, as a possible *Würzburg* radar installation.
AIR 20/1631

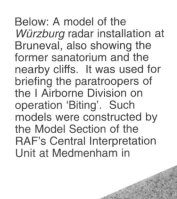

Below: A model of the *Würzburg* radar installation at Bruneval, also showing the former sanatorium and the nearby cliffs. It was used for briefing the paratroopers of the I Airborne Division on operation 'Biting'. Such models were constructed by the Model Section of the RAF's Central Interpretation Unit at Medmenham in Buckinghamshire. They were large but made of rubber so that they could be rolled up and transported.

DEFE 2/102

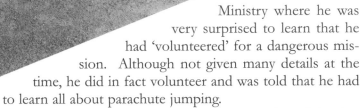

Ministry where he was very surprised to learn that he had 'volunteered' for a dangerous mission. Although not given many details at the time, he did in fact volunteer and was told that he had to learn all about parachute jumping.

Cox arrived a few days later at No 1 Parachute School at RAF Ringway, near Manchester. Here he was told that he had to help bring back a radiolocation device from somewhere in France. He began an intensive course of jumping, firstly from balloons and then from Whitleys, in company with some very tough but likeable soldiers. More training followed with I Airborne Division at RAF Netheravon in Wiltshire and at RAF Thruxton in Hampshire. Meanwhile, the RAF's Central Interpretation Unit at Medmenham in Buckinghamshire prepared a photographic mosaic of the target. On 20 February, Cox and an Army officer went to the Air Ministry to inspect these and be told about the operation.

At 22.00 hours on 27 February 1942, the order to emplane was given at RAF Thruxton. Wing Commander Pickard was impressed with the qualities of the 120 paratroopers, most of whom came from Scottish regiments. They marched round the perimeter track to the sound of pipes, before each section of ten men entered one of the twelve black Whitleys. The paratroopers cheered when the aircraft took off at around 22.15 hours and began to play cards or sing. Cox was in aircraft No 6 and gave a rendition of *The Rose of Tralee*.

The Whitleys formed up in sections of four over Selsey Bill and flew low over the Channel, reaching the French coast at Fécamp. Accurate tracer from cannon fire came up to them, and three aircraft were hit. There was no serious damage but some aircraft lost formation during evasive

Left: One of the magnificent photographs brought back by Flight Lieutenant Tony Hill on 5 December 1941, showing the *Würzburg* radar installation beside the former sanatorium at Bruneval. The British photo-interpreters named it a 'bowl-fire' radar, owing to its appearance.

AIR 20/1631

Below: The five-man crew of an Armstrong Whitworth Whitley, checking the aircraft preparatory to taking off.
INF 2/42

action. Meanwhile, aircraft of Bomber and Fighter Commands made diversionary sorties.

In Cox's Whitley, Major Frost passed round a flask of rum while the men checked their static lines. The order to jump was given at 00.20 hours and the ten men went quickly through a hole in the floor from which the retractable 'dustbin' turret had been removed. Equipment containers were also dropped. The aircraft was at only 600 feet and Cox soon landed on snow-covered ground. The men assembled in moonlight and unpacked the containers. They moved towards the assembly point, pulling trolleys intended to carry dismantled equipment. From there, they went on to the radar station.

There were two other sections of paratroopers. One was ordered to secure a nearby beach for withdrawal by sea, but the men were dropped almost two miles out of position and they had to make their way to the operational area. The other section was ordered to cover the withdrawal and the men attacked trenches and dugouts near the village of Bruneval.

Cox and a sapper set to work on the *Würzburg* apparatus, which was situated in a pit surrounded by a low turf wall.

Above: A stick of paratroopers adjusting their parachute harnesses before entering a Whitley of 295 Squadron at Netheravon in Wiltshire on 2 October 1942, on a training exercise.

INF 2/42

Right: Paratroopers being briefed by Major the Lord Lovat for operation 'Biting'. Lord Lovat, captain of Lovat Scouts, became a legendary leader of Commandos in the Second World War, although he did not take part in this raid.

DEFE 2/103

Right: Seamen on a destroyer cheering the men returning in assault landing craft from the beach near Bruneval, at dawn on 28 February 1942. Most of the men were then taken on board and the craft were towed back to England.

DEFE 2/102

The Bruneval Raid

They used screwdrivers and hacksaws but these proved inadequate, while light from their torches brought a hail of bullets from nearby woods. Most of this fire was too high but the troops soon began to rip equipment out by brute force, at the expense of causing damage. The withdrawal began after only ten minutes, and it was found easier to carry the equipment on shoulders than on the trolleys. Wounded men were also helped in the retreat. A timed explosive was left in the radar installation, which duly blew up.

The beach chosen for the evacuation was about 750 yards away but the defences were still occupied by Germans. However, the third section of paratroopers arrived and attacked with the warcry of the Seaforth Highlanders, capturing the guardroom and strong point after a stiff fight, while the other soldiers gave covering fire.

Before these engagements took place, the Infantry Assault Ship HMS *Prins Albert* and five motor gunboats had arrived twenty miles off Bruneval, having left Portsmouth at

Below: Paratroopers returning
from the raid on Bruneval.
DEFE 2/102

Above: The two German
prisoners being searched.
DEFE 2/103

Below: The transmitter/receiver of the *Würzburg* radar brought back from the raid on Bruneval.

17.15 hours. Eight landing craft had been lowered and thirty-two officers and men from the Royal Fusiliers and South Wales Borderers entered these, to cover the withdrawal. They beached at 03.15 hours and Bren guns opened up on a German position on the cliff top. The paratroopers waded out and embarked with five wounded, leaving behind two dead and six missing. They brought with them the aerial framework, the transmitter/receiver, the intermediate frequency amplifier and the pulse generator. There were two prisoners, one of whom was a radar operator. The RAF records state that there had been one other prisoner, a woman operator in the Luftwaffe, who was 'given a good spanking and then released'.

There were no casualties among the boat parties. It was estimated that the Germans lost 30–35 dead, but enemy records indicate that this was exaggerated. The troops boarded the motor gunboats and the landing craft were taken in tow. All arrived home at about 16.35 hours, under relays of protection from Fighter Command.

The German equipment was examined and a scheme to confuse its signals was devised. Labels on parts of the equipment enabled the British to determine places of manufacture and probable output. Operation 'Biting' was classed as a great success. Among those decorated was Flight Sergeant Cox, who received a Military Medal. 'Bruneval' became the first battle honour awarded to the Parachute Regiment.

9 Bombing Policy

On 9 July 1941 the Air Officer Commanding-in-Chief of Bomber Command, Air Marshal Sir Richard Peirse, received written instructions to the effect that his Command was to concentrate firstly on disrupting the German transportation system and secondly to destroy the morale of the civil population, including the industrial workers. For some months the strategic bombing at night was directed primarily at German industrial cities in the Ruhr and along the Rhine, with occasional diversions to U-boat bases in France and the German warships in Brest.

This directive coincided with the introduction of new heavy bombers, the twin-engined Avro Manchester and the formidable Short Stirling and the Handley Page Halifax,

Below: After heavy losses on daylight operations during the first months of the war, Vickers Wellington Is of Bomber Command were confined to night operations. Black undersurfaces were extended partly up the sides of fuselages. By December 1940, this black was extended further to cover three-quarters of the fuselage as well as the fin and rudder. These Wellington Is were photographed en route to Germany.

INF 2/42

Above: 'Sergeant J.A. Ward putting out fire' by unknown war artist

Sergeant James A. Ward, a New Zealander in 75 (RNZAF) Squadron based at Feltwell in Norfolk, was awarded a Victoria Cross for an amazing feat accomplished on the night of 7/8 July 1941. He flew as second pilot in Wellington IC serial L7818 captained by a Canadian, Squadron Leader R.P. Widdowson. This was one of ten aircraft contributed by the squadron to a total of forty-nine Wellingtons despatched by Bomber Command to raid Münster. The raid was carried out successfully but on the return flight the bomber was attacked by a Messerschmitt Bf110 night-fighter which raked the fuselage and wounded the rear gunner, Sergeant A.J.R. Box. Nevertheless, fire from the rear turret sent the enemy down with smoke pouring from an engine.

Soon afterwards, burning fuel from a severed petrol pipe in the starboard engine of the Wellington began to set fire to the surrounding fabric. The crew tore fabric from the fuselage and tried to put out the fire with an extinguisher, but were thwarted by the slipstream. Ward ensured that his parachute was tightly strapped, tied round his waist a rope which was held by another crew member, and removed the astrodome cover. Then he clambered down the side and out to the wing by kicking footholds in the fabric, and tried to beat out the flames with a cockpit cover. This was partially successful but he needed all his remaining strength against the slipstream to re-enter the Wellington. Fortunately, the fire died out, since most of the surrounding fabric had been destroyed.

Widdowson managed to nurse the Wellington back to England, where he made an emergency landing at Newmarket in Suffolk. The aircraft was so badly damaged that it was written off. Widdowson was awarded a DFC, Box a DFM, and Ward's Victoria Cross was gazetted on 5 August 1941. Ward was killed on 15 September 1941 when the captain of Wellington X3205 which failed to return from a raid on Hamburg.

INF 3/434

although at this stage there were only a few of these and they were suffering from technical problems. Most of the night bombing was still carried out with the older Whitleys. Hampdens and Wellingtons. Tactical daylight bombing continued with 'Circus' operations against targets in France and the Low Countries, and in July 1941 the Douglas Boston began to replace the Blenheim as the standard light bomber. This was a more suitable aircraft, with better armament and a heavier bomb load, but casualties on daylight operations were always severe, in spite of swarms of fighter escorts.

The strategic bombers also began to suffer heavier casualties, primarily from the increased number and effectiveness of German night-fighters. Most of these were based in the Netherlands where their commander, General Josef Kammhuber, had placed a continuous belt of searchlights behind the coast, ready to illuminate the bomber streams. He also began to install a system of ground control stations which directed the night-fighters, by then fitted with airborne radar sets.

Moreover, in late August 1941 a very disturbing report was presented to the Air Ministry and the War Cabinet. This was an analysis of the strategic bombing campaign compiled

Left: 'Bombs falling on dockside shed at Lübeck' by war artist Roy Nockolds

A major raid took place against the Baltic port of Lübeck on the night of 28/29 March 1942 when Bomber Command despatched 234 aircraft, including Wellingtons, Hampdens, Stirlings and Manchesters. This painting shows one of the Stirlings. Twelve aircraft were lost, but the raid caused the destruction of 62 per cent of the buildings in the ancient Hanseatic port.
INF 3/1607

military production and achieving negligible results. On 13 November 1941, Sir Richard Peirse was ordered to limit his winter campaign while the matter was discussed. By this time, however, the war had widened to include the USA and Japan, and Britain had to play her part. The Chief of the Air Staff, Air Chief Marshal Sir Charles Portal, managed to convince the War Cabinet that if forty-three German industrial cities could be destroyed with an increased bombing force, Germany would collapse within six months. His arguments prevailed, although a request for an increase to 4,000 bombers was rejected as impracticable.

Below: Fornebu airfield, near Oslo, photographed while covered with snow on 9 February 1942. Photo-interpeters were able to pick out the outline of the main runway from A to AA, while the aircraft were identified as Junkers Ju52s, Messerschmitt Bf109s and Focke-Wulf Fw58s, with a Heinkel He111 and a Junkers Ju88.
AIR 34/743

by D.M. Butt of the War Cabinet Secretariat. Based on over 4,000 photographs taken by night cameras during the previous June and July, it showed that only a quarter of the bombs had fallen within five miles of the target on most nights, increased to a third over Germany in full moon periods.

The problem was one of navigation. The crews had no radio beams, while sextants could be used only on clear nights and in any event the best astro fixes were accurate only within a radius of about five miles. The crews depended on dead reckoning navigation and visual observations. Coastlines and rivers could be picked out on clear nights, but a blacked-out city or town was difficult to see. A crew which brought back their bombs could be in disgrace, and the sortie did not count as operational. The bombs were often dropped by time and distance from a pinpoint and seldom hit the target.

This report threw the future of strategic bombing into doubt. It was absorbing a high proportion of Britain's

Below: 'Squadron Leader J.D. Nettleton attacking Augsburg' by unknown war artist

This impression of an attack by Avro Lancasters (bombing at an impossibly low level) followed national publicity of Bomber Command's attempts to use these new machines on a daylight raid against a vital target on 17 April 1942. Six of 44 (Rhodesia) Squadron at Waddington and six more from 97 Squadron at Woodhall Spa, both in Lincolnshire, were ordered to attack the M.A.N. factory at Augsburg, which manufactured diesel engines for the German armed forces. The bombers had to cross 500 miles of enemy territory to reach their target, flying at 500 feet. Four of 44 Squadron's Lancasters were brought down by Messerschmitt Bf109s but Squadron Leader John D. Nettleton, a South African in the RAF, led the rest to Augsburg, with his own aircraft riddled with holes. All bombed the factory but three more were shot down. The attack was in the late afternoon, and the surviving five Lancasters flew home in the dark. Machine-tool shops, a forging shop and the main assembly shop were damaged, but Bomber Command's experiment with daylight raids against Germany was discontinued.

The Victoria Cross to Nettleton was gazetted on 24 April 1942 while other survivors received the DSO, the DFC or the DFM. Wing Commander Nettleton was killed on the night of 13 July 1943 while commanding 44 (Rhodesia) Squadron during a night raid on Turin. His Lancaster was shot down by a night-fighter over the Channel on the return flight.

INF 3/451

Above: The Renault Works at Billancourt, west of the centre Paris, photographed on 4 March 1942 after a raid by 235 aircraft of Bomber Command during the previous night. This was the largest concentration of bombers so far deployed in the war. Experienced crews went in first, thus marking the target for the others. Over 300 bombs fell on the factory, causing widespread devastation including the destruction of almost 2,300 trucks. Unfortunately, some of the bombs fell on nearby dwellings and killed 367 French people. Only one aircraft was lost.

AIR 34/743

Left: Twenty-two Douglas Bostons from 88 and 107 Squadrons bombed ships at Le Havre on 26 March 1942, scoring several hits but losing one of their number. They were escorted by five squadrons of Spitfires, which claimed eight enemy aircraft destroyed. Two Spitfires were lost.

AIR 37/47

Above: Twelve Bostons of 88 Squadron carried out an accurate attack against Mondeville power station, about four miles east of Caen in France, on 14 April 1942. No bombers were lost. They were escorted by eight squadrons of Spitfires, which claimed three enemy fighters destroyed for the loss of two of their number.

AIR 37/47

On 14 February 1942, Bomber Command was directed to concentrate its efforts on the built-up areas of these German cities, in order to destroy factories and the morale of the workers. This modification of the directive of 9 July 1941 inaugurated the policy known as 'area bombing'. Sir Richard Pierse was replaced with Air Marshal Arthur Harris, a trenchant and single-minded commander whose name became identified with the policy he was ordered to implement.

Above: As part of the diversion for the daylight raid by Lancasters against Augsburg on 17 April 1942, six Bostons from 88 Squadron bombed the shipyards at Grand Quevilly from 10,000 feet, scoring hits on ships. Nine squadrons of Spitfires accompanied the Bostons but there were no combats and all returned.

AIR 37/47

Above Right: Four attacks took place on the Baltic port of Rostock: 161 aircraft on 23/24 April 1942, 125 aircraft on the following night, 128 on the night after that, and the last on 26/27 April. These resulted in the destruction of about sixty per cent of the main town area and gave rise to the expression 'terror raids' used by the Germans until the end of the war. A total of only eight aircraft was lost on these four raids. Some of the bombers were sent to the Heinkel Works in the southern suburbs of the town. This photograph shows hits through the roof of main assembly shop, with other damage to nearby buildings and sheds.

AIR 34/741

By this time, the new four-engined Avro Lancaster was beginning to enter service. Harris could muster only about 450 night bombers, but the heavy element with its greater bomb-carrying capacity was on the increase. Equally important, in March 1942 the airborne aid known as Gee was introduced, a radar device which enabled the navigator to plot his position accurately on a special map, provided the aircraft was within about 245 miles of the transmitters.

Harris tried one daylight raid with the new Lancaster, against Augsburg on 17 April 1942, but this was not a success. But his attacks at night against Lübeck on 28/29 March, Essen in March and April, and Rostock in April, resulted in enormous devastation. The continuation of Bomber Command, with growing power and effectiveness, became assured.

10 Fighter Sweeps

After the success of Fighter Command in the Battle of Britain, the new Air Officer Commanding-in-Chief, Air Chief Marshal Sir Sholto Douglas, expected that his squadrons would have to fight a similar defensive battle in the spring and summer of 1941. The German invasion of Russia on 22 June altered the circumstances, for it became apparent that there was no possibility of a major attack against Britain. Fighter Command was on the offensive.

By this time, many of the Hurricane squadrons had been re-equipped with Spitfires while others were converting to fighter-bomber duties. Two Hurricane squadrons were sent to Russia where the pilots operated over the Eastern Front before handing over their aircraft to their Allies. By the end of 1941, most home-based fighter squadrons were equipped with the Spitfire VB, introduced during the previous February as an improved version of the Mark I and designed mainly for defensive duties.

The Spitfire VB was powered by a Rolls-Royce Merlin 45 engine and armed with two 20mm Hispano cannons plus four .303 inch Browning machine guns. With a more powerful engine than the Mark I, it was designed to give battle to new German aircraft expected to have improved performance at higher altitudes. It was originally intended as a stop-gap, awaiting a version with a pressurised cabin, but became the main production version after the invasion of Russia.

During the Battle of Britain, the main adversary of the Spitfires and Hurricanes had been the Messerschmitt Bf109E, but in late 1940 the Luftwaffe began to receive a new fighter. This was the Focke-Wulf FW190, a fast and manoeuvrable aircraft with an excellent performance at both high and low altitudes. Several variants of this outstanding fighter were produced and the Spitfire pilots learned to respect its qualities, including the firepower from the two 20 mm cannons and four machine-guns of the FW190A-3. This variant was powered by a BMW 801D engine achieving 1,700 hp in combat.

The exact performance of this new fighter was not known by the RAF until one landed in error at RAF Pembrey in Carmarthenshire on 23 June 1942. Given RAF markings, it was tested during the following month by the

Above: 'British and Russian Fighters' by war artist Jobson

On 7 September 1941, Hurricanes of 81 and 134 Squadrons flew from the aircraft carrier HMS *Argus* and landed at Vaenga in North Russia, where they formed the RAF's No 151 Wing and operated with the Russian Air Force. This painting shows a Junkers Ju87 going down in flames, with Russian fighters overhead. The Hurricanes were handed over to the Russians a few weeks later and the RAF men returned to Britain in November.

INF 3/1622

Above: Pilots attending an early morning briefing prior to a sweep by a fighter wing over enemy territory. The room displays photographs, maps and models of aircraft for recognition purposes.

INF 2/45

Below: An armourer checking one of the cannons of a Spitfire VB, which was armed with two 20 mm Hispano cannons, each with 60 rounds, and four Browning .303 inch machine-guns, each with 350 rounds.

INF 2/45

Above: Bicycles were in very common use at RAF stations, mainly because of the long distances around the airfields and the dispersal of aircraft. Ground crews used them to and from the aircraft they serviced while pilots could park them near their crew rooms.

INF 2/45

Below: Pilots wearing their 'Mae West' life-jackets and flying boots, waiting for the order to take off.

INF 2/45

Air Fighting Development Unit at Duxford in Cambridgeshire, in mock combat with a Spitfire VB. It was found to be faster than the Spitfire at all levels, to have better acceleration, a better rate of climb and dive, and superior manoeuvrability except in tight turning circles.

Another problem with the single-engined RAF fighters was their inability to escort bombers sufficiently far into enemy territory. Unarmed photo-reconnaissance Spitfires, fitted with extra fuel tanks in the wings and known as 'flying petrol bowsers', could fly as far as Prague and back, but these could not operate as bomber escorts. The need for such escorts prompted Winston Churchill to write to the Chief of Air Staff, Air Chief Marshal Sir Charles Portal, on

Below: A pilot saying what he hopes is *au revoir* to a black dog mascot before starting the engine. Black dogs were considered lucky.

INF 2/45

Right: A pilot checking his R/T and flying controls, attended by a ground mechanic.

INF 2/45

Above: Section after section leaves the airfield on the operation.

INF 2/45

Left: Destruction of a Focke-Wulf FW190 on 4 May 1942 on a sweep over Ambleteuse in France, showing the pilot baling out. The photograph was taken by the gun camera of Spitfire VB serial BM155 of 435 (RNZAF) Squadron at Kenley flown by Flight Sergeant A.R. Robson.

AIR 41/49

26 May 1941, requesting a further report on lengthening the range of fighters. Portal replied stating that drop-tanks under the wings of Hurricanes extended their range to 1,050 miles or more. He also said that the Beaufighter had an endurance of 5.2 hours and the new Mosquito would have an endurance of 4.8 hours. No mention was made of the Spitfire.

Churchill was not happy with this response and on 2 June urged Portal to take more steps in the matter. Portal replied the next day stating that the long-range Beaufighter could not operate successfully against the enemy short-range fighter and that bomber escort by Hurricanes and Spitfires deep into enemy territory was not possible. Churchill replied stating that 'This closes many doors of hope and opportunity'.

The matter resurfaced when the Japanese conquered Malaya in February 1942, using long-distance fighters to escort bombers. Churchill wrote to Portal on 1 March 1942, requesting comparative ranges of Japanese and British fighters. He received a table two days later, which included figures showing the range of the Spitfire VB as 440 miles with the standard tanks, increased to 670 miles with a smaller drop-tank or 1,000 miles with a larger one. In fact, thirty and forty-five gallon 'slipper' tanks had been fitted under the fuselage of the Spitfire VB in the summer of 1941, but these did not enable it to penetrate deep into enemy territory. At the end of 1941, a ninety gallon slipper tank was introduced, used primarily in the Mediterranean theatre.

The Spitfire IX, which was fitted with a Merlin 61 engine and entered squadron service in June 1942, proved a match for the Focke-Wulf FW190. But even this new version was not capable of escorting bombers deep into German territory. The matter was not resolved until the US Eighth Air Force and the RAF began to employ the North American

Above: The intelligence officer and the black dog wait for the sound of the returning Spitfires.
INF 2/45

Left: With undercarriages lowered and flaps down, the first section of four Spitfires comes in to land.
INF 2/45

Left: 'The Fighting Cock' by Charles J Thompson

Soon after noon on 25 April 1942, Hurricane IIC serial BN230 of 43 Squadron (known as the Fighting Cocks) was sent off on an air test from Acklington in Northumberland. It was flown by a Belgian in the RAF, Squadron Leader Danny Le Roy du Vivier. While in the air, he heard over the R/T that a section of Spitfires from 88 Squadron at Ouston in Durham had been scrambled to intercept a Junkers Ju88 reconnaissance aircraft sent to photograph the shipyards of the Tyne. He headed towards the position at full boost. The Junkers came in over the sea, swept over the target and headed east at 32,000 feet. Du Vivier approached it, dead astern, but could not close the gap and opened fire with his four 20mm cannons from long range. Return fire shattered his armour-plated windscreen, causing slivers to hit the right spectacle of his goggles and lacerate his face. One bullet passed through the shoulder of his 'Mae West' life jacket and hit the armoured plate behind his seat. But the Junkers appeared to have been damaged and slowed down. Du Vivier fired another burst from 300 yards and smoke poured from the starboard engine of the Junkers, which then burst into flames. One crew member baled out but the others were still on board when the bomber dived vertically into the sea.

Left: This Focke-Wulf FW190A-3 of 7./*Jagdgeschwader* 2 based at Morlaix in Brittany was flown by *Oberleutnant* Armin Faber in an air battle with Spitfires of the Exeter and Portreath Wings on 23 June 1942. Faber then flew in error on a reciprocal course (a fairly common error with the compasses in use at the time) and mistook RAF Pembrey in Carmarthenshire for a base in France, where he landed. The machine was given RAF roundels, the letter P for prototype, the serial number MP499, and tested in mock combat with Spitfires.

AIR 41/49

P-51 Mustang long-range fighter in December 1943. This superb aircraft had a range of over 1,170 miles with drop-tanks. Its combination of range, speed and manoeuvrability made it the most effective fighter in the last two years of the war.

11 Disaster at Dieppe

By the spring of 1942, political elements in Britain were demanding the opening of a 'Second Front' on mainland Europe to help the hard-pressed Russians fighting the Wehrmacht. Although conditions were not yet ripe for a full-scale invasion of the Continent, the Cabinet and Chiefs of Staff were aware of the need to experiment with a limited operation as a prelude to later Allied landings. It was decided in April to land troops at Dieppe under operation 'Jubilee', and planning commenced at Combined Operations Headquarters commanded by Admiral the Lord Mountbatten. The main force was to be drawn from the Canadian Army, which was already in England and becoming restive from inactivity.

Right: The Bristol Blenheim IV entered RAF squadron service in March 1939 as a light day-bomber but in 1942 was being superseded in this role by more modern aircraft. Nevertheless, Blenheims of Bomber Command's No 2 Group were employed on the Dieppe raid of 19 August 1942. This Blenheim was photographed on 18 August 1941, with its camouflage merging with the fields when haymaking was in progress.
AIR 34/235

Left: The Douglas DB-7 entered RAF squadron service in July 1941. It was named the Boston III and gradually replaced the Blenheim IV as a light day-bomber. Squadrons of Bostons in Bomber Command's No 2 Group were employed on the raid on Dieppe of 19 August 1942. This Boston was photographed over France when approaching the target.

DEFE 2/338

Above: Four squadrons of the North American Mustang Is from the RAF's Army Co-operation Command were employed on the Dieppe raid. This was a new aircraft, which first flew operationally in May 1942. Fitted with an Allison engine of 1,120 hp, it was intended as a fighter but did not perform well at high altitudes. Thus it was converted to the photo-reconnaissance role, with a camera fitted obliquely on the port side. The main task of the Mustang Is at Dieppe was to keep watch on German reinforcements approaching the port, but they also took photographs of the action. The later version of the P-51 Mustang, known as the Mustang III by the RAF, was fitted with a Packard Merlin engine of 1,680 hp, and from December 1943 achieved fame as a long-distance fighter escort as well as a fighter-bomber.
AIR 34/238

Left: A Douglas Boston laying a smoke screen over the beaches of Dieppe on 19 August 1942. Some of these aircraft were fitted with four L-shaped pipes protruding from the closed bomb-bay for this purpose.
AIR 41/49

Disaster at Dieppe

Dieppe was chosen partly as it was within range of RAF fighters. The objectives were to embarrass the enemy by destroying military objectives such as port installations and shipping, heavy gun batteries, a radar station and a nearby fighter airfield. However, Dieppe was a very hard nut to crack, for it was heavily defended and covered by high cliffs

Below: RAF operations during the raid on Dieppe of 19 August 1942.

DEFE 2/551

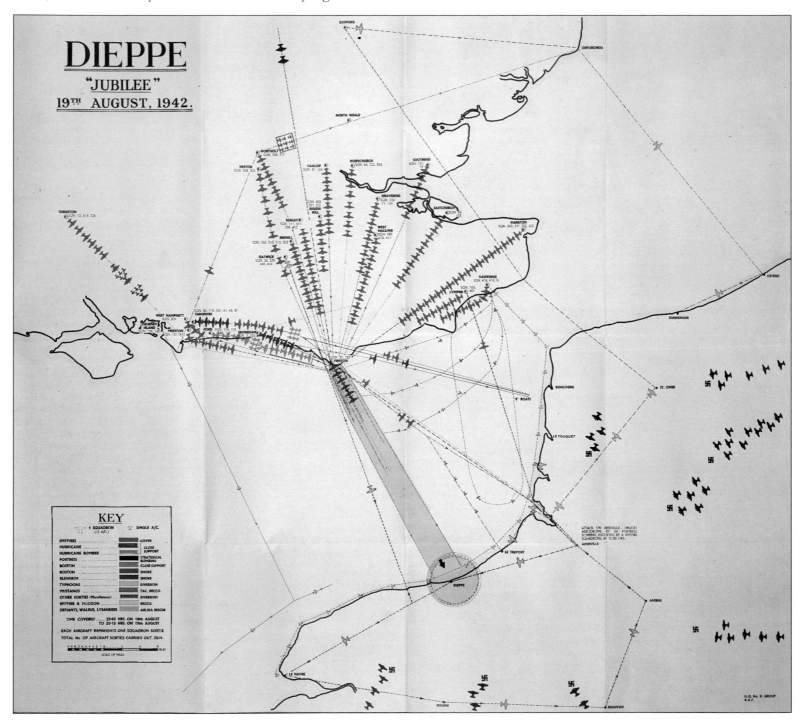

Left: Smoke from a fire burning on the front at Dieppe during the operation of 19 August 1942, with more smoke from battle drifting over the beaches.
DEFE 2/338

Below: Smoke from explosions on the beaches of Dieppe during the height of the battle, when many men of the Canadian Army were being mown down by the defenders. An assault landing craft is in the left foreground.
DEFE 2/338

with few openings and only narrow beaches. Nevertheless, planning went ahead and the operation was scheduled for 19 August. Eight destroyers, nine 'landing ships infantry', thirty-nine coastal craft and 179 assault landing craft were detailed to transport 4,961 men of the Canadian Army, 1,057 commandos and a few men of the U. S. Rangers. Fifty-eight Churchill tanks were also taken on the operation. An original plan to employ airborne troops was cancelled and the commandos were substituted.

The RAF contribution, under Air Vice-Marshal Trafford Leigh-Mallory, consisted of fifty-six fighter squadrons of Hurricanes, Spitfires and Typhoons, as well as four squadrons of the new Mustang reconnaissance aircraft. Five Blenheim and Boston squadrons from Bomber Command's No 2 Group also came under Leigh-Mallory's command for close support and smoke-laying, but preliminary night bombing of positions was prohibited for fear of causing French civilian casualties and alerting the enemy.

All the initial arrangements went according to plan. Embarkation of troops and tanks took place and the expedition sailed from Portsmouth, Newhaven and Shoreham on the evening of 18 August, preceded by minesweepers. Three landings were to be made at dawn on the flanks of Dieppe and two on a frontal assault. At about 03.00 hours in the following morning, the assault landing craft were lowered and the troops embarked. However, some of the craft carrying commandos to the eastern outer flank ran into a German coastal convoy and became disorganized. Surprise was lost and the enemy was alerted. About twenty heavy gun emplacements, anti-aircraft batteries and numerous machine-gun posts were manned, while Luftwaffe fighters and bombers took off.

The enemy fire directed at the landing parties was murderous. Casualties were appalling on the eastern inner flank, with 485 men killed, wounded or captured from the 545 men of the Royal Regiment of Canada who landed. The commandos on the western outer flank, under Lieutenant-Colonel the Lord Lovat, were far more successful, capturing the enemy battery and withdrawing in good order. However, the main assault in the centre was a disaster. The men were mown down by withering fire, while the tanks could not cross a defensive ditch. A withdrawal became imperative and the Royal Navy did its best to bring off the survivors. The rescue operation ended soon after midday, when the last of the rearguard was taken off the beaches. The Canadians left

Below: A naval motor-launch and four smaller craft returning with survivors of the Dieppe operation.

DEFE 2/338

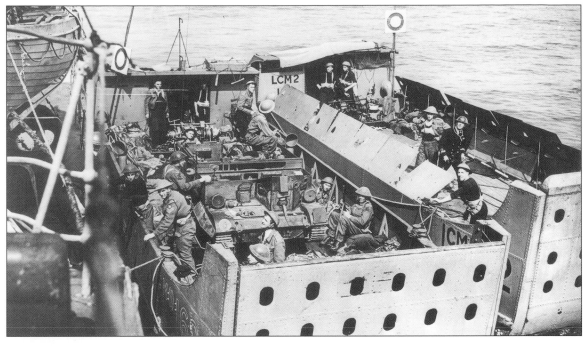

Right: Two tank-landing craft, one containing a Bren-carrier, coming alongside a destroyer after the Dieppe operation. Every tank that landed on the beaches was lost.
DEFE 2/338

Left: Survivors of the Dieppe operation. The soldier in the foreground has had a trouser leg cut off, perhaps to dress a light wound.
DEFE 2/338

behind 3,363 casualties, 68 per cent of their force, while the commandos lost 247 men, just over 23 per cent. Every tank was lost.

While this tragedy was in progress, RAF bombers attacked enemy gun positions – with limited success – and laid smoke screens to cover the operation. Fighters were engaged in fierce battles with increasing numbers of enemy fighters and bombers, but the price was also heavy. The RAF lost 106 aircraft for only forty-eight of the enemy destroyed and twenty-four damaged. Moreover, the Luftwaffe succeeded in damaging the destroyer HMS *Berkeley* so badly that she had to be scuttled, while other destroyers were also hit.

The Germans were jubilant at their success but astonished at the failure of the British to bomb the defences heavily or to employ airborne forces in the rear before seaborne troops were launched in a suicidal frontal attack. The British learnt – or perhaps relearnt – that command of the air was essential in combined operations, as were airborne troops and heavy bombardment of enemy defences from both air and sea. These fundamental mistakes were not repeated in the major landings in North Africa, Sicily, Italy and Normandy.

12 Atlantic Lifeline

The Battle of the Atlantic was one of the bitterest and hardest-fought of the Second World War. Of course, the main responsibility for keeping open Britain's lifeline to her Commonwealth and America fell on the Royal Navy, but the RAF's Coastal Command made an increasingly effective contribution. At first, the Command was ill-equipped with aircraft and equipment, but these defects were gradually rectified.

German U-boats and a handful of Italian submarines had been able to operate with impunity from attacks by shore-based aircraft in the 'Atlantic Gap', where they took an appalling toll of merchant supply ships in convoy. The British acquired bases in Iceland when their forces landed at Reykjavik on 10 May 1940, forestalling the Germans, while Coastal Command controlled an RAF Group in Gibraltar after the Italians entered the war. Hudsons and Sunderlands were able to operate from Iceland during the early part of the following year, but the range of these aircraft was insufficient for the tasks they faced. 'Very long range' aircraft were required and this need was met gradually by the arrival of Consolidated Catalinas in March 1941, Consolidated B-24 Liberators the following June, and Boeing B-17 Fortresses in January 1942.

However, major successes were not yet being achieved, for during the year ending June 1942 Coastal Command sank only eight U-boats or Italian submarines. But improvements were under way. New versions of air to surface-vessel radar were coming into service; powerful depth charges with pistols designed to explode near the surface were being fitted to bomb racks. From June 1942 some Wellingtons based in Britain and then Gibraltar carried the remarkable Leigh Light, a brilliant beam which could be switched on when airborne radar picked up submarines during the night, at a time when these came to the surface to recharge their batteries.

Above: 'U-boat surrendering to British aircraft'
by war artist W. Krogman

On 27 August 1941, a Hudson of 269 Squadron flown by Flying Officer William J.O. Coleman was on patrol from Kaldadarnes in Iceland when a U-boat was sighted about 150 miles to the south. Coleman attacked but his depth charges did not release. He called in a second Hudson, flown by Squadron Leader James H. Thompson, who dropped four depth charges while his crew fired their machine-guns. The U-boat began to dive but then surfaced and the crew waved a white flag. The depth charges had caused chlorine gas to be released. It was a Type VIIC, *U-570*, commanded by *Kapitänleutnant* Hans Joachim Rahmlow.

INF 3/1533

Left: British warships arrived and the U-boat was boarded by Lieutenant H.B. Campbell from the trawler HMS *Kingston Agate*, who crossed in a dinghy with another seaman. The U-boat was towed to Iceland, where it yielded some useful intelligence information. She was recommissioned as HMS *Graph*.

AIR 34/236

Right: Bomber Command did not find the Boeing B-17C Fortress suitable for its operations after a few entered squadron service in May 1941. In the following January they were transferred to Coastal Command. An improved version, the B-17E, arrived in July 1942 and was known as the Fortress IIA. With a range of up to about 2,500 miles, the Fortresses in Coastal Command formed part of the 'Very Long Range' aircraft which helped to close the 'Atlantic Gap' where enemy submarines had been able to operate with impunity from shore-based aircraft. This Fortress IIA, photographed on 4 August 1942, was on the strength of 206 Squadron based at Benbecula in the Hebrides.

AIR 34/235

Above: On 3 September 1942, Whitley V serial Z6978 of 77 Squadron based at Chivenor in North Devon and flown by Flight Sergeant A.A. MacInnes was on patrol about 400 miles south-west of Lands End when a U-boat was sighted on the surface. Depth charges released from about fifty feet straddled the U-boat, which also received machine-gun fire from both front and rear gunners. MacInnes turned, made a second attack and the U-boat sank. She was *U-705*, a Type VIIC, commanded by *Kapitänleutnant* Karl-Horst Horn and on her first patrol, having left Kiel on 1 August.

AIR 34/234

These technical improvements, coupled with the increased ability of the Government Code and Cypher School at Bletchley Park to decrypt enemy signals and locate the probable positions of U-boats at sea, resulted in a dramatic increase in successes. During the year ending June 1943, Coastal Command aircraft sank seventy-one enemy submarines, and damaged many more. It is also evident that the sight of the aircraft in the skies was enough to deter U-boats and cause them to crash-dive, at times when they could have fired torpedoes at merchant ships.

While the Atlantic became much safer for Allied ships, it became far more dangerous for the Kriegsmarine. So many U-boats were being sunk or damaged at night in the Bay of Biscay by Leigh Light Wellingtons that the head of the Kriegsmarine, Admiral Karl Doenitz, ordered his crews to make their passages on the surface by day and to fight it out with any attacking aircraft. By May 1943, destruction of U-boats in this area and the North Atlantic had become so numerous that Doenitz was compelled to order his U-boats

Right: This photograph of Lorient was taken on 26 September 1942.
Photo-interpreters were able to identify (1) two completed U-boat shelters (2) five pens under construction (3) three floating docks camouflaged with netting, probably used as workshops.

AIR 34/743

Right: This Type VIIC U-boat, *U-442*, was commanded by *Korvettenkapitän* Hans Joachim Hesse on its second war cruise when it was spotted at 14.02 hours on 12 February 1943 by the crew of Hudson VI serial EW910 of 48 Squadron, flown from Gibraltar by Flying Officer G.R. Mayhew. The U-boat was on the surface about 100 miles west of the south-west tip of Spain, returning to St Nazaire, when Mayhew dived to attack from the stern and dropped his depth charges while firing his front guns. The U-boat fired back, as shown in this photograph, and the rear gunner in the Hudson also opened fire. Three depth charges then exploded round the U-boat, which sank with all hands, leaving debris and oil in the water.

AIR 34/236

Left: This Type IXC U-boat, *U-189*, was attacked on 23 April 1943 by Liberator III serial FL923 of 120 Squadron, flown by Flying Officer J.K. Moffat from Reykjavik in Iceland on convoy escort duties. Two U-boats were sighted about 450 miles south-west of Iceland and Moffat dived on the nearest and dropped four depth charges. The U-boat opened fire before these exploded. Moffat circled and dropped two more. The U-boat began to sink, leaving many of the crew in the water. She was commanded by *Kapitänleutnant* Helmut Kurrer and had left Kristiansund in Norway twenty days before on her first war cruise. This photograph of the depth charges splashing in the water was taken during the first attack.

AIR 34/237

Right: The Focke-Wulf Condor, adapted from a civil airliner, hunted for Allied shipping from French and Norwegian bases after the Fall of France, delivering bombing attacks and sometimes working in concert with U-boats. This machine crashed with its undercarriage up in the summer of 1943, probably somewhere close to its base of Mérignan, near Bordeaux. The guns have been removed from the wreck.

AIR 34/239

to move away and concentrate on the Central Atlantic for the time being. The rate of sinkings of Allied ships fell substantially.

The conquest of North Africa, the invasion of Sicily and the capitulation of Italy brought some additional relief to the RAF's anti-submarine squadrons by September 1943. In the following month, Lagens airfield in the Portuguese islands of the Azores became available to Coastal Command, so that a squadron of Fortresses with another of Hudsons began to operate from mid-Atlantic.

Left: 'For Valour'
by Charles J. Thompson

One of the least favoured bases of the RAF in the Second World War was Yundum, near Bathurst in The Gambia, from which aircraft flew on patrols over the Central and South Atlantic. Early on 11 August 1943 a New Zealander in the RAF's 200 Squadron, Flying Officer Lloyd A. Trigg, took off with his crew of eight in Consolidated Liberator serial BZ832. At 09.45 hours they spotted a surfaced U-boat about 240 miles south-west of Dakar and went into the attack. The crew of the type VIIC U-boat, *U-468* from La Pallice, opened fire with two 20mm cannons and hit the Liberator, setting it on fire. Nevertheless, Trigg continued his run and dropped six depth charges from about fifty feet. The Liberator hit the sea and exploded, killing all nine men. The U-boat suffered enormous damage and began to sink. Many Germans jumped overboard but all perished except the captain, *Oberleutnant zur See* Clemens Schamong, the first lieutenant and five seamen. These managed to inflate and clamber into the Liberator's dinghy, which had been thrown clear. This was located the next day by a Sunderland of 204 Squadron based at Bathurst, which dropped supplies and guided the corvette HMS *Clarkia* to the rescue. The Germans were taken to Britain, where they reported the bravery of the Liberator crew. Trigg was awarded the Victoria Cross posthumously, exceptionally on testimony from enemy officers.

Left: 'Sunderland over Gibraltar'
by Charles J. Thompson

After the fall of France, Hitler decided to send U-boats into the Mediterranean to operate with Italian submarines. Some were sunk en route but several passed through the Strait of Gibraltar. In November 1941, No 200 Group in Gibraltar, which controlled only one RAF squadron, was abolished. RAF Gibraltar was then formed, with additional squadrons which could operate over the western Mediterranean as well as the Atlantic.

Below Left: The German blockade runner *Alsterufer* of 2,729 tons left Kobe in Japan on 4 October 1943 loaded with essential war supplies. She passed through the southern Atlantic and was heading for the Gironde in France when she was spotted on 27 December by a Sunderland of 201 Squadron. The crew homed in a Sunderland of 422 (RCAF) Squadron which made an attack under fire, but the bombs missed narrowly. The first Sunderland was then ordered to attack from medium height, but the bombs also missed.

Another Sunderland of 201 Squadron arrived and homed in Liberator V serial BZ770 of 311 (Czech) Squadron, flown by Pilot Officer O. Dolezal from Beaulieu in Hampshire. This Liberator was armed with rockets and bombs and went into the attack under intense fire. Five of the eight rockets struck home and two bombs hit the stern. The ship caught fire and the crew abandoned her, as shown here. Shortly afterwards, the burning hulk was sunk by bombs from two Liberators of 86 Squadron.

AIR 34/239

Below: At 07.19 hours on 24 May 1944 a Catalina IV flown from Sullom Voe in the Shetlands by a South African serving in the RAF's 210 Squadron, Captain F. W. L. Maxwell, attacked a U-boat about 300 miles north of the Faroe Islands. The U-boat opened fire but six depth charges were dropped and she spun round and sank. Then she reappeared with her bows and forepart out of the water, and sank again. She was the Type VIIC *U-476*, commanded by *Oberleutnant zur See* Otto Niethmann, which had left Bergen on 20 May. Some of her crew were rescued by *U-990* but in turn this was sunk by a Liberator of 59 Squadron on the following day. Some of the survivors were rescued by a German escort vessel, *Vp5901*.

AIR 15/277

By the beginning of 1944, Coastal Command was provided with modern aircraft and the latest equipment. There were over 100 Liberators in its establishment, while many of the Hudsons had been phased out or converted to air-sea rescue work, a task they performed admirably in combination with RAF high-speed launches around the coasts of Britain. In the year up to June 1944, the Command sank a total of 114 U-boats, in addition to many more damaged. At the same time, Royal Navy vessels were sinking an increased number. Bomber Command continued to hammer at the U-boat bases in Germany and the occupied territories, as well as at the factories manufacturing parts of the vessels, which had been dispersed inland. Deaths of German submariners became proportionally the highest of those in all branches of the country's armed services. The Kriegsmarine was sustaining losses which it could not replace, either in terms of new vessels or experienced crews.

13 Thousand Bombers

In May 1942, the strength of Bomber Command's night force with operational crews and the radius of action to reach targets in Germany still stood at about 450 aircraft. But Air Marshal Arthur Harris was determined to assemble 1,000 bombers for a single raid, partly to impress the War Cabinet but also to persuade the British public that the war could be won by air power alone. He knew that there were many bombers with pilot instructors in operational training units or conversion units, and he also hoped that bombers from Coastal Command would join in such a mass attack.

Thus it seemed that this great force could be gathered, but there remained the problem of organizing such a mass of aircraft to a single target. Collisions on dark nights happened all too frequently. It was necessary to devise a bomber stream in which all aircraft flew to the target at the same speed although at different altitudes. Fortunately, the radar device of *Gee* had been installed in some aircraft, reducing the difficulties of navigation. A full moon period was also required, to ensure that the crews could keep a good lookout for other bombers as well as identify the target. This stream should be as compact as possible, to minimize attacks by enemy night-fighters, swamp the flak defences

Left: The first operation by de Havilland Mosquitos of Bomber Command took place on 31 May 1942 when five were despatched in daylight to take photographs of Cologne and drop some more bombs. One was hit by flak and crashed in the North Sea on the return journey. This photograph was taken from 26,000 feet.

AIR 37/47

Above: Bomber Command despatched 960 aircraft to Bremen on the night of 25/26 June 1942, while Coastal Command contributed 102 and Army Co-operation Command sent five more. The force was thus larger than that of the first 1,000 bomber raid on Cologne of 30/31 May and the second against Essen two nights later. Much damage was caused but forty-eight aircraft of Bomber Command and five of Coastal Command were lost. This photograph of a Lancaster with its bomb doors open was taken over the target.

AIR 34/745

Above: On American Independence Day, 4 July 1942, twelve Bostons of 226 Squadron were despatched on low-level attacks against four airfields in the Netherlands. Six aircraft were crewed by men from the US Eighth Air Force, this being the first operation of the new force. This photograph showing bomb bursts was taken over the airfield of Bergen-Alkmaar. On the left of the control tower is part of a Focke-Wulf FW190, a fighter/bomber being used for hit-and-run raids over southern England. Three Bostons were lost, two of them crewed by Americans.

AIR 34/745

Right: Twenty-four Bostons were despatched to bomb the port of St Malo and Abbeville airfield on 31 July 1942, escorted by ten squadrons of Spitfires. The bombs which fell on St Malo, as shown in this photograph, hit the target area and caused extensive damage to port facilities and industrial property. All the Bostons returned safely. The fighter pilots claimed six Messerschmitt Bf109s and five Focke-Wulf FW190s, but nine Spitfires failed to return.

AIR 34/743

over the target itself, and overwhelm the enemy fire services dealing with great showers of incendiaries.

Harris's first choice was Hamburg, in the last week of May, but the weather proved unsuitable and he decided on Cologne, the second choice. In the event Coastal Command was unable to contribute any aircraft, but on the night of

30/31 May Harris managed to despatch 1,047 aircraft, consisting of Lancasters, Halifaxes, Stirlings, Manchesters, Wellingtons, Whitleys and Hampdens. Of these, 369 came from the training units. 'Tour-expired' operational crews were mustered and a great effort was made to attain maximum serviceability of the aircraft in all squadrons and units. Forty-one aircraft were lost but about 2,500 fires were started in Cologne, over 3,300 buildings destroyed and almost 10,000 damaged, over 500 people killed and 5,000 injured. About a quarter of the remaining population fled the city.

The news of the first 1,000-bomber raid astonished the British public, most of whom grimly supported the action after their own experiences in the Blitz. It seemed the best method of bringing Germany to her knees, keeping Allied casualties to a minimum and freeing those people suffering in the occupied countries. The policy of area bombing was taking a toll which lasted to the end of the war. This great raid was followed by a string of others against German cities during the next few months, although not on quite the same scale.

However, Bomber Command was suffering a high rate of attrition in this period, with average losses rising to over four per cent per raid. With each crew expected to complete thirty bombing missions, it was obvious that few could expect to survive their tour. Of course, not all those shot down were killed and the RAF element in the PoW camps in Germany was growing steadily. But the crews would have

Above: 'Night raid view from bomber cockpit' by war artist Edward Osmond

A Short Stirling over enemy docks, with the co-pilot flying. The pilot is holding a target map and what appears to be the bomb release switch. Both are wearing the RAF's standard sheepskin Irvin jackets. The artist was probably allowed access to photographs in the 'Pilot's and Flight Engineer's Notes'

INF 3/852

Below: Four Mosquitos of 105 Squadron took off from Leuchars in Fife on 25 September 1942 to bomb the Gestapo headquarters in Oslo, as a boost to Norwegian resistance. They were attacked by Focke-Wulf FW190s at low level and one was shot down. Four bombs were dropped on the target but failed to explode. The interpreters of this photograph assumed that it was taken just prior to explosion.

AIR 37/47

Left: On 17 October 1942, Bomber Command despatched ninety-four Lancasters on a daylight attack against the huge Schneider factory at Le Creusot in east central France, which manufactured heavy equipment for the German war machine. There was no fighter escort and the Lancasters flew around the Brittany peninsula and then at low level for about 300 miles across France. They bombed from medium level but many of the bombs fell short and destroyed housing. Only one aircraft was lost, from a crash at low level. Forty-five Lancasters can be counted in this photograph taken on the outward journey, over Montrichard on the river Cher, a tributary of the Loire.

AIR 34/743

Below: 'Mass bomber raid on Cologne' by war artist W. Krogman

The artist's impression of the RAF's first 1,000 bomber raid, which took place against Cologne on the night of 30/31 May 1942.

INF 3/1603

Above: On 6 December 1942, the Philips radio factories at Eindhoven in the Netherlands was raided by forty-seven Venturas, thirty-six Bostons and ten Mosquitos. Nine Venturas, four Bostons and one Mosquito were shot down, but the works were so severely hit that full production was not resumed for six months. Unfortunately some of the bombs killed Dutch civilians. The target was too far inland for fighter escort but three squadrons of Spitfires and one of Typhoons covered the withdrawal, without combats.

AIR 34/47

Below: 'Flight Sergeant R.H. Middleton wounded' by war artist Oliphant

Flight Sergeant Rawdon H. Middleton was an Australian in the RAAF who flew Short Stirling Is in three RAF squadrons. At 18.14 hours on 28 November 1942 he took off in Stirling serial BF372 of 149 Squadron, based at Lakenheath in Suffolk. It was his twenty-eighth operation and his Stirling was one of 228 aircraft despatched by Bomber Command to attack the Fiat Works in Turin.

Middleton crossed the Alps and came down to 2,000 feet for the attack when the aircraft was hit twice by flak. He was hit in the eye, face, chest, side and legs, and slumped over the controls. The co-pilot, Flight Sergeant Leslie Hyder, was also wounded but managed to take over and finish the bomb run, until Middleton recovered sufficiently to order him back to have his wounds dressed. The wireless operator, Pilot Officer Norman Skinner was wounded in the leg. The Stirling was in a parlous state, with the windscreen shattered, but Middleton decided to make for England in spite of his severe wounds. The pilots skirted round the Alps while the crew dumped all possible equipment, but were picked up by searchlights over southern France and fired at over the north coast. Reaching the Kent coast near Dymchurch, Middleton ordered his crew to bale out. Hyder was helped out and followed by the other six members of the crew. Sergeants James Jeffery and John Mackie landed in the sea and were drowned, their bodies being washed ashore. Middleton's body was not washed ashore until 1 February 1942. All five surviving crew members were awarded a DFC or DFM. A posthumous Victoria Cross to Pilot Officer R.H. Middleton was gazetted on 12 January 1943. His commission had come through before his last flight.

INF 3/465

Above: On 23 March 1943, fifteen Mosquitos bombed the St Joseph locomotive works three miles north-west of Nantes. They attacked in two waves, one at 1,000 feet and the other at very low level. This photograph shows extensive damage, with roof covering stripped and scattered by blast. All aircraft returned safely.

AIR 34/236

Below: This photograph of the Luftwaffe's experimental station at Regensburg-Obertraubling, taken on 5 April 1943, shows a twin-boomed Heinkel He219 taking off, as arrowed. The other aircraft are six-engined Messerschmitt Me323 transports, which were assembled at Regensburg.

AIR 34/236

been very obtuse if they had not realized the statistical odds against them, and their morale was an important factor in the campaign.

On 17 August 1942, the new Pathfinder Force (PFF) was formed, against the wishes of Harris. For many months, the more experienced bomber crews had been sent first to the targets, in order to drop flares and guide the main stream. It was intended that this new force would consist of such crews, use *Gee* radar to locate the targets and then drop suitable marker bombs. In fact, four normal squadrons formed the PFF at first, and the techniques took some time to develop.

Another event of importance took place on 17 August 1942, the first raid by heavy bombers of the newly-formed US Eighth Air Force. Only eighteen Boeing B-17 Fortresses participated in this daylight attack: twelve against railway works at Rouen-Sotteville and six on a diversion, all without loss. This was the forerunner of the great combined air offensive against Germany, with the RAF's Bomber Command operating at night and the US Eighth Air Force in daylight.

By the end of 1942, Bomber Command had grown considerably in strength. One of the main reasons was the influx of four-engined bombers coming off the production lines. These were better armed and could carry a far greater tonnage than the Wellingtons, Hampdens and Whitleys they replaced, while their performance was superior, especially at high altitudes. The need to bolster a night-bombing force with aircraft from training units disappeared.

Equally important, two new radar devices came into service. One of these was code-named *Oboe*, designed to tell the aircraft when it was in position to drop its bombs. The transmitting stations could handle only one aircraft at a time, and the first instruments were fitted in the high-flying Mosquitos of the Pathfinder Force. The other device was named H_2S, a small screen with a revolving trace which gave a rather indistinct picture of the ground below, even through cloud. Some of the first were also fitted in the PFF Mosquitos. Apart from these, new 'marker bombs' came into service, specially designed to eject pyrotechnic candles in brilliant colours, which descended slowly and guided the main bomber stream to targets. All these new devices enabled the pathfinder squadrons to develop into an élite force. On 8 January 1943, they were redesignated No 8 (PFF) Group and thereafter grew into a total of nineteen squadrons. This was the main instrument by which Bomber Command located targets with increasing accuracy for the rest of the war.

14 Strike Wings

During the Second World War, Coastal Command came under the operational control of the Admiralty, a system which by and large worked effectively. The Command is always remembered for its part in winning the Battle of the Atlantic and for carrying out air–sea rescues of downed airmen. Less well-known is the fact that from 16 November 1940 it controlled the RAF's strategic photo-reconnaissance units and squadrons, equipped with unarmed Spitfires and Mosquitos, which brought back superb photographs from enemy territory and contributed information of paramount importance to Allied Intelligence.

But there was also another of its activities which has had little recognition, although it was the most dangerous in all RAF squadrons. This was the anti-shipping force which sought to combat the Kriegsmarine and deprive the Germans of the coastal trade which fed the country's war machine. In the first two years after the fall of France, some of these operations were undertaken by Hudsons but the brunt was borne by Beaufort squadrons, usually carrying torpedoes. Most of the attacks took place in daylight, at extreme low level and in the face of withering fire. They were normally carried out by only a few aircraft, without fighter escort, and the losses were extremely heavy.

Below: The new 'Torbeau', a Bristol Beaufighter VI adapted to carry a torpedo in addition to four 20mm cannons and six machine-guns, was developed by the Torpedo Development Unit at Hampshire in July 1942.

AVIA 16/67

Above: The unsuccessful first attack by the North Coates Strike Wing on 20 November 1942 when fourteen Beaufighter VICs of 236 Squadron and twelve Torbeaus of 254 Squadron attacked a convoy near the Hook of Holland. The formation missed a rendezvous with Spitfire escorts and faced intense flak as well as Focke-Wulf FW190s from Schiphol airfield. Three Beaufighters were shot down and others damaged. The only vessel sunk was the naval tug BS4 of 449 tons, although others were slightly damaged.

AIR 28/595

Above: 'The North Coates
Strike Wing'
by Charles J. Thompson

An example of one of the early
attacks made from North
Coates by Beaufighter VICs.

However, in mid 1942 all the Beaufort squadrons were withdrawn from Britain and flown to Malta or the Middle East, where they were engaged on attacks against Axis convoys in the Mediterranean. Their role in Britain was taken up temporarily by Hampden squadrons transferred from Bomber Command and converted to torpedo-bombers.

In the autumn of 1942, it was realized that success could be obtained only if sufficient aircraft were employed to suppress the gunners on the flak ships which accompanied the merchant vessels. The aircraft capable of carrying out this task was the new Beaufighter VIC, armed with four 20mm cannons and six machine-guns, and carrying up to 2,000 lb of bombs or a torpedo. In November 1942, the North Coates Strike Wing was formed in Lincolnshire with two

squadrons of Beaufighters: No 236 in the anti-flak and bombing role and No 254 carrying torpedoes. The first attack took place on 20 November but was not well co-ordinated and the rendezvous with the Spitfire escort was missed. Almost no damage was inflicted on the enemy convoy while three Beaufighters were shot down and two more crashed on return.

The North Coates Strike Wing was withdrawn for more training and the next attack did not take place until 18 April 1943, by which time the two squadrons had been joined by 143 Squadron in the anti-flak role. On this occasion, everything worked to perfection. Spitfires maintained close escort, the attack was concentrated into four minutes, the main merchant vessel was torpedoed and sunk, escort vessels were shattered by cannon fire, and all aircraft returned. Such attacks then continued, with great success.

In June 1943 the Beaufighters were equipped with a new and deadly weapon in their armoury. This was the rocket projectile, fitted with a solid-shot warhead designed to punch holes in hulls below the waterline. After some problems in aiming these new weapons, eight of which were carried on rails under the wings, the rocket proved more effective in sinking vessels than the torpedo, which was dropped from a greater distance and frequently missed the target.

These successes prompted the formation of more Strike Wings. The next was formed in October 1943 at Wick in

Above: The second attack made by the North Coates Strike Wing, by twenty-one Beaufighters of 143, 236 and 254 Squadrons, two of Spitfires and one of Mustangs, took place off the Dutch island of Texel on 18 April 1943. The Dutch merchant vessel *Hoegh Carrier* of 4,906 tons was torpedoed and sunk, while four escort vessels were badly damaged. All the RAF aircraft returned safely, in spite of intense flak.

AIR 28/595

Below: The first rocket attack made by the Strike Wings took place on 22 June 1943 when thirty-six Beaufighters from 143, 236 and 254 Squadrons at North Coates, escorted by Spitfires and Typhoons, attacked a convoy off Scheveningen in the Netherlands. The Beaufighters of 254 Squadron still carried torpedoes, all of which missed, and two aircraft were shot down. Rockets and cannon fire damaged several vessels but there were no sinkings.

AIR 28/595

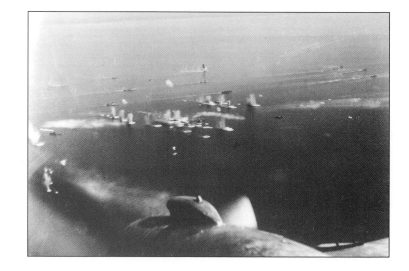

Left: The North Coates Wing made a successful attack, without loss, against a convoy off the Dutch island of Texel on 2 August 1943. Thirty-six Beaufighters took part, some of which were armed with rockets, escorted by four squadrons of Spitfires. Seven flak ships were badly damaged, while torpedoes dropped by the Torbeaus of 254 Squadron sank the merchant vessel *Fortuna* of 2,700 tons and the flak ship *Vp1108* of 314 tons. The Spitfires shot down two Messerschmitt Bf109s.
AIR 28/595

Left: The Leuchars Strike Wing, equipped with the new and more powerful Beaufighter TFXs, attacked a convoy of about sixteen ships off Stavanger in Norway on 6 March 1944. Eight Beaufighters of 455 (RAAF) Squadron were armed with cannons while four Torbeaus of 489 (RNZAF) Squadron carried torpedoes. The German merchant ship *Rabe* of 994 tons was sunk and numerous escort vessels were hit by cannon fire. The Beaufighters came under intense fire from the convoy and shore batteries, and were also attacked by German fighters, but all returned safely.
AIR 28/471

Right: Twenty-four Beaufighters of the Langham Strike Wing, escorted by fighters, attacked a large convoy off the Dutch island of Ameland on 14 May 1944. The Wing had moved down from Leuchars during the previous month. The Dutch merchant vessel *Vesta* of 1,854 tons was torpedoed and sunk, and the minesweeper *M.435* of 750 tons was also sunk. One Beaufighter was shot down.

AIR 15/472

Left: On 29 March 1944, twenty-nine Beaufighter TFXs of the North Coates Strike Wing, escorted by two squadrons of Mustangs, attacked a large convoy near Borkum in the East Frisian Islands. The German merchant vessels *Hermann Schulte* of 1,305 tons and *Cristel Vinnen* of 1,894 tons were torpedoed and sunk, while many other vessels were damaged by rockets and cannon fire. One Beaufighter was shot down.
AIR 28/595

Right: On 20 April 1944 the North Coates Strike Wing, consisting of the Beaufighters of 143, 236 and 254 Squadrons, attacked a German convoy off Borkum. This photograph shows *Sperrbrecher 102* (formerly the merchant vessel *Condor* of 889 tons) under attack with cannon fire and rockets before exploding and sinking. A Swedish supply ship in the German convoy, *Storfors* of 974 tons, was badly damaged.
AIR 34/240

Caithness with 404 (RCAF) Squadron and the RAF's 144 Squadron, both equipped with Beaufighters. These operated over the Norwegian coast, but at this stage of the war there were no long distance fighters capable of escorting them. This was followed by the Leuchars Strike Wing in Fife, formed in March 1944 with Beaufighters of 455 (RAAF) and 489 (RNZAF) Squadrons, both of which had been equipped with Hampden torpedo-bombers.

The Strike Wings did not always remain at the same base. In April 1944, the Leuchars Strike Wing flew down to Langham in Norfolk, and the Wick Strike Wing was posted to Davidstow Moor in Cornwall in the following month.

These moves were in preparation for the D-Day landings.

The Portreath Strike Wing in Cornwall was formed in early June 1944, consisting of 235 and 248 Squadrons. This was equipped with Mosquito VIs and Mosquito XVIIIs, the latter being fitted with a Molins gun which fired six-pound shells, originally anti-tank weapons. Mosquitos had served with Coastal Command's anti-shipping squadrons from the previous October, although not as a Wing. Eventually, some of the Beaufighter squadrons would be re-equipped with these beautiful machines. The Strike Wings in Cornwall would also fly up to Scotland, after France had been liberated, to continue operations along the Norwegian coastline.

15 Dambusting

One of the most famous episodes in the Second World War was Bomber Command's attack on dams in the Ruhr and Weser districts, which took place on the night of 16/17 May 1943. A special unit was formed for this purpose, 617 Squadron at Scampton in Lincolnshire, commanded by Wing Commander Guy P. Gibson. This was equipped with the Lancaster III, a variant of the heavy bomber which had been modified to carry an 'Upkeep' mine invented by Dr Barnes Wallis and known as the 'bouncing bomb'. The dorsal gun turret and part of the ventral turret were removed to make way for the mine and a motor which imparted backspin to the weapon and increased the distance of its ricochet over the surface of the water.

Nineteen Lancasters took off, in three waves. Their targets were four dams in the Ruhr district, the Möhne, the Sorpe, the Lister and the Ennepe, and two in the Weser district, the Eder and the Diemel. They flew at very low level over the North Sea and then for more than 200 miles over enemy territory. Wing Commander Gibson led the first wave of nine aircraft, heading for the Möhne dam. One aircraft was shot down en route and another over the target. Five mines were dropped and the wall of the dam was breached. Five of the surviving aircraft flew on to the next target, the Eder dam, and the remaining three mines breached this dam. Of the surviving seven aircraft, two were shot down on the return journey.

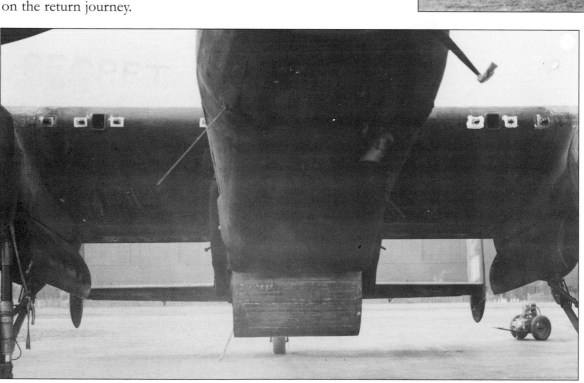

Left: The 'Upkeep' mine fitted to Wing Commander Gibson's Lancaster, serial ED932/G. The crews were trained to drop it at an altitude of 60 feet and at a ground speed of 220 mph, so that it bounced towards the dam wall and 'crawled' down the water side before exploding. It was a cylinder 60 inches in length, 50 inches in diameter, weighed 9,250 lb, contained 6,600 lb of explosive and was fitted with three hydrostatic pistols set to detonate 30 feet below the surface.

AIR 14/840

Left: Lancaster III serial ED825/G, which was not delivered until the morning before the operation.
AVIA 18/715

Below: A German photograph showing the breached Möhne dam protected by balloons after the attack.
AIR 20/4367

Dambusting

The second wave, of five aircraft, headed for the Sorpe dam, but two were shot down on the outward journey while two others were so badly damaged that they were forced to turn back. The wall of the dam did not give way when the fifth pilot dropped his mine.

The third wave also consisted of five aircraft, but two were shot down en route. Mist had gathered, making conditions very difficult for the attack. One pilot dropped his mine on the Sorpe but the wall still held. Another dropped his mine on what he thought was the Ennepe, without any result. The remaining pilot could not identify any target.

Flooding from the breaching of the Möhne and the Eder dams caused enormous devastation and loss of life. Although the Germans repaired the breaches quickly, they were forced to employ about 10,000 men from the armed forces to guard these and other dams for the rest of the war.

Right: A German photograph showing water still pouring through the breach in the Eder dam after the attack.
AIR 20/4367

Below: 'Dambusters' by Mark Postlethwaite

Above: The upper reaches of the Möhne Lake at a point where a road bridge crosses, photographed by the RAF on 17 May 1943. The water has drained away, with the former level clearly seen.

AIR 34/236

Left: The wall of the Sorpe dam did not give way but this RAF photograph of 19 May 1943 shows repair work and road clearance taking place on the damaged crown. Thirteen balloons were flying at medium altitude and seven more were bedded down when the photograph was taken.

AIR 34/236

Above: This German photograph of a Lancaster on a Dutch beach is probably that of Lancaster serial ED877/G, flown by Squadron Leader Henry M. Young, which was shot down near Ijmuiden on the return journey after dropping a mine against the Möhne dam. He and his crew lost their lives.

AIR 20/4367

Right: A mosaic of the Eder valley, photographed by the RAF on 18 May 1943. Water is still pouring through a breach of 190 feet in the wall of the dam. Photo-interpreters annotated the mosaic with (C) houses in the village of Hemfurth washed away or damaged, (D) bridges over the river destroyed, (E) Brinkhausen power station flooded, with the north part of the switch and transformer park washed away, (G) several houses destroyed in the village of Affoldern, (H) a road bridge breached in two places, (I) road bridge from Mehlen to Buhlen destroyed.

AIR 34/236

Above: Wing Commander Guy P. Gibson VC, DSO, DFC, photographed at Scampton in the afternoon of 27 May 1943, the day his Victoria Cross was gazetted. It was also on this afternoon that King George VI and Queen Elizabeth visited Scampton. The King chose a crest for 617 Squadron, showing a broken dam with a flash of lightning above it and the motto *Après Moi le Déluge*.

INF 2/42

The British public and the services were elated at the success of the operation. It boosted morale in Bomber Command and established an enduring reputation for enterprise and efficiency.

Wing Commander Guy Gibson was awarded a Victoria Cross for his successful leadership of the Dambusters and became a national hero. But he did not survive the war. He and his navigator, Squadron Leader J.B. Warwick, were killed when returning to base in a Mosquito of 627 Squadron on the night of 19/20 September 1944. Both men are buried at Steenbergen-en-Kruisland in the Netherlands.

16 Firestorm

In the spring and early summer of 1943, the industrial conurbation of the Ruhr became the main target for Bomber Command, known as 'Happy Valley' by the cynical RAF aircrews. At the opening of this offensive, Sir Arthur Harris could dispose about 600 aircraft, but this number grew rapidly to 800, of which the great majority were new four-engined bombers. The policy remained that of 'area bombing', in which districts of cities were attacked with a combination of blast bombs and incendiaries, obliterating factories and homes alike. The newly-formed No 8 (Pathfinder) Group marked targets with the aid of radar navigational instruments which had a limited range but could cover the Ruhr. The devastation resulting from these night attacks was enormous.

This bombing policy stemmed from a conference held for ten days in January 1943 at Casablanca in Morocco by the Allied Chiefs of Staff, headed by Winston Churchill and Franklin Roosevelt, at a time when Anglo–American armies were clearing the Axis forces out of Tunisia. Resulting from these discussions was the decision that the first objective must be the conquest of Germany, without diminishing the build-up of forces intended to crush Japan. However, in spite of pressure from the Soviet Government demanding the opening of a 'Second Front' which would draw off German divisions from the Eastern Front, it was considered

Below: 'Aircraft factory'
by war artist Rowland Hilder

The noses and the dihedral of the wings indicate Avro Lancasters but the fins and rudders resemble those of Handley Page Halifaxes.
INF 3/803

Right: 'Failed to Return'
by Charles J. Thompson

Right: 'Failed to Return'
by Charles J. Thompson

Handley Page Halifax II of 102 Squadron, serial HR911, took off from Pocklington in Yorkshire at 17.37 hours on 22 October 1943. It was flown by Pilot Officer D.W. Brookes and was one of 569 aircraft despatched by Bomber Command to Kassel in central Germany. It was also one of 43 bombers which failed to return, for it was shot down by a Junkers Ju88 night-fighter after leaving the target. Brookes and three other crew members were killed but the remaining three survived to become PoWs. One of these survivors was the navigator, Sergeant Stan Fautley, who baled out past the two burning engines in the port wing when the order was given. Years later, he commissioned this painting from the artist.

Below: This remarkable photograph of an anti-aircraft shell bursting in the air was taken over Hamburg during the attack by Bomber Command on the night of 24/25 July 1943. The centre of the explosion is shown by the arrow.
AIR 34/238

that the time was not yet ripe for an invasion of France. The alternative was to strike through southern Europe. Sicily followed by Italy were chosen for the next combined assaults.

Meanwhile, Germany had to be hammered from the air. On 21 January 1943, Harris had received the instruction 'Your primary object will be the progressive destruction and dislocation of the German military, industrial and economic system, and the undermining of the morale of the German people to a point where their capacity for armed resistance is fatally weakened'. A similar directive had been sent to Lieutenant-General Ira C. Eaker, who commanded the US Eighth Air Force. The expansion of his daylight bombing force was proceeding at an enormous rate, until it reached the total of 2,000 heavy bombers by the early spring of 1944.

The Battle of the Ruhr, as it became known, resulted in the withdrawal of Luftwaffe fighter units from the Eastern Front and an alarming increase in the losses of both Bomber Command and the US Eighth Air Force. In response, a new directive entitled 'Pointblank' was issued on 10 June 1943. The Americans were to be diverted to the

Left: Hamburg photographed on 25 July 1943 from a B-17 Flying Fortress of the US Eighth Air Force, which despatched 123 of these aircraft to the city in daylight. Fires were still burning from Bomber Command's attack the night before. However, the massive attack took place two nights later, when Bomber Command despatched 787 aircraft and a terrible firestorm was created.

AIR 34/237

Below: Hanover photographed on 8/9 October 1943, when Bomber Command despatched 504 aircraft to the city. A four-engined bomber is flying above incendiary fires. There was extensive damage in the centre of the city and to the west. German records state that about 1,200 people were killed and 3,345 injured. Almost 4,000 buildings were destroyed and over 30,000 damaged. Twenty-seven aircraft were lost.

AIR 14/3696

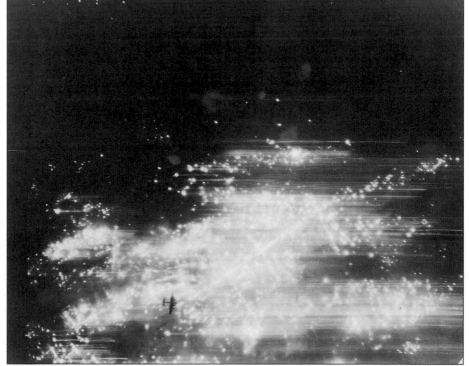

destruction of the Luftwaffe fighters and the industries which supported them. To the dismay of Air Marshal Harris, a new Combined Operational Planning Committee was set up to co-ordinate the activities of both forces. Harris saw this as a potential threat to the progressive destruction of forty major German cities, which he regarded as the most effective way of winning the war.

As it happened, Bomber Command was not diverted from the policy of area bombing at this stage in the war. During June and July, Cologne, Krefeld, Essen, Mülheim, Wuppertal, Gelsenkirchen and Aachen were among the targets attacked by huge numbers of night bombers, laying waste to vast tracts of buildings. Then, on 24/25 July, Hamburg was chosen for a series of massive assaults, although not as part of the Battle of the Ruhr. This target, Germany's principal port and its second largest city, had been attacked many times before, but

not with the ferocity which was now contemplated. The US Eighth Air Force was invited to participate.

The target was easily identified from the coastline, in reasonable weather, and the RAF used a new device for the first time. This was code-named 'Window' and consisted of strips of paper to which aluminium foil was stuck on one side. When dropped in sufficient quantity, it obliterated the radar screens of installations which controlled aircraft and flak guns as well as the airborne radar of night-fighters.

The first of four massive raids took place with 791 bombers of the RAF on 24/25 July. It was accurate and caused great damage to buildings and the air raid precaution system, with about 1,500 people killed. The US Eighth Air Force followed with 118 B-17 Fortresses on the following day, causing further damage to shipyards in spite of heavy cloud. Only fifty-four of these daylight bombers were able to locate and attack U-boat pens on the next day.

But the raid of 27/28 July by 787 aircraft of Bomber Command was the one which caused appalling devastation. The bombing was concentrated and the fires soon combined to create a firestorm which lasted three hours, sucking in surrounding air in conditions where the temperature was already high and humidity low. Nothing could survive this inferno. About 40,000 people died and 16,000 buildings were completely destroyed. Some two-thirds of the remaining population fled the next day. Even then, Bomber Command continued with 777 aircraft on 29/30 July and 740 more on 2/3 August. The first of these caused more destruction but the second achieved little since the force ran into a severe thunderstorm and many aircraft turned back.

Above: A Halifax dropping its bombs on Leipzig during an attack by 527 aircraft on the night of 3/4 December 1943. The target was marked accurately by Pathfinders and the raid was assessed as successful although twenty-four aircraft were lost. The American broadcaster Ed Murrow flew as a reporter on this raid and returned safely.
AIR 34/238

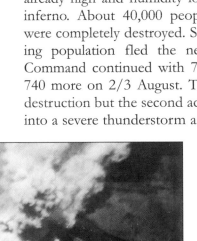

Left: The Gnome and Rhône aircraft engine factory at Limoges in France received a devastating attack on the night of 8/9 February 1944 from twelve Lancasters from 617 Squadron led by their commanding officer, Wing Commander Leonard Cheshire. The target was marked in bright moonlight by Cheshire, who dropped incendiaries. Each of the other eleven Lancasters then dropped a 12,000 lb bomb, ten of which hit the factory precisely. Production came almost entirely to a halt and no Lancasters were lost. This photograph was taken over the target during the raid.
AIR 14/3696

Left: 'A Hard Day's Night' by Charles J. Thompson

De Havilland Mosquito VI of 157 Squadron returning to Predannack in Cornwall in late 1943, after flying an intruder patrol over France and the Bay of Biscay.

Below: On 10/11 May 1944, Bomber Command despatched 506 aircraft to attack railway yards in France and Belgium, as part of the D-Day preparations. Much damage was caused, although thirteen aircraft were lost. This photograph was taken from 8,250 feet over Lille by a Lancaster of 61 Squadron.
AIR 14/3696

During the remainder of August, Bomber Command was diverted to raids on Italian cities, a move which had an alarming effect on the population and hastened the surrender of the country on 8 September. New navigational devices were coming into operation, as well as devices enabling specialized Lancasters to jam or confuse German voice transmissions to the Luftwaffe's night-fighter force. Bomber Command moved back to the German industrial heartland for the next ten weeks and then began a sustained assault on Berlin, which however was beyond the range of most radar navigation aids.

This became the worst period for casualties of bomber crews in the entire war. The German night-fighter force had expanded and become more expert. The longer distance travelled by the bombers gave the Luftwaffe crews a fuller opportunity to practice their skills. RAF bombers were hacked out of the sky in such numbers that the older Stirlings and some marks of Halifaxes had to be withdrawn and turned to less hazardous duties, such as

Left: 'Rear gunner's view from bomber aircraft'
by unknown war artist

This view of an attack appears to have been from a Fraser Nash FN4A tail turret, designed for the Whitley IV and V but also fitted in the Manchester, the early Stirling I and the Wellington III. This turret was armed with four .303 inch Browning guns, as indicated by the four ammunition feeds, although the barrels of only the upper two guns can be seen in the painting.

INF 3/906

Right: This Mosquito Mk IX serial ML897 was on the strength of 1409 (Meteorological) Flight at Wyton in Huntingdonshire. The photograph was taken after its 150th operational flight on 9 November 1944, when it was flown by the commanding officer, Squadron Leader N. Bicknell, with Flying Officer C.N. Saunders as navigator, on a sortie over The Hague, Koblenz and Dunkirk. No 1409 Flight was part of No 8 (Pathfinder) Group of Bomber Command. Although engaged primarily on weather reconnaissance before raids, the aircraft sometimes carried bombs to leave as 'visiting cards'.

AIR 34/241

minelaying in the Baltic or diversionary raids. Morale among the crews fell accordingly and yet Berlin remained the main target until the end of March 1944. There is no doubt that the bombing caused considerable damage to the German capital, but at an unjustifiable cost to the attackers. Then, in April 1944, a new policy was forced on Bomber Command.

17 Allied Expeditionary Air Force

Planning for the eventual re-entry into mainland Europe began soon after Dunkirk, with one of the essential requirements known to be air superiority. The grim experience at Dieppe in August 1942, followed by the successful invasion of the North African coast three months later, provided practical demonstrations of this necessity. The command structure for the invasion of northern France and the eventual conquest of Germany was entitled Supreme Headquarters Allied Expeditionary Force (SHAEF). The overall commander was General Dwight D. Eisenhower, appointed on 16 January 1944. His deputy, Air Chief Marshal Sir Arthur Tedder, was appointed four days later. Both men had successful experience of combined operations in the Mediterranean and of working harmoniously together.

In May 1943, a conference of Allied leaders in Washington set a provisional target date for the invasion, 1 May 1944, at a time when the Allied air forces in Britain were expected to number about 11,400 operational aircraft. But air power alone could not conquer the Wehrmacht defending its 'West Wall'. The massive seaborne and airborne invasion was code-named operation 'Overlord'. In order to give tactical support to these Anglo–American armies, a huge but mobile air force was required. For this purpose the Allied Expeditionary Air Force (AEAF) was formed on 1 June 1943, commanded from 15 November 1943 by Air Chief

Above: A photo-reconnaissance Mustang of the 2nd Tactical Air Force under fire on 28 July 1943 from a flak battery of three light guns on the end of the outer mole at Boulogne. The aircraft was undamaged and continued over its target.
AIR 34/237

Left: Thirty-five Bostons from 88 Squadron at Swanton Morley in Norfolk, 107 Squadron at Hartfordbridge in Hampshire and 342 (Lorraine) Squadron at Great Massingham in Norfolk, attacked the Denain Engineering Works near Valenciennes in northern France on the evening of 16 August 1943. They were escorted by seven squadrons of Typhoons. About thirty-one tons of bombs were dropped, exploding among the assembly shops, foundries and forges, but enemy fighters were encountered as well as intense flak. Six Bostons failed to return from the operation.
AIR 34/237

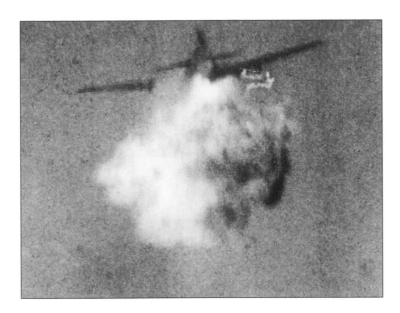

Above: On 19 August 1943 the 2nd Tactical Air Force despatched Marauders to bomb Bryas-Sud airfield in France, escorted by Spitfire IXs of 65 of 112 Squadrons, both from Kingsnorth in Kent.

When a formation of enemy aircraft attempted to attack the Marauders, this Focke-Wulf FW190 was shot down by Flight Lieutenant J.R. Heap of 65 Squadron in Spitfire IX serial MA420.

AIR 34/238

Marshal Sir Trafford Leigh-Mallory. Its RAF component was the 2nd Tactical Air Force (2nd TAF), created from the whole of Fighter Command, temporarily renamed the Air Defence of Great Britain, and the light bombers of No 2 Group, Bomber Command. To these were added the air transports of the RAF's Nos 38 and 46 Groups. From the beginning of 1944, the 2nd TAF was commanded by Air Marshal Sir Arthur Coningham. The USAAF component of the AEAF was the Ninth Air Force under Lieutenant-General Lewis H. Brereton. This was reactivated in the UK on 16 October 1943, after serving in the Mediterranean theatre, and numerically it was even larger than the 2nd TAF.

Thus the AEAF was an integrated Anglo–American body, capable of transporting numerous airborne forces, providing close support to troops over their front lines, and making tactical attacks behind enemy lines. Apart from the AEAF, the Allied air strength in the UK included two great strategic forces. These were the heavy bombers and fighter escorts of the US Eighth Air Force and the heavy and light bombers of the RAF's Bomber Command, engaged on 'round the clock' bombing of the enemy's heartland and positions in occupied countries. The long-distance fighters

Left: Ten Bostons of 342 (Lorraine) Squadron were despatched in the early evening of 2 September 1943 from Great Massingham in Norfolk to bomb the marshalling yards at Serqueux, north-east of Rouen. The Free French squadron was escorted by four squadrons of Typhoons and bombed the target from low level with great precision. The bombs burst from the northern to the southern end of the yard and also hit a fuel storage tank, which exploded. One Boston was shot down but crash-landed successfully and the crew became prisoners-of-war.

AIR 34/237

Right: 'RAF day raiders over Berlin's official quarter' by war artist Jobson

This poster depicts the first occasion when Berlin was bombed in daylight, on 30 January 1943. Only six Mosquitos from Marham in Norfolk participated, in two sections. Three aircraft of 105 Squadron bombed in the morning at exactly the same time Goering was due to address a Nazi rally, causing the speech to be delayed for an hour. Three aircraft of 139 Squadron followed at the time Goebbels made his speech, but one was shot down and both crew members were killed.

INF 13/123

of the Eighth Air Force were also winning a war of attrition with enemy fighters, at a time when the Luftwaffe was unable to replace its experienced pilots. After some discussion it was decided that these heavy bombers could be called upon to assist in operation 'Overlord' whenever required by the supreme Allied commander of the great enterprise.

Of course, the RAF and the USAAF did not wait for D-Day before striking at the enemy. The main targets were identified by Leigh-Mallory's Bombing Committee in what

Left: On 19 February 1944, nineteen Mosquitos of the 2nd Tactical Air Force took off to attack the wall of a jail at Amiens where French Resistance fighters were being held prior to execution. Supported by fighter escort, they swept in at low level and breached the wall so effectively that 258 prisoners were able to escape, although many were recaptured. Unfortunately, 102 prisoners were killed in the bombing attack. The leader of the Mosquitos, Group Captain P.C. Pickard, was shot down by Focke-Wulf FW190s; he and his navigator, Flight Lieutenant J.A. Bradley, lost their lives.

AIR 34/241

Right: On the night of 3/4 May 1944, Bomber Command despatched 352 aircraft to bomb a German military camp and training area at Mailly-le-Camp, south-east of Paris. After some initial difficulties with communication from the Controller, the main force released about 1,500 tons of bombs on the target, causing great destruction of barracks, transport sheds and ammunition stores. Over 200 German soldiers were killed and many injured. Over 100 vehicles, including tanks, were destroyed. But German night-fighters had time to arrive and forty-two Lancasters were shot down. This photograph was taken on 6 May 1944 from 26,000 feet by a photo-reconnaissance Spitfire.

AIR 25/792

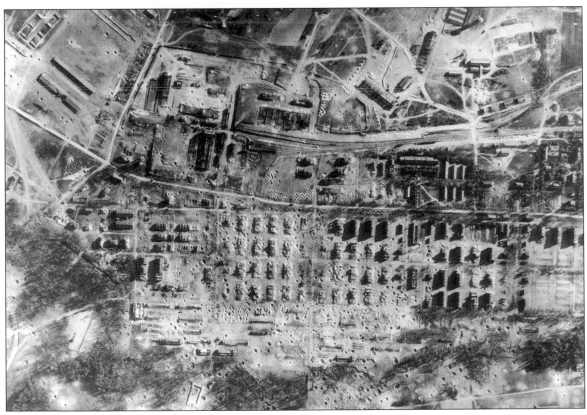

Above: Two Mosquitos of 21 Squadron, 2nd Tactical Air Force, were returning on 21 March 1944 to their base at Hunsdon in Hertfordshire from an uneventful patrol over the river Loire, when they flew near the fighter airfield of Gael in Brittany. They were Mosquito serial LR381 flown by Squadron Leader H. E. Bodien and serial LR382 flown by Flight Lieutenant D. Taylor, each carrying four 500 lb bombs, and the pilots both decided to attack. They bombed from 100 feet and hit two hangars. On the way out, fire from two camouflaged flak towers in nearby woods opened up on them, and Taylor's Mosquito was hit in the tail, almost severing the main tail spar. Bodien turned and attacked one of the towers with gunfire. Both aircraft returned safely.

AIR 34/240

Right: The 2nd Tactical Air Force made two attacks on a bridge at Courseulles-sur-Seine on 30 May 1944. In the morning, six Mitchells of 98 Squadron and six Bostons of 320 (Lorraine) Squadron from Dunsfold in Surrey, together with six Mitchells of 226 Squadron from Hartfordbridge in Hampshire, made an attack. However, the bombs overshot and the bridge was left intact. In the afternoon, twelve of 98 Squadron, twelve of 320 (Lorraine) Squadron and six of 226 Squadron went to the same target. On this occasion, some of the bombs exploded in a nearby factory, as shown in this photograph, but crews of 320 (Lorraine) Squadron reported that they had hit the bridge.

AIR 37/334

Left: 'Cockpit view of a raid on single target in Holland' by unknown war artist

On 11 April 1944, six Mosquito VIs of 613 Squadron from Swanton Morley in Norflok, part of the 2nd Tactical Air Force, made a daylight attack at low level on a five-storey building in The Hague where Gestapo records were held. Bombs and incendiaries reduced the building to a heap of rubble. A German barracks nearby was also razed to the ground.

INF 3/1465

became know as the 'Transportation Plan'. The railways in Belgium and northern France were to be systematically attacked. These included the servicing and repair centres, even though civilian casualties would be incurred. This first phase of the plan was carried out by Bomber Command from early April 1944, with the US Eighth Air Force joining in the assault later in the month. The attacks were colossal and continued with great success up to D-Day. The Mosquitos, Bostons, Mitchells and Marauders of the AEAF also attacked the transport system as well as other special targets. Photo-reconnaissance aircraft brought back superb shots of these operations and of the entire enemy coastline.

The second phase began nearer D-Day, when all railways, bridges and roads leading towards the chosen beachheads were to be destroyed by bombing, as well as the rolling stock itself. To these were added enemy radar stations in France and the Low Countries, gun batteries along the coastlines, and fighter airfields. To avoid disclosing the probable beachheads, numerous targets outside the chosen area had to be attacked. Many of the daylight operations were carried out by the fighter-bombers of the AEAF, with considerable success but at heavy cost. During the two months before D-Day, the Allied Air Forces lost almost 2,000 aircraft in these preparatory operations. Nevertheless, the air armada mustered for the invasion consisted of about 5,000 four-engined bombers, 1,520 light or medium bombers, and 2,840 fighters or fighter-bombers. To these should be added the squadrons of Coastal Command and the Fleet Air Arm in position for reconnaissance and to guard the flanks of the invasion fleet crossing the English Channel. Opposing this huge force, Luftflotte 3 in northern France possessed only 891 aircraft of all types – fighters, reconnaissance, ground attack, coastal and transport. Of these, only 496 were serviceable on D-Day.

Below: A Mitchell of the 2nd Tactical Air Force flying past flak bursts over the Doullens area of France, near Amiens, on 22 April 1944.

AIR 34/240

18 Coup de Main

The Allied invasion fleet of about 6,500 ships and landing craft formed on the night of 5/6 June 1944 off Littlehampton in Sussex, before sailing due south for the beaches of Normandy. The massive operation had been postponed for twenty-four hours as a result of bad weather but further delays were not practicable.

The invasion beaches had been covered extensively by photo-reconnaissance aircraft, and the troops in every landing craft carried clear photographs of their precise points of landing and the objectives they were to secure. The RAF's

Below: RAF preparations for the D-Day landings of 6 June 1944. The map was drawn by the RAF's Air Historical Branch. AIR 41/24

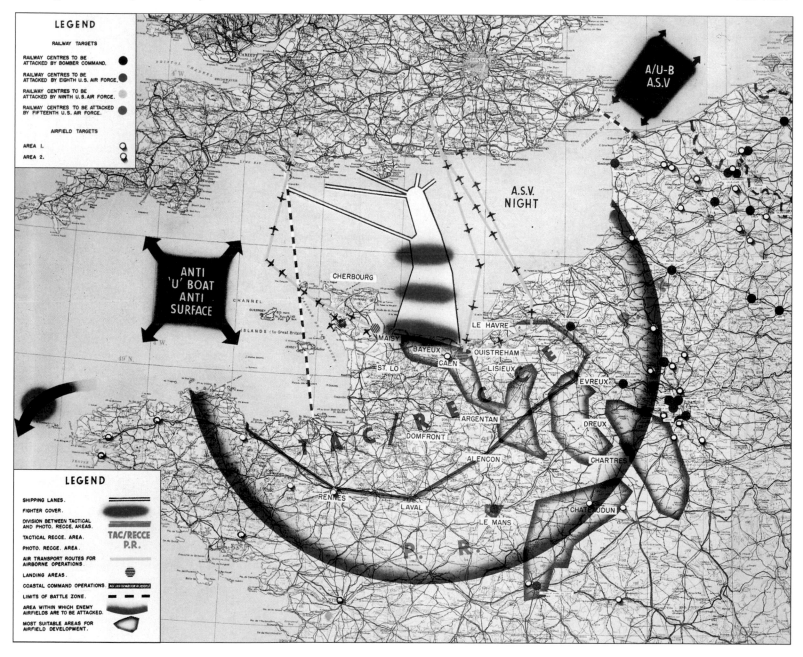

Above: Paratroopers preparing the containers which carried their heavy arms and ammunition, prior to entering a Douglas Dakota of the RAF. This was part of a large-scale exercise held by the British and US Armies on the weekend on 22/23 April 1944 in preparation for D-Day.

INF 2/43

Coastal Command stood guard over the flanks of the invasion fleet, combing the seas for U-boats and making attacks on any German craft which attempted to penetrate their screens.

The RAF's Bomber Command carried out a series of operations while the troops were afloat. Apart from attacks by 1,136 bombers on enemy coastal batteries, some squadrons were engaged on deception plans. False signals

Right: 'What a Way to Go' by Charles J. Thompson

Short Stirling IV of 299 Squadron taking off from Keevil in Wiltshire, towing a troop-carrying Airspeed Horsa glider. Rows of gliders are waiting their turn at the side of the runway while more Stirling tugs are taxiing along the perimeter track in the distance.

Above: Paratroopers inside a Dakota, awaiting the order to jump, during the exercise prior to D-Day.

INF 2/43

had already convinced the Germans that the Allies intended to land further east, between Boulogne and Dieppe, and Bomber Command reinforced this deception. Lancasters of 617 Squadron flew between Dover and Fécamp, circling a number of small ships flying balloons fitted with reflectors which German radar could pick up. They also dropped 'Window' aluminium foil, cut into shapes which simulated the approach of ships on radar screens. The whole procession moved towards the French coast at about seven knots, giving the impression of a huge convoy. Lancasters of 218 Squadron carried out a similar operation further east, circling gradually towards Boulogne.

At the same time, Stirlings of 199 Squadron and B-17 Fortresses of the USAAF used airborne devices to jam enemy radar which might have picked the approach of the true invasion fleet. Further to the west, Lancasters of 101 Squadron and Fortresses of 214 Squadron flew between Beachy Head and Paris, dropping 'Window' foil to jam the enemy night-fighter control system. Halifaxes and Stirlings of 90, 138 and 149 Squadrons dropped dummy paratroops, fireworks and rifle-fire simulators over the village of Yvetot,

STIRLINGS TOWING HORSA GLIDERS.

Left: Horsa gliders, carrying about twenty-five airborne troops and two pilots of the Army's Glider Pilot Regiment, under tow by RAF Halifaxes and Stirlings prior to D-Day.

AIR 37/1231

Below: A dummy parachutist with a machine-gun simulator attached, such as those dropped over Yvetot in the early hours of 6 June 1944 by Halifaxes and Stirlings.

AIR 24/281

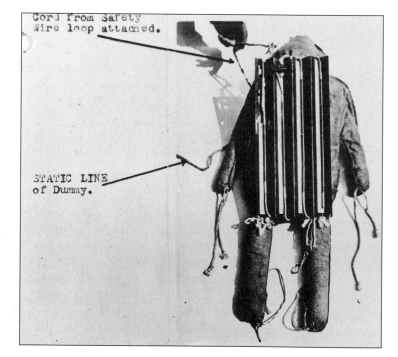

Cord from Safety Wire loop attached.

STATIC LINE of Dummy.

north of Rouen, to deceive the enemy into believing that an airborne operation was taking place in that area. A few men of the SAS were also dropped.

The British Second Army was destined to land between Ouistreham and Graye-sur-Mer in Normandy, on beaches code-named 'Sword' and 'Juno'. In advance, the 6th Airborne Division was given three major tasks to support the landings. Firstly, it had to capture intact two bridges over the Caen canal and the river Orne, so that the seaborne troops could advance and secure their bridgehead. Secondly, the heavily fortified gun battery at Merville, which overlooked the 'Sword' beach, had to be destroyed. Thirdly, it had to blow up five bridges over the river Dives to the east, to prevent German forces moving up on the British flank.

The capture of the two bridges was a combined Army and RAF 'coup de main' operation. Six Halifaxes of 298 and 644 Squadron took off from Tarrant Rushton in Dorsetshire at about 23.00 hours GMT on 5 June, towing six Horsa gliders flown by Army pilots of C Squadron, Glider Pilot Regiment. The gliders carried 138 soldiers of the 2nd Battalion, Oxfordshire and Buckinghamshire Light Infantry, thirty men of the Royal Engineers, medical staff and a liaison officer from the 7th Parachute Battalion, all under the command of Major R. John Howard. The formation arrived at the French coast shortly before midnight and the tows were released.

Above: The three gliders which landed at 00.16 hours on D-Day, 6 June 1944, near the bridge over the Caen canal, photographed later in the day. From top to bottom: Horsa No 91, flown by Staff Sergeant James Wallwork; Horsa No 93, flown by Staff Sergeant Geoffrey Barkway; Horsa No 92, flown by Staff Sergeant Oliver Boland.

DEFE 2/429

Right: Horsa gliders in Normandy, photographed on 9 June 1944. The fuselages were detachable for ease of unloading. They broke away sometimes, on landing.

AIR 14/3650

One Horsa, flown by Staff Sergeant A. Lawrence, was mistowed and came down too far to the east, but the other five gliders came down near their targets with remarkable accuracy. At 00.16 hours the glider flown by Staff Sergeant James Wallwork slid through the perimeter wire at the eastern side of the canal bridge. Fifteen yards behind, the glider flown by Staff Sergeant Geoffrey Barkway slewed round

Above: Landing craft and shipping on the beach at Graye-sur-Mer, where part of the British Second Army landed in the early morning of 6 June 1944. The photographs were taken at low tide in the afternoon and formed into a mosaic.

AIR 34/240

Right:The concrete caissons designed to form part of the 'Mulberry' artificial harbours in Normandy were floated on D-Day, 6 June 1944. Towing across the English Channel then began.

AIR 34/241

and broke in half. The third glider, flown by Staff Sergeant Oliver Boland, landed about ten yards away in marshy ground and was badly damaged, with one soldier drowned. The remaining two gliders, flown by Staff Sergeants R. Howard and S. Pearson, landed close to the river bridge. Air Chief Marshal Sir Trafford Leigh-Mallory of the AEAF described these achievements as 'one of the finest pieces of airmanship thus far in World War II'.

The German troops defending the river bridge dropped their weapons and ran away, but there was a bitter fight for the canal bridge. The position was taken at the cost of several casualties and held until reinforced by paratroops of the 7th Parachute Battalion, who had dropped slightly to the east. Several German counter-attacks were repelled, and then at 13.30 hours the defenders were relieved by seaborne commandos of the 1st Special Service Brigade led by Brigadier the Lord Lovat.

The Merville battery was taken by the paratroops at terrible cost. It was intended that 600 men would assault the strong defences after ninety-nine Lancasters and Halifaxes had delivered a bombing attack, but the weather closed in and most of the bombs fell to the south of the battery. Many 'Eureka' homing beacons dropped with paratroop 'pathfinders' were damaged, and men from the main parties remained widely scattered. All the gliders carrying heavy equipment and more troops missed the correct dropping zones. By 02.50 hours only 150 men of the 9th Parachute Battalion assembled for the assault, the same number as the defenders. They lost sixty-five, killed in a desperate fight, with 100 Germans killed.

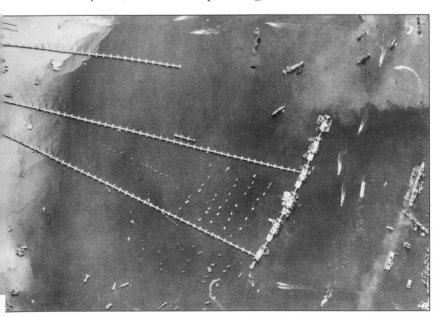

Left: Floating roadways connected to the pierhead of concrete caissons to the shore. This photograph was taken on 30 June 1944.
AIR 34/241

Above: German prisoners under escort marching across the floating roadway for embarkation to England.
AIR 34/241

The third task of blowing five bridges over the river Dives was accomplished by the attacking airborne troops, after a series of spirited actions. With all three tasks completed, the men took up defensive positions to await the arrival of seaborne troops. These landings were accomplished by about 57,500 troops of the US 1st Army on 'Utah' and 'Omaha' beaches and by about 75,000 British and Canadian troops on 'Gold', 'Juno' and 'Sword' beaches. They were preceded by about 27,000 airborne troops who descended by parachutes and gliders.

A stream of seaborne reinforcements followed, many of whom landed with their supplies at the ingenious 'Mulberry' harbours which were assembled from the caissons, roadways and blockships brought over the English Channel.

19 British Bridgehead

The Allied Expeditionary Air Force continued to be based in England during the first four days of the invasion. Spitfires, Mustangs, Typhoons, Mitchells, Mosquitos and Tempests of the 2nd Tactical Air Force ranged over the beachheads and beyond, seeking enemy aircraft and ground targets to attack. The Luftwaffe remained elusive but troop movements on roads were detected and devasting attacks on armed columns were made, albeit at some expense to fighter-bombers blasting them at close range.

Units of the RAF's Servicing Commandos and Construction Wings came ashore on 7 June and worked with the Royal Engineers on new airfields, usually under fire. The first was completed at Ste Croix-sur-Mer on 10 June and three squadrons of RCAF Spitfires began to operate from it, defended by detachments of the RAF Regiment. By 12 June,

Below: Bomber Command despatched 1,065 aircraft on the night of 6/7 June 1944 to bomb transport centres behind the Allied beachheads. Cloud affected accuracy but considerable damage was done to several targets. This photograph of the burning town of Caen was taken from 800 feet by a photo-reconnaissance Spitfire during the following day.

AIR 25/792

Above: A Giant Würzburg radar, demolished at Douvres La Delénerance, a few miles south of the beaches where British troops landed.
AIR 20/2207

Below: Spitfires at a forward airfield in Normandy, revving up ready to taxi out to the runway and take off on an evening patrol.
DEFE 2/502

Above: Men of an RAF Servicing Commandos and Construction Wing unrolling steel wire mesh for constructing a runway.
DEFE 2/502

the American and British/Canadian beachheads had linked up to form a front fifty miles long and about ten miles deep. As this area gradually expanded, thirty more airfields were built in the British zone while fifty were constructed by the Americans in their zone.

Attacks by Mosquitos, Bostons and Mitchells of the 2nd Tactical Air Force, combined with bombers of the US Ninth Air Force, were made against enemy airfields and enemy reserves approaching the battle zone. Many movements by rail and main roads were brought to a halt and the Germans began to use secondary roads at night in an attempt to filter through. Mosquito crews became particularly skilful in picking out the glint of armoured vehicles in moonlight and delivering their attacks. Some German units took about a fortnight to reach the front line, their strengths depleted by these continual air operations.

After three weeks, the number of Allied squadrons based on airfields hastily constructed in the beachheads had increased to thirty-one. In addition, fighter squadrons based in England continued their patrols over the coastal area.

Heavy bombers of the US Eighth Air Force and Bomber Command were also called upon to make attacks behind enemy lines, and did so with devastating effect. Allied aircraft dominated the battleground while the Luftwaffe fighters could do little more than attempt to defend their own airfields. German bombers were seldom able to pierce the

Allied defences and instead were relegated to the task of dropping mines at night in the English Channel.

Light bombers of the 2nd Tactical Air Force, escorted by Mustangs, ranged further afield. Typhoons and Spitfires formed 'cab ranks' over front lines, awaiting calls by Army liaison officers before swooping down on enemy columns and strongpoints. The air was full of these deadly RAF aircraft and the roads were strewn with wrecked German vehicles and their dead occupants. Rockets proved the most effective weapons in these ground attacks and the German soldiers soon learnt to detest Typhoon and Spitfire fighter-bombers. There were instances of columns becoming immobilized on roads by smashed vehicles at their head and rear, so that the aircraft could then range along the whole length and finish off all those remaining. Field Marshal Erwin Rommel, who commanded Army Group 'B' in the west, was badly injured in a fighter-bomber attack on 17 July; he survived only to meet his end in an enforced suicide on 14 October.

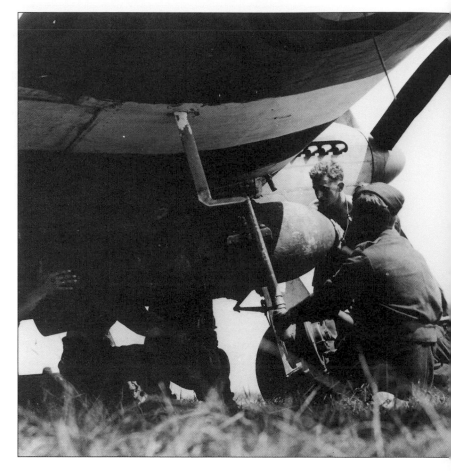

Left: 'Blaze of Rockets Ahead' by Charles J. Thompson

An impressionistic painting of a Hawker Typhoon making a rocket attack after D-Day.

Above: An RAF Mustang at a forward airfield in Normandy, being armed with two 1,000 lb high-explosive bombs, at a time when the squadron was engaged on 'barge-bashing' against enemy river transport and jetties on the Seine, mainly in the area of Rouen. Other targets were road and rail transport. The airmen winching up the bomb under the mainplane are recorded as (left to right) Corporal S.R. Powell, Aircraftman J. Taylor and Corporal W.H. Glover.
DEFE 2/502

Left: Rocket-firing Typhoons of
the 2nd Tactical Air Force.
AIR 34/241

Right: A damaged Hawker
Typhoon IB of 184 Squadron
on an airfield in Normandy. A
rocket projectile had been fired
by accident and hit the ground
nearby. The starboard side
of the aircraft was riddled
while the blast had caused
misalignment of the main
member of the fuselage.
AIR 20/2207

Meanwhile, the British 1st Army was stalled outside for-tified villages around the city of Caen. Field Marshal Sir Bernard Montgomery, who commanded the land forces, decided to call for a series of heavy bomber attacks much closer to the front line. The first was delivered by 467 aircraft of Bomber Command on 7 July, resulting in the devastation of the northern suburbs. The British and Canadians were able to advance and enter the outskirts of the city. But the Germans still held the area to the east and in early morning of 18 July an even greater number, 942 aircraft, mounted a colossal attack. This was followed on the same day by 977 heavy and medium bombers of the US Eighth and Ninth Air Forces. These had a paralysing effect on the defences and an armoured breakthrough seemed imminent.

Above: A German armoured troop carrier, destroyed by rocket projectiles which struck a front track after being fired by an RAF Typhoon.

AIR 20/2207

Below: A train of oil tank wagons on the railway line between Beauvais and Méru, north of Paris, burning furiously after an attack by fighter-bombers of the 2nd Tactical Air Force. The photograph was taken from 6,000 feet on 8 June 1944 by a photo-reconnaissance Spitfire.

AIR 25/792

Left: A German Panther tank, burnt out and abandoned after air attack.

AIR 20/2207

Right: The results of a rocket attack by Typhoons on enemy headquarters, being studied by pilots after its capture.

AIR 34/241

Allied reinforcements continued to pour over the English Channel and on 23 July sufficient Canadians had arrived to form the Canadian 1st Army, fighting on the left of the British 2nd Army. On the right flank, the US 1st Army continued its pressure. Yet the Germans still held firm, in spite of the overwhelming strength they faced on the ground and in the air. Of course, they were under orders from Hitler not to retreat, but it says much for the fortitude and discipline of these soldiers that they did not capitulate and even counter-attacked on occasions. But a time was approaching when they could no longer fight against such odds.

20 The Ninth in Action

The US Ninth Air Force had been set up on 16 October 1943 as a tactical force, capable of moving rapidly across north-west Europe in support of the US 1st Army and indeed the whole enterprise. It was the USAAF's component of the Allied Expeditionary Air Force and the equivalent of the RAF's 2nd Tactical Air Force. Of course these two forces worked in close collaboration with each other, under Air Chief Marshal Sir Trafford Leigh-Mallory. On D-Day, the Ninth Air Force had a strength of about 172,000 men and 2,769 serviceable aircraft. These can be compared with the RAF elements of the AEAF – the 2nd Tactical Air Force, the Air Defence of Great Britain and the Transport Groups – which numbered about 230,000 men and 2,500 serviceable aircraft.

Fighters formed the greater number of aircraft in the Ninth Air Force. Of these, P-47 Thunderbolts predominated, equipping thirteen Fighter Groups (a Group in the USAAF being the equivalent of a Wing in the RAF). Three Groups were equipped with P-38 Lightnings and two with P-51 Mustangs. There were also variants of the Lightnings and Mustangs for the vital role of photo-reconnaissance.

Above Right: Beach defences on the French coast, photographed before D-Day by an F-5 Lightning of the US Ninth Air Force flying at very low level. The tide was out, exposing stakes and ramps to which explosives had been attached.

AIR 40/1959

Right: 'The Bridge-Busters' by Mark Postlethwaite

Martin B-26 Marauders of the 497th Bomb Squadron, 344th Bomb Group, US Ninth Air Force, in action over Normandy, with North America P-51 Mustang fighter escorts in the distance.

Eleven Groups were equipped with the B-26 Marauder medium bomber or the A-20 Havoc light bomber (a variant of the Boston), with the Marauders being the more numerous. Added to these were two Troop Carrier Wings (a Wing in the USAAF being the equivalent of a Group in the RAF). These were equipped with about 1,150 C-47 Skytrains or C-53 Skytroopers, but came under the direct command of the AEAF for operational purposes. In addition to these powered aircraft were the gliders, numbering about 2,750 serviceable aircraft.

In the weeks before D-Day, the Ninth had concentrated on destroying bridges over the Seine, to prevent German reinforcements moving from the east to the landing beaches. On D-Day itself, it gave high cover over the assault area in co-operation with Spitfires of the 2nd Tactical Air Force, provided low cover with fighters of the US Eighth Air Force, gave tactical support to the US 1st Army over its beachheads, and sent its photo-reconnaissance aircraft on tactical missions behind enemy lines. It made over 3,000 operational flights on that day, excluding the airborne troop carriers which flew on over 900 missions. The American

Above Left: Namur railway centre in Belgium was extensively damaged by bombers and fighter-bombers of the US Ninth Air Force by two attacks on 23 April 1944. The first wave consisted of sixty-seven Mustang fighter-bombers escorted by thirty-two Mustang fighters. The second wave consisted of seventy-six Marauders escorted by fifty P-47 Thunderbolts, with five squadrons of RAF Spitfires providing additional cover.
AIR 37/1231

Left: On 26 April 1944, the US Ninth Air Force despatched seventy-four Bostons, escorted by twenty-nine Thunderbolts, to bomb railway targets at Louvain in Belgium. Results were generally good, but some aircraft bombed a target nearby.
AIR 37/865

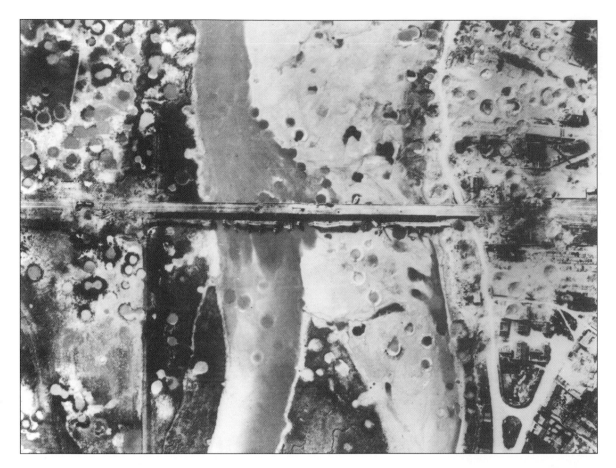

troops landed to the west of the British, on beaches code-named 'Utah' and 'Omaha' and met strong and withering fire on 'Omaha' beach, where casualties amounted to almost 4,000 dead, wounded or missing.

The Ninth maintained the same maximum scale of effort on the second day, but serviceability decreased and operations on the third day were limited to 2,400 sorties, a rate which was still intense. These were centred on disrupting enemy movements on the ground, particularly in the 'Omaha' sector. Elsewhere, there was some duplication of effort with the 2nd TAF, but boundaries between the two forces soon became better defined. However, the British 2nd Army requested an attack on German positions near its front line at Caen. This was accomplished with precision by 250 Marauders of the Ninth in the early morning of 9 June, while its fighters went further afield against roads and railways, earning a signal of appreciation from the British.

During the remainder of the first week after D-Day, the Ninth was engaged on fighter cover and escort, interception of enemy aircraft, attacking enemy gun positions and strong-points, strafing enemy troops and dumps, and troop

Above: Units of the US Ninth Engineer Command landed on 'Utah' beach on D-Day and others landed on 'Omaha' beach the following day. They began constructing an emergency landing strip at St Laurent two days after D-Day. This was rapidly improved until it could be used by transport aircraft.

AIR 37/865

Right: Air evacuation of wounded to the UK began from A-21 St Laurent airstrip on 10 June 1944 by the US Ninth Air Transport Command, employing Dakotas. By the end of the month the Command had transported 7,410 American, 42 Allied and 211 German wounded to England, without any fatalities en route.

AIR 37/865

carrier or transport missions. The ground attack Thunderbolt, when fitted with ten 5-inch rockets, had a devastating effect on German armour. The Lightning fighter-bomber, with a bomb-carrying capacity of up to 2,000 lb, was employed on destroying bridges and troop movements from low level. Both these fighter aircraft achieved extraordinary results, but losses in such point-blank work were sometimes heavy. The Havocs and Mitchells were mainly

Above: The Port du Gravière railway bridge over the river Seine, photographed from 5,000 feet on 11 June 1944 from an F-5 Lightning of the US Ninth Air Force. The northern half of the bridge had been seen to have collapsed six days earlier after extensive bombing of bridges over the Seine.

AIR 25/792

Above: Beaugency railway viaduct, to the south-west of Orléans, was cut in two places on 14 June 1944 by fifty-one tons of bombs dropped by thirty-six Marauders of the US Ninth Air Force, escorted by Thunderbolts and Mustangs.
AIR 37/1231

Below: Two sections of the railway bridge at Tours-la-Riche over the river Loire were destroyed by the US Ninth Air Force. Forty-seven P-47 Thunderbolts made an attack on 13 June 1944, thirty of them dropping seven tons of bombs.
AIR 37/1231

engaged on attacking marshalling yards and bridges to the immediate south of the American bridgehead. These operations were mounted against numerous targets, but each was on a small scale compared with the huge attacks on single targets made by the US Eighth Air Force.

It had been intended that bridges and the traffic further south would be destroyed by the heavy bombers of the US Eighth Air Force and Bomber Command, but a combination of poor weather and other commitments prevented execution of this task. The Ninth began bombing railway bridges over the river Loire on 13 June and within four days had destroyed all of them, causing considerable hindrance to enemy reinforcements moving up from the south.

On the ground, the US 1st Army fought against stubborn defences and suffered considerable casualties, but on 14 June one division broke out across the Cotentin peninsula, cutting off three German divisions and joining two other US divisions in an attack on Cherbourg. This port fell on 3 July and enabled the Allies to bring the 'Pluto' oil pipeline ashore and start providing 250,000 gallons of fuel a day to their armies. To the south, however, the German lines still held and a major breakthrough had not yet been achieved.

21 Breakout

In the course of July 1944 sufficient reinforcements were brought over from England to form the US 3rd Army under Lieutenant-General George S. Patton, but to conceal this increased strength from the enemy the various Corps served for the time being as part of the US 1st Army, under General Omar Bradley. By 22 July this Army had suffered over 60,000 dead or wounded while the British and Canadian casualties were almost 35,000. The German Armies had lost about the same number as the Allies but were unable to bring up sufficient reinforcements to maintain their strength.

It was air power which paved the way for the Allies. In the period 1-18 July the Allies lost 312 aircraft over Normandy in the course of 55,747 sorties while the Luftwaffe lost 355 during only 8,840 sorties. Thus in terms of sorties the Luftwaffe losses ran at about seven times the rate of the Allies. Moreover, it could not replace these losses. Even if new aircraft could be brought to the west, few competent pilots were available.

The Allies put their control of the skies to overwhelming use. On 18 July a massive attack by Bomber Command, the US Eighth Air Force and the Allied Expeditionary Air Force dropped 7,700 tons of bombs on Colombelles, a suburb on the east of Caen. Although the German wall did not give way, Field Marshal Günther von Kluge, who by then had taken over from Field Marshal Gerd von Rundstedt as German Supreme Commander in West, could see that the British and Canadians would attempt to break out southwards from their hard-won positions in the ruined city towards Falaise. A Panzer division was moved from the

Left: Direct hits on a German strongpoint in a steelworks at Caen-Mondeville. The photograph was taken on 22 June 1944 during an attack by Bostons of 88 and 342 Squadrons and Mitchells of 226 Squadron. These formed No 137 Wing of the RAF's No 2 Group, part of the 2nd Tactical Air Force.

AIR 34/334

Left: The devastated city of Caen photographed on 13 June 1944 after a week during which there were bombardments by the US Ninth Air Force, Bomber Command and the US Eighth Air Force. Almost all the buildings were wrecked, debris blocked the roads and the bridges over the river Orne were destroyed.

AIR 34/240

Right: Bomber Command despatched 467 aircraft in the evening of 7 July 1944 to assist in the Normandy land battle. The main targets were enemy strongpoints north of Caen, which were holding up the advance of the British 2nd Army and the Canadian 1st Army. The bombing was concentrated and only three aircraft were lost, two of which crashed behind Allied lines. This photograph of a Halifax over the target area was taken from 15,000 feet.

AIR 14/3696

Below: A German fuel dump east of Argentan, in Normandy south of Caen, under attack on 6 July 1944 by Bostons of the RAF's 88 and 342 Squadrons.

AIR 34/334

American sector to bolster the German defences, while an Army which had been held in reserve in the Pas de Calais on Hitler's orders was at last committed to the defence of Falaise. By this time there were three times the number of Germans facing the British and Canadians than the Americans. In fact, this accorded exactly with the strategy of General Sir Bernard L. Montgomery, the Commander-in-Chief of the Allied Armies.

By then, the American line stretched from Caumont in the east to Lessay on the west coast of the Cotentin peninsula. In the clear morning of 25 July, a great offensive opened in the centre of his line, in open country near St Lô. It began with 600 fighter-bombers of the US Ninth Air Force attacking the enemy's forward positions, some of them dropping napalm bombs. These were followed by waves of the US Eighth Air Force's heavy bombers, amounting to 1,500 in all, dropping 3,400 tons of high-explosive and fragmentation bombs. Then came waves of medium bombers of the US Ninth Air Force, dropping more bombs on targets further south. The US 1st Army advanced through the devastation, supported closely by fighter-bombers of the Ninth while medium bombers continued to attack behind the lines. These assaults continued for three more days, supported by the Ninth, and by then the German line was broken.

Left: The railway marshalling yards at Châlons-sur-Marne and Nevers were attacked by 229 aircraft of Bomber Command during the night of 15/16 July 1944. Interpretation of photographs of Châlons-sur-Marne, such as this taken on 17 July, showed that serious damage had been caused in the sidings. All the lines had been cut and over 100 goods wagons destroyed, damaged or derailed.

AIR 14/3663

Below: 'Thunderbolts and Lightning over St Lô' by Charles J. Thompson

A great offensive by the US Eighth and Ninth Air Forces took place on 25 July 1944, under operation 'Cobra'. It included about 600 fighter-bombers of the US Ninth Air Force which made low-level attacks with high explosive and napalm on forward positions of the German LXXXIV Corps along the River Vire on the west of the Normandy beachhead, opposite the US VII Corps. The Germans lost over half the men killed or wounded and much of their equipment. The US 1st Army was able to break through on the next day.

This painting shows P-47 Thunderbolts of the 81st Fighter Squadron of the 50th Fighter Group, one with the 'razor back' fuselage, one with the 'tear-drop' canopy. The P-38 Lightning is from the 429th Fighter Squadron of the 474th Fighter Group.

On 30 July, Bomber Command and fighter-bombers of the 2nd Tactical Air Force dropped over 2,500 lb of bombs to support the British 1st Army south of Caumont, where a new offensive was opened. However this was a far more difficult area, known as the *bocage*, consisting of a jumble of trees, hills and narrow winding roads enclosed by high banks and hedges. Progress was slow against stiff enemy resistance. Nevertheless, von Kluge advised Hitler that a withdrawal to the east had become necessary. However, at a conference the next day the Führer refused, in a rambling and incoherent speech. He was suffering from injuries sustained in a bomb attack eleven days before.

By 1 August, the Americans had consolidated their gains in the Cotentin peninsula and General Patton, with his US 3rd Army officially constituted, was ordered to advance to the Loire and also send forces westwards to invest the Breton ports of St Malo, Brest and Lorient. Six days later, on 7 August, a strong force of German tanks attacked the American lines at Mortain, at a point where it was thought the US 1st Army could be taken in the flank. Some early

Left: Two bridges had been built over the river Sienne at Gavray, alongside the bridge shattered by Allied bombing. The photograph was taken by the US Ninth Air Force on 29 July 1944, during the advance of the US 1st Army from the Cotentin peninsula.
AIR 37/865

Below: A very effective raid was made in daylight on 31 July 1944 when 127 Lancasters and four Mosquitos of Bomber Command attacked the railway yards at Joigny-La-Roche, south-east of Paris. One Lancaster was lost.
AIR 14/3696

gains were made but it was not long before rocket-firing Typhoons of the 2nd Tactical Air Force appeared. After two hours of attacks, about half the German armour was destroyed, while the US Ninth Air Force dealt with communications to the rear and prevented the Luftwaffe from interfering. Swarms of Typhoons came again during the following day and the Germans were forced to pull back, with heavy losses.

By then, the Wehrmacht had lost the Battle of Normandy. General Patton had send three Corps of his US 3rd Army south and south-east. Le Mans was taken on 8 August and one of these Corps then drove northwards, intending to join up with the British and Canadians advancing towards Falaise. General Bradley also sent his US 1st Army in a pincer movement, circling to the south of the German forces and then north towards the British and Canadians. These moves threatened to trap sixteen German divisions in a huge pocket. At last, on 13 August, Hitler gave the German forces permission to retreat behind the Seine, but by then it was too late.

The Germans caught in the trap fought desperately but their armour was steadily destroyed by rocket-firing aircraft of the Allied Expeditionary Air Force. Some remnants of the shattered forces managed to flee to the east, pursued relentlessly by four armies, two American, one British and one Canadian, all co-ordinating with the Allied Expeditionary Air Force. The advancing troops were heartened by waves of aircraft blasting a way for them, but the morale of the Germans finally cracked. Some might have compared their plight with the success of their *Blitzkrieg* against France in May 1940.

In a lightning movement, the US 3rd Army reached Angers on 11 August and continued to Orléans five days later. To add to the tribulations of the Germans, the US 7th Army made an amphibious landing on 15 August, between St Raphael and Le Lavandou on the French Riviera, under the code-name of operation 'Dragoon'. The troops progressed rapidly beyond the beachhead and pushed northwards. Von Kluge, who had been given an impossible task, committed suicide on 18 August.

In the north, the Canadian 1st Army raced along the coast, bypassing Boulogne, Calais and Dunkirk, which

Below: In the early morning of 2 August 1944, Mosquitos of No 2 Group, part of the 2nd Tactical Air Force, attacked Château Trevarez, a rest centre used by U-boat crews on the river Aulne east of Brest. Although the Mosquito crews saw no activity when dropping their delay-action bombs and destroying the building, a message from the French Maquis stated that over 400 of the U-boat men were there at the time, sleeping off the effects of a heavy party the night before. This photograph was taken by a ciné-camera fitted to one of the Mosquitos.
AIR 34/241

Below: Mosquitos of the 2nd Tactical Air Force ranged further east on 31 August 1944 to attack these school buildings at Vincey, south of Metz, which were reported to be the headquarters of 2,000 SS troops. This photograph does not show the full effect, as the bombs were delay-action, but one building was completely destroyed and the other suffered much interior damage.
AIR 34/241

Left: An enemy ammunition dump at Montreuil-Belfroy was blown up by accurate bombing from Bostons and Mitchells of the 2nd Tactical Air Force on 2 August 1944.

AIR 34/241

Below: The oil storage depot at Bec d'Ambes, under attack by Bomber Command on 4 August 1944. The photograph was taken from 8,000 feet by a Halifax III of 51 Squadron, based at Snaith in Yorkshire, which dropped eight 1,000 lb and two 500 lb bombs.

AIR 14/3696

Right: Bomber Command despatched 288 Lancasters on 4 August 1944 to attack oil storage deports at Pauillac and Bec d'Ambes, near Bordeaux. It was followed the next day by attacks on Pauillac, Blaye and Bordeaux by 308 Lancasters. This photograph of the inferno at Pauillac was taken shortly after the second attack.

AIR 37/1231

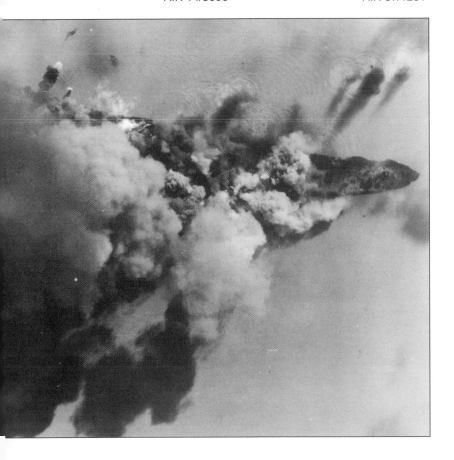

remained for the time being as German 'fortresses'. Some miles to the south, the British 2nd Army crossed the Belgian border on 2 September and liberated Brussels the following day. On their right flank, the US 1st Army left Paris to be liberated on 25 August by a French Armoured Division and then reached Liège and Luxembourg on 8 September. On the far right of the Allied advance, the US 3rd Army streaked across France, to reach Metz and Nancy on 15 September. It linked up with the US 7th Army, driving up from the south, six days later. They were in sight of Germany itself.

The Wehrmacht in France had lost almost 300,000 men since D-Day, together with most of its equipment. The breathless pace of these Allied successes in August and September was enough to convince the more optimistic in the West that 'it will all be over by Christmas'. They were to be proved wrong. On 6 August, Lieutenant-General Lewis H. Brereton of the US Ninth Air Force had been replaced by Major-General Hoyt S. Vandenberg, to form and command the new 1st Allied Airborne Army. There was much fighting ahead for this new Command.

22 Hitler's Secret Weapons

When the tide of war began to flow strongly against his country, Hitler tried to bolster morale by hinting darkly of deadly 'wonder weapons' which he would unleash against the Allies to bring victory to the Third Reich. Of course, he was referring to the flying bombs and rockets which were being developed and tested. In fact, the British had known for some years of such possible weapons and were alert to the danger. Their suspicions began to crystallize from December 1942 when reports were received of tests with long-range rockets taking place at Peenemünde on the Baltic coast. Photo-reconnaissance aircraft were sent out and in April 1943 brought back definite evidence of the weapon. Other possible launching sites were located in the Pas de Calais.

The first action of the RAF was to launch a heavy attack against the site at Peenemünde, on the moonlit night of 17/18 August 1943. Bomber Command caused much damage but lost heavily from night-fighters operating in clear conditions. Soon afterwards, the British became aware from intelligence decrypts, agents, resistance fighters in France and photo-reconnaissance that there were two types of weapons, a 'pilotless aircraft' known as the V-1 and a rocket which was named the V-2. In the late autumn of 1943 a directorate was set up to collate information on these and recommend countermeasures, under operation 'Crossbow'.

Many launching ramps for V-1s were located in woods or orchards between the Seine and Cap Gris Nez, becoming

Right: The German rocket establishment at Peenemünde near the Baltic coast, where research into V-2 rockets was taking place, photographed before the raid by Bomber Command.

AIR 14/3671

Left: The effect of the raid on the night of 17/18 August by 596 aircraft of Bomber Command on Peenemünde, during which considerable damage was caused but forty bombers were lost.

AIR 14/3671

Right: 'Diver Patrol'
by Mark Postlethwaite

The code-name given by the British to the V-1 flying bomb was 'Diver'. This painting shows a Hawker Tempest V of 3 Squadron manoeuvring to attack one of these bombs. The squadron shot down 258 of them before the launching sites were overrun by the Allied armies.

known as 'Noball' sites. Attacks on these began in December 1943, by fighter-bombers and light bombers of the 2nd Tactical Air Force, medium bombers of the US Ninth Air Force, and heavy bombers of the US Eighth Air Force and Bomber Command. Attacks on single sites were usually carried out by only a small number of aircraft, but by May 1944 it was estimated that 103 had been destroyed out of 140 located. While these operations were in progress, the Germans responded by designing a simpler and prefabricated form of ramp for the V-1 which could be rapidly assembled. These were camouflaged to resemble farm buildings, but some were identified and also attacked.

The first V-1 flying bombs were fired against London on 12 June 1944, six days after D-Day. Only seven left the ramps and none reached England. The Germans managed to overcome their technical problems and by the end of the month 2,000 had been launched. The bomb was armed with a warhead containing 1,870 lb of high-explosive and propelled by compressed air from spherical containers in the rear fuselage. The tank held 150 gallons of low octane fuel which gave the weapon about 40 minutes of flying time at about 400 mph. Direction was maintained by gyroscopes

but the bomb was not accurate, even at short range, being affected by wind velocity as well as technical imperfections. Beyond 120 miles, accuracy was very poor indeed.

The response of the British was a combination of defence and offence. Standing fighter patrols were flown over home counties southeast of London and over the Channel between Beachy Head and Dover. Between these and a balloon barrage on the outskirts of London a belt consisting of numerous anti-aircraft guns was installed. At the same time, co-ordinated bombing attacks were delivered by Bomber Command and the US Eighth Air Force on the sites.

These measures achieved some results but were not completely successful. The heavy bombers could not be diverted completely from their assaults in the Battle of Normandy. The V-1 was a small target for ground gunners and fighters had only a slight margin of speed over it. Fortunately many of those which were not brought down by the defences fell on open ground. A change of policy on 14 July involved the movement of the anti-aircraft guns to the coast, improving the rate of 'kills'. But it was the overrunning of the sites by the Canadian 1st Army which brought the main phase of the V-1 assault to an end on 5 September.

Above: In the morning of 6 July 1944, Bomber Command despatched 551 aircraft to attack five sites in the Pas de Calais believed to contain V-2 weapons. Four targets were clear and good results were obtained. This Halifax III was photographed over Sirancourt.

AIR 34/240

Right: The site at Sirancourt after the attack, showing the concrete structure damaged in several places, with the service roads and railways obliterated by hundreds of bombs. The photograph was taken from 100 feet the day after the attack by an F-5 Lightning of the US Ninth Air Force.

AIR 25/792

Left: Another site attacked on 6 July 1944 was at Marquise-Mimoyecques, not far from the coast. This Halifax III was photographed over the target.
AIR 34/240

Above: The site at Marquise-Mimoyecques, showing the concrete structure hit by a heavy bomb and the surrounding area turned into a lunar landscape. The structure was found later to hold sections of barrels for long-range guns. These guns were to be 500 feet long and set at an angle to fire 6-inch shells at London. The project, which was probably technically impracticable, was abandoned by the Germans after the bombing.
AIR 34/240

Thereafter, a few were launched from Heinkel He111s operating at night from airfields in the Netherlands, but these were shot down in increasing numbers by RAF night-fighters. Others were launched in the Low Countries and these continued until 28 March 1945, although there was no accuracy. During the whole of the campaign, almost 4,000 V-1s were brought down by the defences. Those which arrived caused over 6,000 deaths and 17,000 seriously wounded, almost entirely among the civilian population.

The V-2 rocket was the forerunner of the intercontinental ballistic missile which became part of the nuclear armoury

FLYING BOMB ON LAUNCHING PLATFORM

Above: A V-1 Flying Bomb in position on the bottom of a ramp, ready for launching, with the control building barely discernable among trees.

AIR 34/240

Right: Eleven 1,000lb and three 500lb bombs dropping from a Lancaster of 582 Squadron, based at Little Staughton in Huntingdonshire, at 15,000 feet above a V-1 Flying Bomb site on 19 July 1944. Bomber Command despatched 144 aircraft on that day. Most of the targets were covered with cloud but it was believed that they were hit. No aircraft were lost.

AIR 14/3696

of nations post-war. It was launched vertically from a pad, had a range of about 200 miles, was radio-controlled during flight, and the warhead contained about a ton of high-explosive. The first fell on England on 8 September 1944. About seventy-five of these weapons then fell haphazardly on London and the Home Counties in the next four weeks. Some caused little damage but there were civilian casualties and the attacks gave rise to consternation. The V-2s descended without warning from high level and exploded, and there was no defence against them save the bombing

Right: This site at Wizernes, designed for V-2 rockets, was photographed by a Mosquito after a successful attack by Bomber Command, which despatched 369 aircraft to six V-weapon sites on 20 July 1944. Several 12,000lb bombs had hit this target, which had been built into the edge of a quarry. Most of the works buildings were underground, topped by a massive concrete dome. The attack had damaged this dome and also caused much of the cliff face to collapse, blocking several tunnels leading to underground workings. The Todt Organisation was working on the site at the time, using a 100 ft hammerhead crane to repair damage caused by another attack by Bomber Command three days earlier.
DEFE 2/502

Left: A Halifax III of 433 (RCAF) Squadron, based at Skipton-on-Swale in Yorkshire, flying at 15,000 feet over Forêt de Nieppe in northern France on 3 August 1944, during an attack on V-1 flying bomb stores. The evening sun cast a shadow of the fuselage and mid-upper turret over the port wing. Bomber Command despatched 1,114 aircraft against flying bomb storage sites on that day, and six Lancasters were lost.
AIR 14/3647

of launching pads and the production centres or storage depots.

By mid October launching pads had been discovered south of The Hague, and attacks were mounted against German transport facilities and liquid oxygen factories in the area by fighter-bombers and medium bombers of the Allied Expeditionary Air Force. There was some diminution in the number of V-2s reaching England, and for a while the weapons were aimed against Antwerp, which had fallen to the Allies. But the rockets continued to fall on England until the Germans in the west of the Netherlands had been cut off from Germany by the advancing Allies. The last of 1,115 to arrive in England was launched on 27 March 1945. By this time they had caused almost 3,000 deaths and over 6,000 seriously wounded.

23 One-Way Ticket

In the last fortnight of September 1944, the Allied Air Forces played a prominent part in forcing the surrender of German garrisons holding out in Hitler's 'fortresses' on the French coast. Le Havre gave up the unequal struggle on 12 September and Boulogne followed a fortnight later. Calais lasted out until the end of the month. Meanwhile a major operation was conceived by Field Marshal Sir Bernard Montgomery and mounted under the code-name 'Market Garden'. This involved an attempt by Allied forces to out-flank enemy defences and seize bridges by means of a massive airborne attack in the vicinity of Arnhem in the Netherlands. If successful, this would enable the British 2nd Army to cross the Rhine and enter Germany itself. Thus the Wehrmacht in western Holland would be cut off and the Allies could sweep to the right, down into the Ruhr and then to the centre of Germany.

Top Right: Bomber Command despatched 348 aircraft in daylight on 5 September 1944 to bomb positions at Le Havre, where a German garrison was holding out after being bypassed by the Allied Armies. All aircraft returned safely and the weather was clear. This photograph, taken from a Lancaster of 514 Squadron, shows the dock area covered with smoke.

AIR 14/3663

Right: A massive attack by Bomber Command on Le Havre, this time by 992 aircraft on 10 September 1944, destroyed eight different German strongpoints. This photograph shows bomb explosions in the centre of the city. The garrison consisted of 11,300 men, equipped with 115 guns of all calibres and rations for ninety days. Hitler had ordered them to resist to the last. However, they surrendered to the 1st Canadian Army a day after one more attack, by 218 aircraft on 11 September. The Allies needed the port.

AIR 37/1231

Above: British airborne troops waiting by Horsa gliders on Sunday morning, 17 September 1944.

AIR 14/3650

Right: An Armstrong Whitworth Albemarle taking off with an Airspeed Horsa, while others wait their turn.

AIR 14/3650

The Allied airborne forces had been formed on 2 August 1944 into a single army under Lieutenant-General Lewis H. Brereton, the former commander of the US Ninth Air Force. This 1st Allied Airborne Army included the US Eighteenth Airborne Corps, the I Airborne Corps, the US Ninth Troop Carrier Command, and Nos 38 and 46 Groups of the RAF's Transport Command.

According to the airborne 'Garden' part of the plan, the main assault would be made by I Airborne Corps, commanded by Lieutenant-General F.A.M. 'Boy' Browning. Two US divisions would drop in the areas around Grave and Eindhoven, to the south of Arnhem, and capture bridges over the Maas and the Vaal. At the same time, a British division and a Polish brigade would drop near Arnhem and secure bridges over the Rhine. The 'Market' part of the plan involved the relief of the airborne forces by the British XXX Corps advancing from the south.

The operation began on Sunday 17 September, after about ten days of delay. British airborne forces were towed to Arnhem in Horsa gliders by Albemarles, Halifaxes and Stirlings of Transport Command. At the same time, the British 1st Parachute Brigade was dropped near Arnhem by

Left: Paratroopers preparing to jump from the entry door on the port side of a Douglas Dakota.

AIR 14/3650

Below Left: A corner of the main landing ground near Arnhem showing Horsa and Hamilcar gliders. The photograph was taken on 17 September 1944.

AIR 14/3650

Below: Airspeed Horsa and General Aircraft Hamilcar gliders on the main landing ground to the west of Arnhem.

AIR 14/3650

Dakotas of Transport Command and the US Ninth Troop Carrier Command, the latter being employed since the British did not have enough aircraft. Two American airborne divisions landed at Grave and Njmegen. This operation on the first day involved 3,887 British and American aircraft. These included escorting 1,240 fighters, 1,113 bombers making diversionary sweeps, and about 500 gliders. But even this armada carried only half the number of troops required for the operation.

The two American divisions achieved initial successes at Grave and Nijmegen but the British ran into immediate difficulties further north at Arnhem. To avoid flak near their target, they were dropped over seven miles west of the bridges. They were unaware that two Panzer divisions were resting north of their objectives and when one airborne brigade reached Arnhem in the evening, according to plan, it was surrounded. Moreover, their R/T communication did not work, so that the other forces had no up-to-date information. The British XXX Armoured Corps intended to relieve the airborne troops met far stiffer opposition than

Below: Wrecked German vehicles on the northern end of the bridge at Arnhem, photographed on 19 September 1944.

AIR 14/3650

Above: 'Air VC at Arnhem' by Charles J. Thompson

On Tuesday 19 September 1944, Flight Lieutenant David S.A. Lord took off in Dakota III serial KG374 of 271 Squadron from Down Ampney in Wiltshire on an air-dropping mission to the besieged airborne forces at Arnhem. His aircraft was loaded with ammunition panniers and there were four RAF men in the crew as well as four despatchers of the RASC. Together with sixteen other Dakotas of the squadron, they headed for a dropping zone on the north-west outskirts of Arnhem, not knowing that this was still in German hands. When nearing the dropping zone at 15.00 hours and at about 1,500 feet, the Dakota flew into intense flak and was hit in the starboard engine, which burst into flames. Lord continued his run, descending to 900 feet, but ordered his crew to prepare to bale out. The navigator, Flying Officer Harry King, went back with his parachute to help the despatchers kick out the panniers. Lord gave the order to bale out when all but two had been dropped, but then the burning starboard wing broke away and King was thrown through the opening. He managed to pull his ripcord but hit the ground hard and injured himself. The Dakota plunged to earth and exploded, carrying all the other men to their deaths.

After a night in action with paratroopers at Wolfheze railway station, King was captured by the Germans. It was not until he returned to England after the war that he was able to give a full report of the sortie. The posthumous award of a Victoria Cross was gazetted to David Lord on 13 November 1945.

143

expected. A copy of the Allied plan of the whole operation was captured by the Germans in a US glider shot down over their territory, and the defences were organized accordingly. The British Corps made unexpectedly slow progress, in spite of close support provided by rocket-firing Typhoons of the 2nd Tactical Air Force.

To compound the problem, the weather turned against the Allies. The lift on the following day was delayed until the afternoon, by which time the situation at Arnhem had deteriorated further. The Polish Independent Parachute Brigade, intended to support the first wave of troops, was unable to emplane. When these men finally took off, on the third day, the aircraft could not rendezvous with their fighter escort in the cloud and rain. About half were turned back while the remainder suffered heavy casualties from flak brought up by

Left: The flat and unobstructed terrain at Grave, south of Nijmegen, where US airborne forces landed. Some of these troops are standing on a pontoon bridge which they have erected over the broad and meandering river Maas, while a replacement section is moored at the quay.

AIR 34/241

Above: A close view of a Waco Hadrian glider of the US Ninth Troop Carrier Command at Grave. It carried two pilots and thirteen armed troops or equipment. The nose hinged upwards to permit loading and unloading of cargo.

AIR 34/241

Left: Supplies being dropped to troops on the ground during operation 'Market Garden'
AIR 14/3650

Left: The road and rail bridges at Nijmegen, linking the Netherlands and Germany. They were captured by the Allies on 21 September 1944, after heavy fighting.
AIR 34/241

the Germans. Equally disastrously, the zone chosen for the supply drop on this third day was still in the hands of the Germans, unknown to the RAF crews in the aircraft.

By this time, the British XXX Corps had fought its way to the Americans at the Maas and crossed the river and the canals. It reached the Americans at Nijmegen on the third day but another day of fierce fighting was required before the Waal was crossed, where it was stalled by a Panzer Division. The airborne troops at Arnhem were finally over-run on Friday 21 September, having fought against immense odds for three and a half days. There was no option but to order a general withdrawal. The surviving airborne forces had to retreat to Allied lines as best they could.

This operation cost the Allies over 14,700 men from all units killed, wounded or captured, plus all the gliders and many aircraft. The British I Airborne alone lost three-quarters of its total strength of 10,000 men. It was the biggest and longest airborne operation ever mounted by the Allies and the greatest failure, in spite of the heroism of its participants.

24 End of the Kriegsmarine

Coastal Command achieved almost complete superiority over German surface vessels and U-boats during the last year of the war against Germany. The rate of sinkings of U-boats by the RAF and the Royal Navy continued at such a rate that it became impossible for the Kriegsmarine to replace its losses, either with new vessels or trained crews. The campaign against enemy surface vessels also intensified. A new Strike Wing was formed in May 1944 at Davidstow Moor in Cornwall, from detachments of existing squadrons equipped with Beaufighters. In the following month this was joined by another Strike Wing at Portreath, equipped with Mosquitos. These two formidable forces ranged down the west coast of France, destroying warships and armed merchant vessels, and sometimes attacking U-boats when they were spotted on the surface.

On D-Day and during the next few weeks, Coastal Command helped to guard the flanks of the invasion force and the reinforcements and supplies which poured across the English Channel. In collaboration with the Royal Navy, RAF squadrons made effective attacks against those U-boats and destroyers from western France which attempted to interfere with the Allied enterprise. To the east, they dealt with E-boats and midget submarines which tried ineffectually to make attacks.

Below Left: The heavy cruiser *Prinz Eugen* (centre) at Gdynia on 10 October 1943, with an *Emden* class light cruiser above her. The photograph was taken by Mosquito PR IV serial LR248 flown from Leuchars in Fife by Squadron Leader Reginald A. Lenton. The *Prinz Eugen* was taken over by the Allies at Copenhagen at the end of the war. Her end came at Bikini Atoll in the North Pacific in 1946, when she was used by the USA in the atomic bomb tests.

AIR 34/239

Below: This photograph was taken north of Gujon in Spain soon after 03.00 hours on 7 June 1944 from a mirror camera fitted in a Sunderland III serial ML760 of 201 Squadron from Pembroke Dock. The flying boat, flown by Flight Lieutenant L.H. Baveystock, was patrolling near the north coast of Spain in a hunt for a U-boat believed returning from a patrol in the Atlantic when a blip appeared on the air-to-surface vessel radar. Intense fire from the U-boat opened up as the Sunderland approached, but the tracer missed narrowly. Baveystock dived while his front gunner and then his mid-upper gunner fired at the target. Six depth charges were dropped, one of which can be seen exploding near the U-boat illuminated by flares from the Sunderland. The stick straddled the submarine, which sank immediately. It was *U-995*, a type VIIC submarine, commanded by *Oberleutnant zur See* Hans Baden, returning to Bergen from its first patrol. There were no survivors.

AIR 15/613

Left: Twelve Beaufighters of 144 Squadron, each carrying two 250 lb bombs, together with twelve of 404 (RCAF) Squadron armed with rockets, were despatched from Davidstow Moor on 9 June 1944 to finish off the German destroyer *Z-32*. This had been beached by her crew on the Ile de Batz after damage by destroyers of the Royal Navy's 10th Destroyer Flotilla, during a courageous but vain attempt to attack the western flank of the Allied invasion fleet.

AIR 15/613

Right: The Beaufighters, which were escorted by Spitfires, took turns in attacking the stricken destroyer *Z-32*. She was destroyed beyond any possible repair.

AIR 15/472

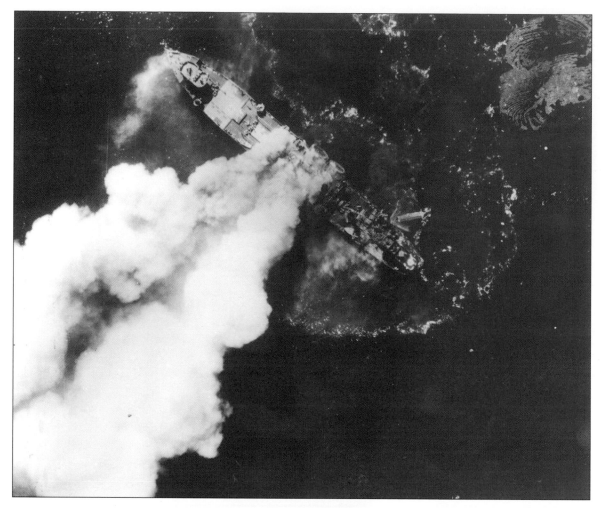

Left: Twenty-four Beaufighters of 236 and 404 (RCAF) Squadrons, part of the Davidstow Moor Strike Wing in Cornwall, took off on 12 August 1944 for a sweep to the mouth of the Gironde. They found the large *Sperrbrecher 7* (formerly the merchant vessel *Sauerland* of 7,087 tons) and left it in flames after a rocket attack.
A further attack was made by a Halifax of Coastal Command. Force 28 of the Royal Navy, consisting of the cruiser HMS *Diadem* and two destroyers, was in the vicinity. The warships closed in at high speed and hit the burning enemy vessel with gunfire, as shown by the arrow in this photograph, taken when she was down by the stern. The vessel sank and there were no survivors.

AIR 34/241

Left: On 24 August 1944, twenty Beaufighters of 236 and 404 (RCAF) Squadrons from the Davidstow Moor Strike Wing attacked the German destroyer *Z.24* and the torpedo boat *T.24* near Le Verdon in the Gironde estuary. These were the only remaining warships of their type active in French waters. This photograph shows both under rocket and cannon attack. The torpedo boat sank immediately and the destroyer capsized early the following morning.

AIR 34/241

When the Allied bridgeheads in Normandy had been established and preparations were being made for a massive breakout, the Strike Wings in Cornwall intensified their operations against enemy vessels operating from ports in the west of France. They sank ship after ship until by the end of August 1944 there were no surface vessels left to attack.

The surviving U-boats could no longer operate from these French ports. They streamed round Ireland and Scotland to continue their unequal struggle from Norway. The introduction of the new *Schnorkel* tube gave some of the new U-boats a temporary advantage, but Coastal Command

Left: Twenty-two Beaufighters of the Dallachy Strike Wing attacked shipping in Midtgulenfjord on 8 November 1944, led by a Mosquito of 333 (Norwegian) Squadron from Banff. They sank with rockets the German merchant vessels *Aquila* of 3,595 tons and *Helga Ferdinand* of 2,500 tons. Unfortunately the Norwegian ferry *Framnes* of 307 tons on her regular run was damaged, and several Norwegians were killed or wounded. Five Beaufighters were hit by flak but all returned.

AIR 27/1786

responded by fitting Liberators with Sonobuoys, devices dropped from aircraft which picked up the noise from propellers and relayed information to the crews. Meanwhile, factories manufacturing parts for U-boats were bombed by the US Eighth Air Force and Bomber Command, while Halifaxes of Coastal Command attacked the ports where the parts were assembled and used as bases by the Kriegsmarine.

By the end of 1944, the strength of Coastal Command had increased to over 1,000 aircraft. This was a modern force which included Beaufighters, Liberators, Halifaxes, Sunderlands, Wellingtons fitted with Leigh Lights, and the unarmed but superbly effective Spitfires and Mosquitos of the photo-reconnaissance squadrons. Some of the increasingly effective Strike Wings moved north to intensify the attacks on ships controlled by the Kriegsmarine bringing supplies to the German war machine. The Banff Strike Wing was formed in September 1944 from the squadrons from Davidstow Moor but in the following month the latter moved to Dallachy in Morayshire, where they were joined by the squadrons previously operating from Strubby in Lincolnshire.

These two Strike Wings created havoc among German shipping in Norwegian waters, while the North Coates Strike

Below: The capsized hull of the battleship *Tirpitz* at Tromsö, photographed on 22 March 1945, after being sunk on 12 November 1944 by 12,000 lb bombs dropped by Lancasters of 9 and 617 Squadrons operating from Lossiemouth in Morayshire. Her hull is covered by snow, but there is a hole on the starboard side. Four salvage vessels lie alongside the wreck.

AIR 34/100

Left: 'Tsetse Attack'
by Mark Postlethwaite

The Mosquito FB XVIII, or Tsetse, was a variant fitted with a Molins gun of 57mm in the nose, where it replaced the four cannons. This weapon carried a magazine of twenty-four rounds and was the equivalent of a six-pounder anti-tank gun. The Tsetse first entered service with a special detachment of 618 Squadron in October 1943, and this served alongside 248 Squadron shortly afterwards on anti-shipping work. The detachment was incorporated into 248 Squadron in May 1944 and the Tsetses continued until their last operation on 15 January 1945. This painting depicts a Tsetse in action in a narrow Norwegian fjord.

Below: On 8 March 1945, the Dallachy Strike Wing despatched twenty-eight Beaufighters of 144, 404 (RCAF), 455 (RAAF) and 489 (RNZAF) Squadrons to attack three merchant ships and three auxiliary ships in Midgulenfjord. They scored rocket and cannon strikes on several of these, the severest damage being to the Danish merchant ferry *Heimdal* of 978 tons, but two Beaufighters failed to return.

AIR 27/1786

Below: Thirty-five Mosquitos of 143, 235 and 248 Squadrons from the Banff Strike Wing took off on 9 April 1945 to attack U-boats in the Kattegat known to be sailing from Kiel in Germany to Horton in Norway. They were accompanied by two Mosquito outriders from 333 (Norwegian) Squadron and one from the RAF Film Unit, and escorted by Mustangs from Peterhead. Two U-boats were seen and sunk by rocket and cannon fire, the Type IX *U-804* and the Type VII *U-1065*, but an explosion from one brought down the Mosquito from the RAF Film Unit, killing the occupants.

AIR 26/597

Left: This U-boat was photographed on 11 May 1945 by Sunderland III serial ML759 of 422 (RCAF) Squadron from Pembroke Dock, when about 180 miles west of Land's End. She had been spotted during the night, on the surface and showing navigation lights. It could be seen in the morning that she was flying the German ensign and a black surrender flag, as ordered on 4 May by the new Chancellor of Germany, Karl Doenitz. Her destination was Loch Eriboll, near Scapa, where the Admiralty had arranged a reception for such U-boats.

AIR 27/1830

Right: The Banff Strike Wing suffered one of its worst days on 15 January 1945 when fourteen Mosquitos of 143, 235 and 248 Squadrons, led by two outrider Mosquitos of 333 (Norwegian) Squadron, attacked shipping at Leirvik. German radar picked up the formation at 11.10 hours and nine Focke-Wulf FW190s took off from Herdla, near Bergen. The German vessels in the fjord consisted of the merchant ship *Claus Rickmers* of 5,105 tons (which had been seriously damaged and run aground in an attack six days before), together with the flak ships *Vp5304*, *Vp5308*, *R63* and *R311*. The outrider Mosquitos reported their presence, but one was shot down by flak. The main force then attacked. This photograph shows rockets exploding on *Vp5308*, which was damaged. Another flak ship, *Vp5304* of 320 tons, was sunk. Two Mosquitos were damaged by flak and turned away, on fire, and one ditched. The remainder of the formation was then jumped by the nine FW190s. In the ensuing air battle, three Mosquitos and three FW190s were shot down. One of these Mosquitos was flown by Wing Commander J.M. Maurice of 143 Squadron, a renowned French pilot whose real name was Max Guedj. He was one of those who lost his life.

AIR 26/597

Wing continued to operate off the coasts of the Netherlands and Germany. Before long, however, the Dutch ports became neutralized with the advances of the Allied armies, and the North Coates squadrons concentrated on the more northerly sector. Enemy convoys could no longer sail anywhere during the day and tried to shelter in Norwegian fjords or ports in Denmark, but they were sought out and attacked in their anchorages. The greatest remaining threat to Allied shipping, the battleship *Tirpitz*, was finally sunk by Lancasters of Bomber Command at Tromsö in Norway on 12 November 1944.

Of course, the long-range aircraft of Coastal Command continued their patrols over the Atlantic from bases in Britain, Iceland and the Azores, finding opportunities in the anti-submarine campaign. As the war reached its inevitable conclusion with the advances of the Russians from the east and the Americans, British, Canadians and French from the west, some of the remaining U-boats in the Baltic began to head north to Norway, in a last desperate attempt to continue their struggle. These came under attack from the Strike Wings. On 4 May 1945, all surviving U-boats on war cruises in the oceans were ordered to surrender by Admiral Karl Doenitz, who had been appointed Chancellor of Germany after Hitler killed himself on 30 April. They were ordered to surface and head for bases in Scotland, flying black flags in token of submission. By this time, Coastal Command alone had sunk almost 200 of their number and damaged many more.

25 The Roads to Germany

During the build-up to Arnhem and its unsatisfactory conclusion, changes in the command structure of SHAEF took place. On 1 September 1944, General Dwight Eisenhower assumed direct control of the Allied armies in France and passed on to his deputy, Air Chief Marshal Sir Arthur Tedder, the task of co-ordinating all air operations. In mid-September 1944, SHAEF demands on Bomber Command and the US Eighth Air Force lessened, although they still came under the overall control of Allied planning. On 25 September, both were directed to concentrate attacks on the German petroleum industry as their first priority, followed by the transport system and the manufacture of tanks and other military vehicles.

The setback at Arnhem dashed all hopes of ending the war by Christmas. Lines of communication from Normandy to the front lines were lengthy, and fuel and ammunition

Left: The Opel Works at Fallersleben in central Germany, burning after a daylight attack by 137 B-17 Flying Fortresses of the US Eighth Air Force on 20 June 1944. This was the *Volkswagenwerke* (People's Car Factory) but had been transferred to aircraft repairs and the production of war material. This is an enlargement of a photograph taken from 35,000 feet by a photo-reconnaissance Spitfire later in the day.

AIR 25/792

Right: Bomber Command despatched 646 aircraft to bomb German positions around Calais on 20 September 1944. The weather was clear and very accurate results were achieved, as shown in this photograph. Another heavy attack followed five days later and yet another two days after that. The garrison of over 9,000 men surrendered on 2 October 1944.

AIR 14/3696

Left: The railway bridge at Zutphen in the Netherlands, south-east of Apeldoorn, was attacked on 14 October 1944 by thirty-five Mitchells and Bostons of 88, 226 and 342 Squadrons of the 2nd Tactical Air Force. Many bombs straddled the bridge, although some fell on the west bank and others overshot. The bombers were escorted by twenty-two Spitfires and thirty-five Mustangs of Fighter Command.

AIR 37/334

Left: Bomber Command despatched 277 aircraft on 28 October 1944 to attack German gun positions on the island of Walcheren. This photograph was taken from 9,000 feet over Flushing, on the east of the island, from a Lancaster of 186 Squadron based at Tuddenham in Suffolk.

AIR 14/3677

were sometimes in short supply. The vital road bridge at Nijmegen over the river Rhine, between the Netherlands and Germany, had been captured intact on 21 September 1944, but the armies on both sides seemed to have reached a stalemate. The Belgian port of Antwerp had been captured on 4 September 1944, but before it could be used the south bank of the Scheldt estuary and the island of Walcheren on the north bank had to be cleared of the enemy. German resistance in the west had stiffened, even though the Wehrmacht was falling back on the Russian front. However, the Allies were strengthened at the end of September 1944 by the arrival of the US 9th Army, which took up positions between the British 2nd Army and the US 1st Army.

The first move in the north was to breach the dyke at Westkapelle, on the western tip of Walcheren, so as to let in the waters of the North Sea and render German positions unusable. This was done by Bomber Command in the afternoon of 3 October, causing the sea to flood in. The dykes of East and West Flushing were breached four days later and German gun positions were also bombed. Infantry of the 1st Canadian Army in assault craft attacked the German forces on the south bank of the Scheldt, under cover of artillery smoke screens and fighter-bombers of the 2nd Tactical Air Force. Further afield, Bomber Command continued to plaster enemy gun positions. When the south bank of the Scheldt was cleared, commandos led the assault on Walcheren, beginning on 1 November, supported by rocket-firing Typhoons and Spitfires. The 2nd Tactical Air Force continued its operations until the last German resistance was quelled on 8 November. There had been over 13,000 Allied casualties, but 40,000 Germans had been taken prisoner. Minesweepers arrived to clear the Scheldt, and the first convoy reached Antwerp on 28 November.

On 15 October 1944, the headquarters of the Allied Expeditionary Air Force were disbanded and absorbed into SHAEF, becoming known as SHAEF(Air). At the same time, the Air Defence of Great Britain reverted to its previous name of Fighter Command. The day before, Leigh-Mallory had been posted to take command of the Allied Air Forces in South-East Asia but lost his life in an air crash en route.

Above: 'Winter Respite' by Charles J. Thompson

Spitfire in snow.

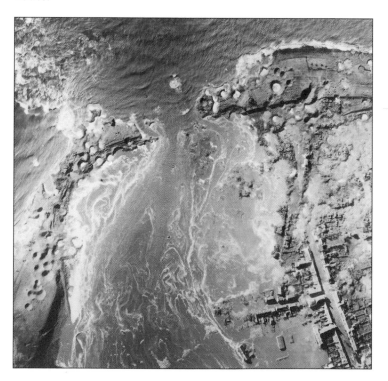

Left: The sea wall at Westkapelle on the western end of the Dutch island of Walcheren was attacked on 3 October 1944 by 259 aircraft of Bomber Command. It was breached with a gap estimated at 100 yards wide and water from the North Sea poured into the reclaimed polder land, which was below sea level. The flooding submerged some German gun batteries and hindered resistance to the Allied ground attack. No aircraft were lost.

AIR 34/241

The weather in the final weeks of 1944 was extremely poor, restricting both land and air operations. The German assault by two Panzer Armies through the Ardennes which began on 16 December did not come as a complete surprise but achieved initial success by driving a deep wedge between the US 1st and 3rd Armies, in what became known as the 'Battle of the Bulge'. The Germans were helped by the low cloud and rain which restricted flying, but when this cleared on 24 December, both the US Ninth Air Force and the 2nd Tactical Air Force delivered remorseless attacks on armoured transport and troops, overwhelming resistance from the Luftwaffe. Then Bomber Command and the US Eighth Air Force were ordered to help. The German thrust, designed to break though to Antwerp and cut the Allied armies in two, ground to a halt. By 16 December, the Panzer armies were in retreat, with heavy losses. They had postponed the Allied offensive into the Ruhr by six weeks, but had not achieved their intended objectives.

Above Left: On 28 October 1944, the 2nd Tactical Air Force despatched 112 Mitchells and thirty-six Bostons to the Netherlands, attacking railway bridges at Venlo and Deventer and a road bridge at Roermond. At the same time, there were patrols by 843 fighters of the RAF – 423 Spitfires, 410 Typhoons and ten Tempests. This Mitchell was photographed over Deventer, on the river Yssel north-east of Arnhem.

AIR 34/241

Above: On 31 October 1944, twenty-five Mosquitos from three squadrons of the 2nd Tactical Air Force, escorted by eight Mustangs, made a low-level attack on the Gestapo headquarters in the town of Aarhus in Denmark. Two four-storey buildings in the university were the targets. Both were destroyed and the records were wiped out, including written evidence of Danish resistance to the German occupation.

AIR 34/241

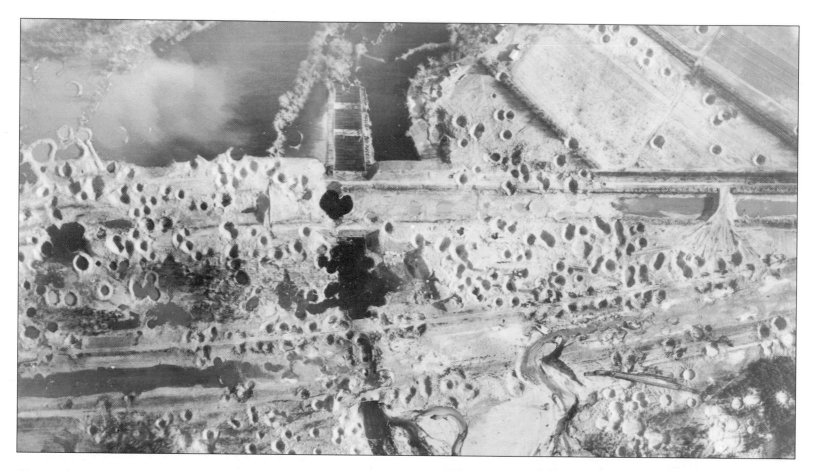

Above: The Mittelland canal between Dortmund and Ems was attacked by 138 Lancasters of Bomber Command on the night of 21/22 November 1944, as one of the objectives of a campaign intended to cut the lines of communication between north-west Germany and the Baltic. For the loss of two aircraft, they completely demolished the aqueduct over the river Glane, breached the embankments on both sides and left thirty miles of the canal dry. It had previously carried over 75 million tons a year. This photograph was taken five days after the attack.

AIR 34/241

Right: The railway marshalling yard at Giessen, north of Frankfurt, received a battering on the night of 6/7 December 1944 when eighty-seven aircraft of Bomber Command were despatched to bomb this transport centre while 168 others bombed the town. Another attack, solely on the marshalling yards, was delivered by 353 B-17 Flying Fortresses of the US Eighth Air Force four days later. The combined attacks put the yards out of action.

AIR 34/241

Right: The Belgian town of Houffalize in the Ardennes was largely destroyed by artillery fire, as well as an attack by 140 aircraft of Bomber Command on the night of 5/6 January 1945. It was a bottleneck in the German supply system during the 'Battle of the Bulge'.

AIR 37/1231

Below: The centre of the Belgian town of St Vith in the Ardennes was shattered by 294 aircraft of Bomber Command on 26 December 1944, during the 'Battle of the Bulge'. This photograph of the snow-covered outskirts was taken on 5 January 1945, when bombs were falling on the railway lines.

AIR 37/46

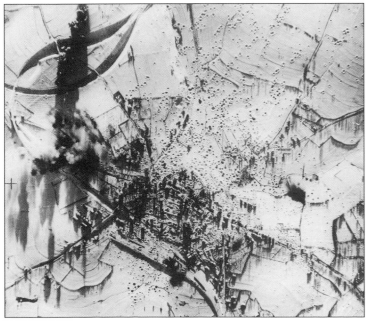

Meanwhile, it had become clear that Air Chief Marshal Sir Arthur Harris of Bomber Command did not agree with the directive issued on 25 September concerning bombing priorities. In response to criticisms that he was not giving these his wholehearted support, he wrote on 1 November 1944 to the Chief of Air Staff, Air Chief Marshal Sir Charles Portal, pointing out that his Command had virtually destroyed forty-five of the sixty major German cities, and asserting that continuation of 'area bombing' was the best policy. The arguments continued in writing. On 8 January 1945, Portal sent to Harris a dossier of 'Ultra' decrypts, demonstrating that the attacks on oil were having a serious effect on Germany's capacity to wage war, particularly in the ability to train new aircrew. This did not induce Harris to change his mind, and on 18 January he offered to resign. Portal backed away from accepting this outcome, which would have been unpopular in the RAF and the country generally. The matter was never resolved satisfactorily.

26 End of the Third Reich

Almost half the tonnage dropped by Bomber Command in the course of the war fell in the last nine months, and much of this on German soil. With the liberation of France, Belgium and part of the Netherlands, much of the enemy's outer defence system had disappeared. The tactics of the RAF's 100 Group, equipped with apparatus for jamming enemy signals, reduced the number of interceptions by night-fighters. RAF ground stations controlling navigation aids such as Gee and GH were moved closer to Germany, giving greater range and accuracy. The presence of long-range fighters, such as the Mustang III of the RAF, enabled Bomber Command to attack targets in daylight, alternating with its usual night attacks. At the same time, the US Eighth Air Force intensified its daylight bombing campaign against synthetic oil production, transport facilities and production of military vehicles. Germany began to reel from these blows, while resisting desperately against attacks by ground forces on both the Eastern and Western fronts.

The last year of the war opened with a determined attempt by the Luftwaffe to destroy the RAF's 2nd Tactical Air Force and the US Ninth Air Force near the front line. About 800 aircraft, drawn from every type of unit, had been gathered for raids against airfields which began in the early hours of New Year's Day. These succeeded in destroying 144 aircraft on the ground in the British sector alone but it seems that about 200 of the attackers were shot down by the

Above: A pattern of searchlight beams taken from 24,500 feet by time exposure during a raid against Kiel on the night of 26/27 August 1944. It was taken from a Mosquito of 608 Squadron based at Downham Market in Norfolk.
AIR 14/3696

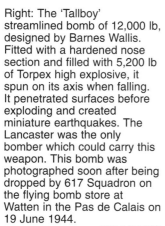

Right: The 'Tallboy' streamlined bomb of 12,000 lb, designed by Barnes Wallis. Fitted with a hardened nose section and filled with 5,200 lb of Torpex high explosive, it spun on its axis when falling. It penetrated surfaces before exploding and created miniature earthquakes. The Lancaster was the only bomber which could carry this weapon. This bomb was photographed soon after being dropped by 617 Squadron on the flying bomb store at Watten in the Pas de Calais on 19 June 1944.
AIR 14/3696

Above: 'Lancasters at Sunset'
by Charles J. Thompson

RAF and the USAAF. This was the last major effort made by the Luftwaffe in the west, and the cost to it was dear in terms of experienced pilots.

Bitter fighting took place during January, primarily between the German, American and French armies along the Rhine, but without major gains of ground. On 8 February, the Canadian 1st Army and the British 2nd Army opened an offensive in the north, supported by the 2nd Tactical Air Force, and entered the German town of Kleve five days later. When German reinforcements were rushed to counter this thrust, the Americans began their offensive further south and linked up with the British. Some 9,000 Allied aircraft attacked enemy communications on 22 February in support of these operations. All the armies suffered heavy casualties during the advances, but the Germans also lost 53,000 prisoners. On 6 March, the Americans entered Cologne. By this time the Allies were across the Rhine in several places, but then the weather closed in and the advances stalled for a short while.

A great breakthrough came on 24 March, under operation 'Varsity'. By this time the Allied 1st Airborne Army had

Left: The effect of a 'Tallboy' bomb on the massive roof of a U-boat shelter at Brest, previously impregnable to air bombardment. These bombs were dropped on the port by Lancasters of Bomber Command on 12 and 13 August 1944. The German garrison at Brest held out against attacks by American ground forces and the US Ninth Air Force, before finally surrendering in the afternoon of 19 September 1944.
AIR 34/241

End of the Third Reich

been rebuilt under General Lewis H. Brereton and a major crossing of the Rhine could take place. This was later considered the best-planned airborne operation of the war. It was preceded by massive attacks from all available squadrons of the Allied air forces against the Wesel sector of Germany, on the confluence of the Rhine with the Lippe. The airborne operation was mounted at the same time as the British 2nd Army crossed the Rhine. Almost 19,000 men were delivered to four drop zones and everywhere the troops were successful, supported constantly by fighter-bombers. The way to the heartland of Germany was opened.

Meanwhile, although Air Chief Marshal Sir Arthur Harris did not believe in the efficacy of attacks against oil targets, Bomber Command and the US Eighth Air Force made systematic raids and succeeded in slowing down output, until by April it had almost stopped. Other targets were factories manufacturing parts for new U-boats equipped with *Schnorkel* or jet engines for new fighters. Some of the effort was still devoted to German cities, although not so much as is generally believed. Such raids occurred mainly when the weather was unsuitable for the pinpoint bombing required for night attacks against relatively small targets.

Above Right: Strips of aluminium foil, known as 'Window', falling over Gelsenkirchen-Buer during a daylight raid on 12 September 1944 against synthetic oil plants. The foil was designed to obscure enemy radar screens. The photograph was taken from a Halifax of 158 Squadron, based at Lissett in Yorkshire.

AIR 14/3647

Right: Darmstadt photographed on 19 September 1944 after an accurate attack by 240 aircraft of Bomber Command on the night of 11/12 September. This was the first effective raid on the city and it resulted in tremendous devastation and the deaths of about 12,300 people – with many injured and 70,000 more rendered homeless – from the population of about 120,000.

AIR 34/241

Left: Medium-capacity bombs of 1,000 lb falling on Cologne from 18,000 feet during a daylight raid on March 1945. There were two attacks, the first by 703 aircraft of Bomber Command, and the second by 155 aircraft. Both caused great destruction and many casualties. The photograph was taken from a Lancaster of 156 Squadron based at Upwood in Huntingdonshire. Cologne was captured by American troops four days later.

AIR 14/3696

Below: The 'Grand Slam' bomb of 22,000 lb, developed by Barnes Wallis. It contained 9,135 lb of Torpex and could be dropped only from a modified Lancaster fitted with more powerful engines. The first operation in which these were dropped was on 14 March 1945 over Bielefeld viaduct in Germany.

AIR 14/3696

Contrary to general belief, the notorious raid made by Bomber Command against Dresden on 13/14 February was not instigated by Harris, although he implemented it. It was initiated by the War Cabinet under pressure from the Russians, who requested such raids to hinder enemy reinforcements being sent to the Eastern Front. Moreover, it was followed by two heavy daylight raids against the same target, made by the US Eighth Air Force on 14 and 15 February.

On the ground, the Allied advances in the west continued remorselessly. The British 2nd Army blasted its way across the north German plain to reach Lübeck on 2 May. The Canadian 1st Army continued to clear the remaining German forces out of the Netherlands. Both the US 9th and 1st Armies reached the Elbe on 19 April, where the latter made contact with the Russians six days later. The US 3rd Army advanced to Erfurt by 12 April and then streaked south-east. The French Army advanced from Strasbourg while the US 7th Army entered Nuremberg on 10 April and then headed south to reach Salzburg on 4 May. With the

Above: The effect of a 4,000 lb bomb with incendiaries from 17,000 feet on Hanover by a Lancaster of 170 Squadron based at Hemswell in Lincolnshire. This daylight raid was one of several which took place on 25 March 1945 against German cities in order to disrupt the railway system leading to the Rhine battle area.

AIR 14/3696

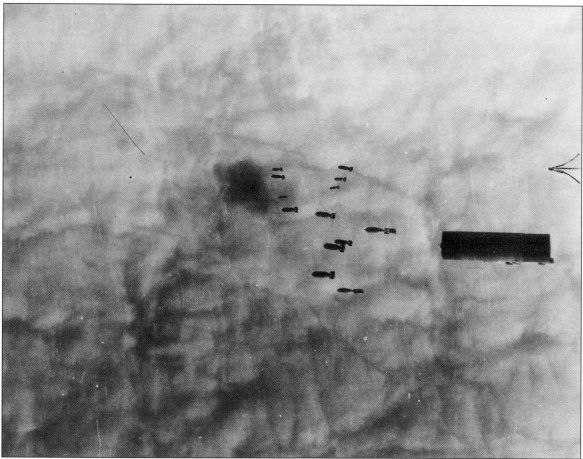

Left: A 4,000 lb blast bomb, known as a 'blockbuster' or a 'cookie', together with incendiaries, falling on Dortmund during a daylight raid on 12 March 1945. Bombing took place through cloud but the target had been marked accurately by the Pathfinder Force and enormous damage was caused by the 1,108 aircraft despatched.

AIR 14/3647

Left: Sea mines were dropped in the river Elbe by eight Mosquitos of Bomber Command on the night of 27/28 March 1945, as part of a plan to destroy the enemy transport system. These weapons descended by parachute and rested on river or sea bottoms, being activated magnetically by ferrous metal in vessels passing above. This photograph was taken from a Mosquito of 627 Squadron, based at Woodhall Spa in Lincolnshire.

AIR 14/3696

Right: After Victory in Europe, the USAAF handed many of its airfields over to the RAF. The Stars and Stripes were lowered and the RAF Ensign raised at Greencastle in County Down on 31 May 1945, the occasion being marked with a goodwill ceremony by the two Allies.

AIR 28/294

Russians at the gates of Berlin, Hitler killed himself on 30 April and his successor, Admiral Karl Doenitz, surrendered unconditionally on 3 May. Victory in Europe was celebrated five days later.

Soon after V-E Day, the author of this book took part in a navigation exercise in an RAF Dakota over Germany, during a long-range conversion course preparatory to flying out to India to participate in the war against Japan. All three on the flight deck – pilot, navigator and wireless operator – were highly experienced in operational flying as well as instructing. We had deliberately crewed up together for a war which we believed would last for at least another year. In the clear early morning, we flew at low level over the Ruhr and were astonished at the spectacle below. There seemed to be hardly a building left standing. The streets were empty and we could see only a few wisps of smoke from domestic fires, with the occasional silver glint of a crashed US bomber. We likened this devastation to the Wellsian fantasy in the pre-war film *The War of the Worlds*. Of course, at the time we knew nothing about the atom bomb.

PART TWO: AFRICA AND SOUTHERN EUROPE

27 Triumph and Disaster

Britain's response to Italy's declaration of war on 10 June 1940, followed by the invasion of southern France, was to despatch thirty-six Whitleys on a raid against Turin two nights later. Most turned back from the Alps in unfavourable weather but nine reached the target and caused some damage to factories and railway yards. This small attack was a prelude to the devastating raids which would be delivered eventually.

Italy's earlier period of expansion had included the acquisition of Libya and the Dodecanese in 1911, the invasion of Abyssinia in 1935, and the seizure of Albania in 1939. In June 1940, her Regia Aeronautica consisted of about 1,700 aircraft, of which some 500 were based in her overseas territories. Facing the latter, the RAF had a strength of about 300 aircraft, stationed mainly in Egypt, the Sudan, Kenya and Palestine. All were immediately brought under RAF Middle East, with its headquarters in Cairo and commanded by Air Chief Marshal Sir Arthur Longmore, apart from Gibraltar which was transferred to the home-based RAF Coastal Command. Some of these aircraft were obsolescent, but fortunately plans for their replacement had been devised. Aircraft without the range to fly to the Middle East via Gibraltar and Malta, such as Hurricanes, were crated and shipped to Takoradi on the Gold Coast, where they were assembled and flown in stages across Africa to Egypt.

Above: The shadows of Blenheim Is of 211 Squadron passing over Shell Mex installations in Egypt on 7 May 1940. The squadron was based on El Daba at this time and had been equipped with these light bombers for a year. After the introduction of the Blenheim IV, they were known as the 'short-nose' version.
AIR 27/1311

Left: One of the early casualties of the war in the Middle East was the old cruiser *San Giorgio* of 9,232 tons in Tobruk harbour, which was badly damaged during a raid by the RAF on the night of 12 June 1940. She was beached and converted into a flak ship but was hit again and set on fire, as shown here, shortly before the advancing British began to enter the port on 21 January 1941. The Italians scuttled her to prevent capture.
ADM 244/10

Left: This wrecked Vickers Vincent biplane bomber was photographed in the Sudan. It was probably one of two destroyed in an Italian air attack of 16 October 1940 on the advanced airfield of Gedaref, together with eight Vickers Wellesleys. The RAF had responded to the Italian invasion of Sudan from Abyssinia by forming No 203 Group, consisting at first of the Gloster Gladiators of No 112 Squadron and 1 (SAAF) Squadron, the Vickers Wellesleys of 14, 47 and 223 Squadrons and the Vickers Vincents of No 430 Flight. The photograph was taken after the Battle of Gallabat of 6-8 November 1940, when the Italians were driven back into Abyssinia by the 5th Indian Division.

CAB 44/76

Right: Bombing up Wellington ICs on a desert airfield. The first to operate with these long-range bombers in the Middle East was 70 Squadron, on 18 September 1940 when based at Kabrit in Egypt.
AIR 41/50

On the fighting fronts, matters went well for the British and Commonwealth forces after some initial reverses. The only fighter defences in Malta were three Gladiators which, after heroic actions by RAF pilots, were supported from the end of June by Hurricanes flown off carriers to the island. The fortress of Malta was to prove a severe thorn in the flesh of the enemy when attempting to bring supplies from Italy to North Africa.

Enemy forces in Abyssinia, Eritrea and Italian Somaliland greatly outnumbered the British in East Africa, who were put on the defensive. But troop reinforcements soon began to arrive while biplanes of the fledgling Southern Rhodesia Air Unit moved north and were followed by squadrons of the South African Air Force (SAAF). When more British troops arrived in East Africa in January 1941, advances were made into Italian territory. By the following

Above: The port of Valona (Vloré) in Albania, photographed from 5,500 feet at midday on 29 December 1940 by a Blenheim I of 211 Squadron based at Menidi near Athens. Italy had seized Albania on 7 April 1939 and declared war against Greece on 28 October 1940. Valona was bombed on several occasions by 112 Squadron, after the aircraft were based at Menidi from 22 November 1940.
AIR 27/1311

Above: Bombs from a Blenheim I of 211 Squadron falling from 10,000 feet on Italian positions near the Albanian town of Tepelinë on 6 February 1941. This squadron was forced to begin withdrawing from Greece on 19 April 1941, after the invasion of the Wehrmacht via Bulgaria. Its records of operations in Greece were destroyed, but some photographs survived.
AIR 27/1312

Left: This crashed Heinkel He111-H was spotted by the British about forty-five miles south of Sollum after they began their advance into Libya on 9 December 1940. On 29 January 1941, a party from No 103 Maintenance Unit at Aboukir in Egypt flew to Sollum in a Vickers Valenta troop-carrier and then set off by road to locate the enemy machine in the desert. They found it three days later and wrote detailed technical reports. The Heinkel was coded IH+JP, works number 3765, of the 6th *Staffel* of II./KG 26 *'Löwengeschwader'*. Tracks of four men in the sand were followed and these showed that the enemy crew had walked about twenty miles westward and reached Fort Maddelena.
AIR 23/7574

Right: The abandoned Italian supply ship *Pietro Querini* of 1,004 tons photographed near the Kerkenna Islands of Tunisia on 24 June 1941 from a Blenheim IV of 82 Squadron, flown from Luqa in Malta by Flight Lieutenant J.T. Hanafy. The vessel had left Trapani in Sicily at 02.00 hours on 22 June 1941 as part of a convoy of three escorted merchant vessels headed for Tripoli in Libya, but was torpedoed at 15.00 hours on the same day by the submarine HMS *Union*. The remaining vessels in the convoy put into the Italian island of Lampedusa and did not resume their journey until 2 July, under stronger escort.

AIR 37/47

April these had reached the port of Massawa in Italian Eritrea. Mopping up continued, but some Italians held out in mountainous areas until November 1941. By then, the whole of East Africa had been cleared of the enemy.

Meanwhile, the dictator Benito Mussolini decided to match Hitler's occupation of Romania in October 1940. At the end of that month he declared war on Greece and attempted to invade that country from Albania. RAF Middle East sent three squadrons of Blenheims and three of Gladiators to support the Royal Hellenic Air Force, while the Italians suffered humiliating reverses from the Greek Army.

Matters also went well for the British and Commonwealth troops when on 9 November 1940 they

C.I.U. MOSAIC Nº 338
ABADAN

Left: A mosaic made up from photographs taken on 5 August 1941 by long-distance Hurricane PR1 serial V7423 of No 2 Photographic Reconnaissance Unit flown from Heliopolis in Egypt by Flight Lieutenant R.G.M. 'Johnny' Walker. It shows the oil refinery and storage tanks at Abadan on an island in the Shatt-al-Arab delta in south-west Persia. This was one of the largest of such complexes in the world and of vital importance to British forces in the Middle East.

AIR 34/744

Wehrmacht invaded Yugoslavia and Greece with overwhelming strength, wiping out the Royal Yugoslav and Royal Hellenic Air Forces and dealing crippling blows against the RAF squadrons. The six Commonwealth divisions sent to Greece were forced to retreat and by 20 April had been taken by the Royal Navy to Crete, leaving their armour and much equipment behind. The few remnants of the RAF squadrons flew to the island.

On 3 April 1941, the British faced an insurrection in Iraq, led by the politician Rashid Ali. This was a country in which they were responsible for security. It was also apparent to British Intelligence that Hitler intended a strategic pincer movement, attacking through Syria and Iraq to the Persian oil wells and through Egypt to the Suez Canal. This would threaten southern Africa and India. At the end of April, a large force of Rashid Ali's troops invested the RAF's large training base of Habbaniya, near Baghdad, and opened artillery fire on the airfield. The RAF responded with an epic

Left: '*Dhasamen* or gondoliers looking up at aircraft' by war artist Oliphant

The artist's impression of an episode in the long air assault on the island fortress of Malta.
INF 3/1613

Below: Wellingtons based in Egypt were able to use Malta as an advanced base to attack ports in southern Italy. This photograph of Naples, taken on 25 September 1941, shows severe damage to a section of railway track, with many administrative buildings demolished or heavily damaged.
AIR 34/743

launched an attack in the Western Desert under the command of General Sir Archibald Wavell, supported by increased numbers of RAF squadrons. In about two months they advanced over 600 miles, took about 130,000 Italian prisoners, and reached the Gulf of Sirte. It seemed certain that the Italians would be cleared out of Africa, but the Deutsches Afrika Korps, let by General Erwin Rommel, landed in Tripoli during February 1941. At the same time, the Luftwaffe's *Fliegerkorps X* arrived in Sicily and began a ferocious bombardment of Malta, which possessed only a single squadron of fighters among its sixty aircraft. RAF Middle East could do little to reinforce the defenders, for by then the Wehrmacht had entered Bulgaria and was on the borders of Greece. All available RAF squadrons had to be sent to this new theatre of operations.

Rommel launched a co-ordinated attack against the overstretched British forces in Libya on 1 April 1941, and advanced with astonishing speed. In two weeks, the British were back in Egypt, leaving only a contingent to hold an enclave around the port of Tobruk. On 6 April, the

Above: Aircrews of No 203 Group being briefed with a model of the target area during an assault of 1-12 February 1941 on Italian positions at Keren, north-west of Asmara in Eritrea. The Group consisted of about seventy-five Blenheim, Wellesley, Hardy, Vincent and Gladiator aircraft, many of them obsolete. Asmara, Keren and the port of Massawa were captured shortly afterwards.
CAB 44/78

Below: A Kittyhawk taxying out to take off from an airfield in the Western Desert, raising a cloud of the all-pervading dust.
AIR 41/50

Above: Pilots of 112 Squadron in front of one of their Curtiss Tomahawk IIBs with the 'Shark's Tooth' insignia, photographed after the squadron claimed 100 enemy aircraft destroyed over the Western Desert. Armed with six .303 inch machine-guns, Tomahawks first arrived in this squadron in July 1941 and were employed on fighter sweeps until replaced by Curtiss Kittyhawk fighter-bombers in the following December.
INF 1/244

defence, using converted biplane trainers as fighters and bombers, and within about four weeks put the attackers to flight. Rashid Ali's forces were then defeated by a British column advancing from the Persian Gulf, and the rebellion was crushed.

On 20 May, a huge force of German airborne troops descended on Crete, consisting of about 700 transports and gliders, accompanied by about 650 escorts. Only about twenty-four aircraft of the RAF and FAA were available to combat them, while the troops lacked equipment. The outcome remained in the balance for some days but the airborne troops wore down the defenders. The Royal Navy came to the rescue and evacuated many to Egypt, losing three cruisers and six destroyers in the process.

28 Seesaw Battles

Land operations in the Western Desert were like a piece of elastic. As one side advanced over vast distances, so the elastic stretched and needed to contract. The gain of desert territory was of less importance than the destruction of enemy forces and the acquisition of ports, as both sides depended on lengthy supply routes for fuel and ammunition. In this respect the British in Egypt were better placed, for convoys could pass round the Cape while aircraft could be assembled in Takoradi and flown to maintenance units. But the only supply routes for the Axis forces were across the Mediterranean, where British submarines operated and the island fortress of Malta stood in the way.

Air Marshal Sir Arthur Tedder was appointed Air Officer Commander-in-Chief Middle East on 1 June 1941. One of his first actions was to support operation 'Battle-axe', a major attempt on 14 June to relieve Tobruk, but this

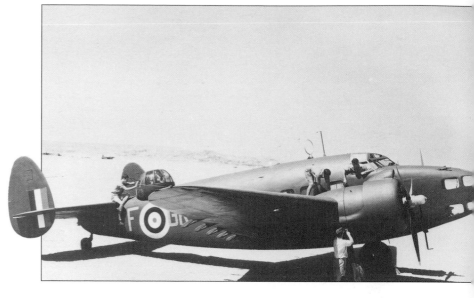

Below: The Hurricane IID, fitted with two 40 mm Vickers 'S' guns, first entered service on 6 June 1942 with 6 Squadron in the Western Desert. It made some very effective attacks at low level against Axis armour, being known as the 'tankbuster'.
AIR 41/50

Above: Ground crews working on a Hudson III of 459 (RAAF) Squadron, which was formed on 10 February 1942 as a maritime reconnaissance squadron at Burg el Arab in Egypt, under No 201 (Naval Co-operation) Group.
INF 2/42

Below: The French battleship *Jean Bart* of 43,293 tons protected by booms at Casablanca in French Morocco. The oblique photograph was taken on 11 April 1942, looking north-west along the Quai Delande. This battleship left St Nazaire on 19 June 1940, before the surrender of France, and was regarded as a potential menace by the Royal Navy.
AIR 34/234

was repulsed with heavy losses by a strong concentration of enemy tanks. However, in another respect Tedder was fortunate, as in this period the Luftwaffe was beginning to withdraw some of its units for the German invasion of Russia on 22 June. Moreover, the RAF was increasing its strength and overtaking that of its adversary. By the following

Left: This Italian merchant vessel, *Vettor Pisani* of 6,339 tons, left Taranto on 23 July 1942, bound for Tobruk with a cargo of fuel, ammunition and military vehicles. She was part of a convoy escorted by three torpedo boats and two motor-torpedo boats. At dawn the following day, while off the Greek coast, the convoy was attacked by six Beauforts of 39, 86 and 217 Squadrons from Luqa in Malta, escorted by nine Beaufighters of 235 Squadron. Three Beauforts were shot down by intense flak but the *Vettor Pisani* was torpedoed, set on fire, and eventually beached on the Greek coast.

AIR 41/50

Right: A night raid in August 1942 on Tobruk in Libya, with the target illuminated by flares. The raids by Wellingtons and Halifaxes on this port were so regular that they were known as the 'milk run'.

AIR 41/50

Above: A fighter attack at low level on enemy trucks on the Egyptian coast road in August 1942.

AIR 41/50

November, the RAF and the FAA numbered about 660 aircraft in the Western Desert and 120 in Malta, while the Axis possessed about 540 in North Africa. British Intelligence played a vital part, for by then it could decrypt signals relating to the strength of the Deutsches Africa Korps as well as those giving details of enemy convoys. The latter were attacked with regularity by Blenheims based in Malta and by submarines. In November 1941, about two thirds of the supply ships which sailed to North Africa from Italy were sunk.

Operation 'Crusader', under General Sir Claud Auchinleck with his recently re-christened 8th Army, began on 18 November 1941, after the enemy positions had been heavily strafed and bombed by the RAF's newly formed Western Desert Air Force, under the command of Air Vice-Marshal Arthur Coningham. Matters went well in the first

Below: A map drawn by the RAF's Air Historical Branch showing the terrain of the seesaw battles between the British 8th Army and the Axis forces. Operation 'Crusader' was in progress on the date shown. The 8th Army under the overall command of General Sir Claud Auchinleck had relieved the garrison at Tobruk and was attacking the enemy under General Erwin Rommel at Gazala. The Western Desert Air Force under Air Vice-Marshal Arthur Coningham was attacking enemy positions and supply lines.

AIR 41/25

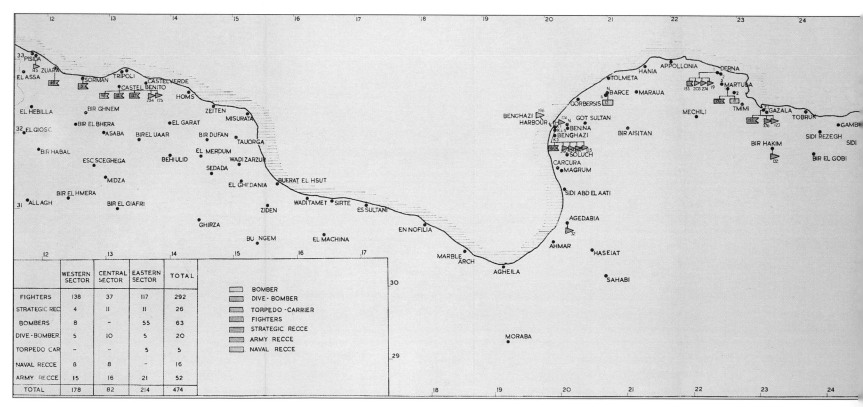

	WESTERN SECTOR	CENTRAL SECTOR	EASTERN SECTOR	TOTAL
FIGHTERS	138	37	117	292
STRATEGIC REC	4	11	11	26
BOMBERS	8	–	55	63
DIVE-BOMBER	5	10	5	20
TORPEDO CAR	–	–	5	5
NAVAL RECCE	8	8	–	16
ARMY RECCE	15	16	21	52
TOTAL	178	82	214	474

BOMBER
DIVE-BOMBER
TORPEDO-CARRIER
FIGHTERS
STRATEGIC RECCE
ARMY RECCE
NAVAL RECCE

Right: This Italian merchant vessel, *Rosolino Pilo* of 8,326 tons, was part of a convoy which left Naples on 17 August 1942, bound for Tripoli with a cargo of 112 military vehicles and 101 German personnel. On the following day, she was torpedoed south of the island of Lampedusa during an attack by three Beauforts of 86 Squadron from Luqa in Malta, escorted by three Beaufighters of 252 Squadron and four Spitfires of 126 Squadron. All the attackers returned but the vessel was left ablaze and the crew and passengers took to the lifeboats. She was torpedoed and sunk on 19 August by the submarine HMS *United*.

AIR 41/50

Below: A poster showing Spitfires shooting down Heinkel He111s over the Western Desert, painted by the war artist Frank Wootton.
INF 13/213

few weeks. The defenders at Tobruk were relieved at last and the Panzerarmee Afrika (as Rommel's force had been renamed) was driven back in a fighting retreat as far as Agedabia. Fuel and ammunition remained the main problem for the Axis forces but this was suddenly relieved in December when two large convoys evaded attacks and reached Tripoli. Rommel was able to counter-attack and the British were pushed back once more, until on 6 February 1942 they formed a new line at Gazala, west of Tobruk.

Then Malta became neutralized for several months. During January 1942, about 400 German aircraft had arrived in Sicily and the island was subjected to a prolonged bombardment. The defending Spitfires were whittled down in combat or attacks on airfields until by March only six remained serviceable. Forty-seven were flown off the US aircraft carrier *Wasp* on 20 April but most were destroyed on the ground during the next day. Supplies from Italy streamed across the sea to Tripoli, and Rommel found he was in a favourable position for another assault, on this occasion expecting to reach Cairo.

The attack which Panzerarmee Afrika opened on 26 May was outstandingly successful. The British and Commonwealth troops were routed and driven out of Libya, without holding on to Tobruk on this occasion. The Axis forces took 45,000 prisoners and captured quantities of fuel and other supplies. But once again they were brought to a halt with their extended supply lines. The port of Tobruk needed much clearance before it could be used and Tripoli was about 800 miles away by road. The advance faltered and the British took another stand in early July at the little village of El Alamein in Egypt, about 150 miles from Cairo. With the aid of intense operations by the RAF's Western Desert Air Force, which remained in strength, the line held.

Right: A dust-storm on a desert landing-ground. The diurnal variation could be huge, with intense cold overnight.

AIR 41/50

Left: The Halifax II entered service with the newly-formed 462 (RAAF) Squadron in September 1942, based at Fayid in Egypt.

AIR 41/50

Left; The Italian supply vessel *Davide Bianchi* of 1,477 tons, part of an Axis convoy nearing Tobruk, was torpedoed at 02.50 hours on 4 September 1942 by a Wellington IC of 38 Squadron flown by Sergeant N. Jones from the advanced airfield LG226 in Egypt. She was carrying 1,095 tons of petrol which was set ablaze, and she soon sank. The Wellington ICs in 38 Squadron had been adapted to carry two torpedoes and the crews were trained to attack at night.
AIR 41/50

Below Left: Bombs dropped by Bostons in September 1942, exploding on a concentration of enemy vehicles in the Western Desert.
AIR 41/50

During a period of stalemate, the British were able to reinforce their ground troops and the RAF. Malta had received sixty-two Spitfires flown from two carriers on 9 May, and this marked a turning point in the defences of the island. In this period, all the Beaufort squadrons in the UK were ordered to fly to Ceylon to meet a threat from the Japanese Navy, but they were held in Malta en route and thrown against the Axis supply route, escorted by Beaufighters. Other attacks were carried out at night by Wellingtons based in Malta while more were made from Egypt by Beauforts and Wellingtons. In spite of severe losses, numerous merchant ships in the Axis convoys were sunk.

Another event in May 1942 was the arrival at Fayid in Egypt of B-24D Liberators of the USAAF, commanded by Colonel Harry A. Halverston and code-named 'Halpro Force'. Thirteen of these aircraft raided the oil refineries at Ploesti in Romania on 12 June, and then landed at various locations in the Middle East. Halpro Force was the nucleus for the US Army Middle East Air force, which was formed on 28 June with Liberators and Fortresses as part of RAF Middle East.

29 Desert Victory

General Sir Harold Alexander took over from General Sir Claud Auchinleck on 15 August 1942 and appointed Lieutenant-General Bernard Montgomery to command the 8th Army. Montgomery's determination to build up overwhelming strength for an assault coincided with a reversal of fortunes for the Wehrmacht on all fronts. The bombardment of Germany by Bomber Command and the US Eighth Air Force was compelling the return of men and resources from the Russian Front, while a German army of 278,000 men had advanced to Stalingrad and would eventually be utterly destroyed. The Battle of the Atlantic was going badly for the Kriegsmarine, for the sinking of U-boats exceeded its capacity to replace crews and vessels.

Rommel attempted a pre-emptive strike on 30 August 1942 against the growing strength of the British forces in Egypt. Rommel's armour came up against deeply entrenched gun positions and tanks, and could make no headway. Many of the Luftwaffe's bombs fell on dummy aircraft provided for this purpose on landing grounds, while RAF fighters swamped the Axis attackers and its bombers hammered Axis positions. Fuel expected

Above: Transport of the 8th Army moving westward along the coast road after the victory at El Alamein.

AIR 41/50

Right: Retreating enemy transport caught by sticks of bombs along the coast road in Egypt between El Dava and Fuka, in the first week on November 1942.

AIR 41/50

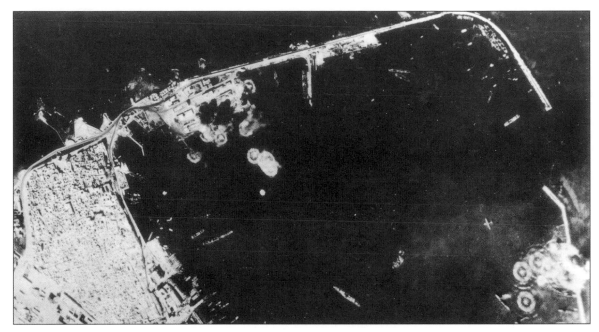

Left: The US Ninth Air Force, part of RAF Middle East, despatched B-24 Liberators on daylight attacks against Tripoli on 21, 26 and 29 November. On this occasion, hits were scored on or near the Spanish quay and the Karamanli mole, damaging vessels.

AIR 29/260

Below: Tobruk photographed one hour after the 8th Army reoccupied the port on 13 November 1942.

AIR 41/50

from Italy did not arrive and the Panzerarmee was forced to pull back.

Malta had been reinforced until 300 RAF aircraft defended the island or tackled Rommel's supply line. Montgomery bided his time until he knew from Enigma decrypts that Rommel had been so badly weakened that he possessed little more than four days of fuel for his Panzerarmee under full battle conditions. By the following October, RAF Middle East controlled ninety-six operational squadrons in Egypt, numbering 1,200 aircraft. They faced under 700 in the Axis forces, many of which were unserviceable. The 8th Army possessed 165,000 men, 2,275 guns and 600 tanks. The Axis forces numbered 93,000 men, 1,450 guns and 470 tanks.

The assault of the 8th Army at El Alamein opened on 23 October 1942 with an enormous artillery barrage and the greatest air bombardment of enemy forces witnessed in North Africa. As a deception, dummy tanks and dumps had been constructed in the south, followed by an initial thrust. Then the main assault began in the north, accompanied by intense strafing by fighter-bombers. Holes were punched in the enemy lines, through which tanks passed, but the enemy did not break, and even counter-attacked. The battle raged until 3 November, when the enemy was seen to be in full retreat along the coast road.

Above: (Centre) Derelict Messerschmitt Bf110E-1, coded 3U+DT, works number 2354, of the 9th *Staffel*, III./*Zerstörergeschwader* 26 *'Horst Wessel'*. (Left) Derelict Bf109E, 'Black 3' of an unknown unit. These machines were found on a landing ground near Sollum in Libya in November 1942.

AIR 41/50

Right: Armoured cars of the 8th Army receiving ammunition unloaded from a Halifax II used as a transport in November 1942.

AIR 41/50

Above: These derelict Luftwaffe machines were photographed in November 1942 on a flooded airfield near Maturba in Libya. In the foreground is a Messerschmitt Bf109E-7/Trop of *Jagdgeschwader* 27. Behind are the remains of a Junkers Ju52/3mg4e-S (*Sanitätsflugzeug*, or air ambulance), works number 311.

AIR 41/50

Above Right: The waterfront at Benghazi in Libya, photographed when the 8th Army entered the port on 20 November 1942.

AIR 41/50

Rommel had almost run out of fuel, ammunition and food, and could not continue the fight. The merchant ships in the last convoy to approach Tobruk had been sunk on 26 October by RAF Beauforts, Bisleys and Wellingtons operating from Egypt, and no replacements could break through. The remaining fuel supplies were being used in a retreat, in spite of Hitler's ridiculous orders to hold on to the last man. Rommel left behind 30,000 prisoners and huge quantities of derelict equipment, but he was not beaten.

Right: The ploughed-up landing ground at Ghindels in Libya, photographed in the third week of November 1942.

AIR 41/50

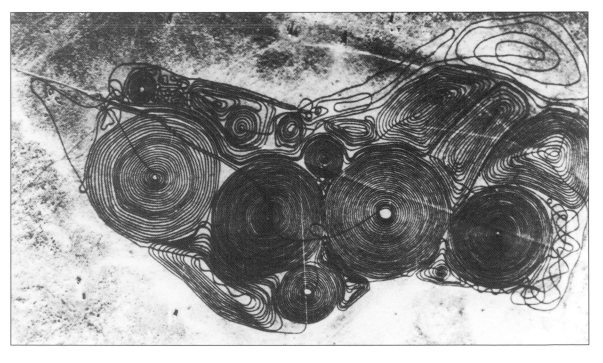

Fortune favoured the Panzerarmee in its retreat, for the heavens opened on 6 November and prevented the RAF from strafing the fleeing columns, while much of the British armour became bogged down. But then Rommel learned that he was caught in a form of pincer movement that Hitler had envisaged for advances on Egypt through Libya and Iraq. Anglo–American forces landed in French North Africa on 8 November and were ready to greet him in the west.

The pursuit by the British rolled across the desert, but Montgomery was careful not to outrun his means of supply, knowing that Rommel was shortening his lines by approaching Tripoli. On 12 November, the US Army Middle East Air Force, within RAF Middle East, became the US Ninth Air Force under Major-General Lewis H. Brereton. The 8th Army entered Tobruk on 13 November and reached Benghazi six days later, with the Desert Air Force moving forward to new landing grounds. Malta was at last relieved on 20 November when four merchant ships arrived, heavily escorted by the Royal Navy, bringing supplies of fuel and ammunition. The Axis air assault on the island petered out.

Rommel reported to Hitler that his motorized formations in the rearguard of the retreat were immobilized for lack of fuel. The Panzerarmee made a stand at El Agheila

Above: 'Beat-up'
by Charles J. Thompson

Bristol Beaufighter Is appeared in the Western Desert in April 1941, when they were employed mainly on strafing enemy road convoys and airfields. The fire-power from four Hispano-Suiza 20 mm cannons in the nose and four .303 inch Browning machine-guns in the wings proved shattering. The Italians named the aircraft *il flagello di Dio* (the scourge of God).

Flying low over the desert caused a local dust storm, in addition to the sandstorms which occurred naturally. The sand could also play havoc with the paintwork.

Below: A Bristol Bombay on the airfield at Marble Arch in Tripolitania, photographed when the 8th Army was advancing towards Tripoli in late 1942. This reliable bomber-transport, which first entered service in November 1939, could carry up to twenty-four troops. Only three squadrons were equipped with them, two in the Middle East and one at home.

AIR 41/50

Right: The Ilva Steel Works, south-east of the port of Trieste, photographed on 23 December 1942. This was the most important of its type in the region, comprising coke ovens, three blast furnaces, steel-making plant and the manufacture of various by-products.

AIR 34/237

Left: Sappers at work on an advanced airfield in Tripolitania on the day before the RAF arrived in January 1943. They were then helped by RAF and RAAF groundcrews.

AIR 41/50

and succeeded in halting the 8th Army until mid December, by which time some fuel had reached Rommel. It was not until 23 January 1943 that the 8th Army entered Tripoli and clearance of the port began. The Panzerarmee reached the French protectorate of Tunisia at the end of January where it was able to man the pre-war defences of the 'Mareth Line' between the mountains and the sea, near Medenine. A stiff and bloody fight lay ahead.

30 The End in Africa

By comparison with the débâcle of the landings at Dieppe on 19 August 1942, the Anglo–American invasions of French Algeria and Morocco the following November under operation 'Torch' were examples of meticulous planning and precise co-ordination. The enterprise took place in the early hours of 8 November, with landings at Oran and Algiers carried out by American forces brought from Britain in vessels of the Royal Navy, supported by the Fleet Air Arm. The British 1st Army followed the Americans at Algiers. In the west, there were landings near Casablanca in French Morocco. These were entirely American, arriving in vessels direct from their home country.

The supreme commander for operation 'Torch' was General Dwight Eisenhower. His ground commander was a

Right: General view of the beaches near Oran in Algeria, where the Centre Task Force landed in the early hours of 7 November 1942, under Operation 'Torch'. The photographs were taken at noon after the landings.
DEFE 2/609

Left: Major-General George C. Patton, with his famous pearl-handled revolvers, demanding from a Naval Staff Officer that supplies and troops be landed at the harbour of Arzeu near Oran. Patton was the ground commander of operation 'Torch'.
DEFE 2/609

Right: 'Squadron Leader Hugh G. Malcolm'
by war artist O'Connell

On 4 December 1942, eleven Blenheim Vs of 326 Wing flew to a forward landing ground at Souk-el-Arba in Algeria to provide close tactical support for the British 1st Army in the front line. This type of Blenheim, which had more powerful engines and increased armour protection, was known as the Bisley. In the afternoon, they were ordered to attack a landing strip in the Chougui area, occupied by the Luftwaffe. Ten were able to take off, led by Squadron Leader Hugh G. Malcolm in serial BA875 of 18 Squadron. One suffered engine trouble and crash-landed soon after take-off. No fighter escort was available. On approaching the target area, the nine Bisleys were beset by swarms of Messerschmitt Bf109s of *Jagdgeschwader* 2 (not Focke-Wulf FW190s as guessed by this artist) and one by one were hacked out of the sky until only three were left, including Malcolm. These were forced to turn back and all crash-landed in Allied territory, but Malcolm's aircraft burst into flames and the three crew members were killed. He was gazetted with a posthumous Victoria Cross on 28 April 1943.

INF 3/467

fellow American, Major-General George C. Patton. Air support was provided by two newly-created air units, the US Twelfth Air Force under Major-General James Doolittle and the RAF's Eastern Air Command under Air Marshall Sir William Welsh. Gibraltar, with its runway extended to 1,400 yards, played a prominent part in the air cover.

Left: Naval transports alongside the jetties at Arzeu. This harbour was captured by Allied forces by 07.45 hours on 8 November 1942, so that supplies and more troops began arriving on D-Day +1.

INF 1/244

Below: 'Aircraft formation over the Alps' by war artist Gordon Nicoll

This representation of Lancasters and Stirlings bombing a city in Italy may have been inspired by an occasion on 20/21 November 1942 when Bomber Command despatched 232 aircraft which included Lancasters, Stirlings, Halifaxes and Wellingtons to bomb Turin. Large fires were started but one Halifax, one Stirling and one Wellington were lost. Raids on industrial cities in Italy at this time supported the landings in North-West Africa and the advance of the 8th Army through Libya.

INF 3/1618

The landings in Algeria went reasonably well, with the surrender of Algiers and the capture of airfields. There was determined opposition in Oran, but the nearby harbour of Arzeu was quickly captured and the town fell within two days. Casablanca proved far more difficult and stiff fighting lasted for three days. But the reaction of the Germans was swift. In the mainland of Europe, troops began to enter Vichy France on 14 November, only to find that almost the whole of the French Fleet in Toulon had been scuttled. To counter the landings in North-West Africa, troops were flown from Sicily across the 100 miles which separated the island from Tunisia, where they were welcomed. These were rapidly built up by air and sea until they became a formidable force.

As the threat in Tunisia developed, the Anglo–American forces moved eastwards as quickly as possible, while on 12 November commandos and paratroops seized the Algerian port of Bone near the border. The British 1st Army pressed on and entered Tunisia but in early December the fresh enemy troops, who by then numbered about 15,000, struck back and repulsed the forward elements. In the absence of suitable advanced airfields, there was insufficient air cover to counter the Luftwaffe, which appeared in strength.

The British 1st Army built up its numbers, but so did the enemy. By mid December, the Germans and Italians in

Below: The municipal airport of Tunis-El Aouina was one of the main bases through which the Axis forces in Tunisia were supplied. This reconnaissance photograph of part of the airfield, taken on 12 November 1942, shows Junkers Ju52s and a Savoia-Marchetti 82. The arrow shows a crashed Bloch 174 of the Vichy Air Force.

AIR 34/234

Above: A Boston of the SAAF photographed on 25 March 1943 over southern Tunisia while en route to bomb a landing ground at Djebel Terbaga. Both 12 (SAAF) and 24 (SAAF) Squadrons were equipped with Bostons at this time and based at Zuara in western Tripolitania.
AIR 34/236

Below: Spitfire VBs of 417 (RCAF) Squadron flying over Tunisia in April 1943, acting as top cover to a bomber escort.
INF 2/42

Tunisia were estimated as 42,000 men, and the British became bogged down in torrential rain, with extended supply lines. Maintenance of Allied aircraft proved a problem and there was little co-ordination between the activities of the US Twelfth Air Force and the RAF Eastern Air Command. In early December, Eisenhower appointed Major General Carl Spaatz as the temporary commander of these two forces.

On 14 January 1943, Roosevelt and Churchill with their Chiefs-of-Staff met at Casablanca for a conference which lasted nine days and determined the course of the war in the West. Among other matters, it was decided that the next major move would be a thrust into the 'underbelly' of Europe, for which there would be a unified air control with a new Mediterranean Air Command under Air Chief Marshal Sir Arthur Tedder. This came into being on 17 February and consisted of RAF Middle East under Air Chief Marshal Sir Sholto Douglas, RAF Malta under Air Vice-Marshal Sir Keith Park, and a new Northwest African Air Force under Major-General Carl Spaatz. The latter was created by the amalgamation of the US Twelfth Air Force and the RAF's Eastern Air Command, together with certain tactical units from RAF Middle East; its three main fighting divisions were a Strategic Air Force under Major-General James Doolittle, a Tactical Air Force under Air Marshal Sir Arthur Coningham and a Coastal Air Force under Air Vice-Marshal Sir Hugh Pugh Lloyd. Command of the land forces was given to the highly experienced General Sir Harold Alexander.

Meanwhile, the fighting in Tunisia continued. The German reinforcements became sufficient to form the new 5th Panzerarmee under General Hans-Jurgen von Arnim. By 13 February 1943, this numbered 110,000 men, including

Above: Hurricane IID 'tankbusters' of 6 Squadron preparing to take off at Gabes in Tunisia in the early afternoon of 6 April 1943 for an attack on enemy armoured forces.

INF 2/42

Right: A Beaufighter TFX of the RAF's 328 Wing, based at Protville II near Tunis. This was a long-range torpedo-carrying aircraft, rated for low-level flying. Nos 39, 47 and 144 Squadrons began to operate from this airfield in June 1943, on anti-shipping sorties in preparation for the invasion of Sicily.

INF 2/42

Right: The Italian light cruiser *Bari* of 3,250 tons sunk in shallow water at Leghorn (Livorno) by USAAF bombers on 28 June 1943. She was broken up by the Germans after the following September. The US 5th Army entered Leghorn on 19 July 1944.

AIR 23/8572

Left: The Model Section of the Northwest African Central Interpretation Unit constructing a model on a scale of 1:5,000 of south-east Sicily, from air photographs and maps, in preparation for operation 'Husky'. The model-maker is transferring roads and railways from a map. Two of these models were made for the planners of the operation.
AIR 34/737

Below Left: A vertical of part of the model, covering the bay between Punta della Formiche and Isola delle Corrente, where units of the British 8th Army were destined to land. Low-level oblique photographs of the model were taken, to assist the naval forces and landing parties.
AIR 34/737

33,000 Italians as well as Luftwaffe and Kriegsmarine personnel. Thus there were two German armies in Tunisia, with the advantage of operating on interior lines and with a short supply route to Sicily. The overall command was nominally under von Arnim.

Eisenhower attempted to split these two armies by thrusting a combination of American and newly-constituted French forces between them, but on 14 February these received a mauling near Kasserine from two Panzer divisions. However, a further attack by Rommel was thwarted, with the aid of the Anglo–American air forces, and on 23 February the Germans began to retreat. Rommel also struck against the British 8th Army near Medenine on 6 March but was bloodily repulsed and retreated back to the Mareth Line. He became ill and flew to Germany for medical treatment. From 22 March, Montgomery succeeded in outflanking this line, with the air of the Western Desert Air Force. The Germans who could escape raced north, pursued by the 8th Army, while the British 1st Army with the American and French forces continued to fight their way from the west.

By 1 May the Axis armies were bottled up in a bridgehead around Tunis, with a defensive line some 100 miles long. Here they were subjected to an immense air bombardment, while their supply line to Tunis came under increased and continuous attack from sea and air. They put up a determined resistance but finally were forced to surrender on 14 May. It had been a costly campaign for the Allied forces, with almost 50,000 soldiers killed or wounded. But the Axis forces also suffered huge casualties and about 250,000 of their men became prisoners. Their losses were almost equivalent to those at Stalingrad.

31 From Sicily to Rome

The team of top air commanders appointed to the Mediterranean Air Command on 17 February 1943 joined in the planning for the invasion of Sicily, under the code-name operation 'Husky'. The invasion force consisted of the American 7th Army under General Patton and the British 8th Army under General Montgomery, with General Alexander as Deputy Commander-in-Chief to the supreme commander, General Eisenhower. The naval force was commanded by Admiral Sir Andrew Cunningham, with some 2,000 vessels available as well as new amphibious landing craft. The troops were destined to land in the south-east corner of the island, where they could be covered by tactical aircraft from Malta.

As a prelude to the invasion, sustained attacks on enemy airfields in Sicily, Sardinia and southern Italy took place from northern Africa and Malta, while Bomber Command in Britain laid waste to targets in the industrial north of Italy. It was estimated that about 1,850 German and Italian aircraft were based in these airfields, but many were unserviceable,

Below: Amphibious landing craft taking troops of the British 8th Army ashore on the south-east tip of Sicily during the landings of 10 July 1943.
DEFE 2/1411

Above: An attack in daylight on 17 July 1943 against the marshalling yard at Naples, while the heavy fighting in Sicily was continuing. It caused much damage to rolling stock, sheds, oil storage installations and an oil refinery.
AIR 34/237

Below: A Messerschmitt Me323 *Gigant* transport aircraft under attack near Corsica in August 1943 by a Marauder of 14 Squadron based at Protville in Tunisia. The six-engined machine made a forced landing on the coast.
AIR 34/238

Above: On 7 September 1943, twenty-four Baltimores from 223 and 55 Squadrons took off from Sigonella-Gerbini III in Sicily, escorted by Kittyhawks from Lentini, to bomb Catanzaro in the south of Italy. The purpose was to block transport routes leading to the shores of Calabria where the 8th Army had landed. Cloud forced the Baltimores to descend to 4,800 feet for their bombing runs, and explosions were photographed on the main road and railway sidings.
AIR 27/1381

Left: The Type VIIC U-boat *U-617* under attack on 12 September 1943 by bombs dropped by a Hudson of 48 Squadron flown from Gibraltar by Wing Commander T.F.U. Lang. The submarine had beached at Cape Tres Forcas in Spanish Morocco after being attacked by two Leigh Light Wellingtons of 179 Squadron from Gibraltar, and the crew had abandoned her. She was also attacked by Swordfish of the Fleet Air Arm and shelled by warships of the Royal Navy.
AIR 27/472

Below: Twenty-four Baltimores of 53 and 223 Squadrons took off from Sigonella-Gerbini III on 15 September 1943, escorted by twelve Curtiss P-40 Warhawks of the US Twelfth Tactical Air Command. Their mission was to bomb enemy troop concentrations on hills at Albanella, inland from Salerno where American and British forces had landed six days earlier. Photographs showed bombing patterns exactly on the targets.
AIR 27/1381

there was a shortage of experienced crews, and liaison between the Luftwaffe and the Regia Aeronautica was poor. The Allies could mount 267 squadrons for the enterprise, under a unified command.

Nevertheless, the invasion began with tragedy. American and British airborne troops took off on the night of 9 July 1943 in gliders towed by Dakotas, Albemarles and a few Halifaxes. The crews had been given a complicated flight plan and a gale blew up so that errors in navigation took place. Many gliders were released too early and over half crashed in the sea while most of the others came down in the wrong places. Of about 130 gliders, only twelve landed near their objectives. Paratroops also fared badly, with Dakotas carrying the British dispersed in the extreme turbulence, so that the men became scattered on the ground. Those carrying the Americans encountered intense flak, and

Above: Two Spitfire XIs of 241
Squadron, serials MA425 and
MH653, flying past Mount
Vesuvius on 27 January 1944.
The squadron was based at
Madna in southern Italy
and engaged tactical
reconnaissance as well as
ground attack duties.

INF 2/43

many Dakotas were shot down while the others also became scattered.

The seaborne landings went well, apart from troops becoming sick in the heaving seas. After a heavy bombardment from sea and air, the American and British forces landed on separate beaches at 04.00 hours on 10 July 1943, with the British on the right. By the early afternoon, the whole of the south-east corner of Sicily was in Allied hands, while sappers and RAF servicing commandos began herculean efforts to restore enemy airfields. Allied aircraft were flown in and supported the armies as they fought their way across the island. These met strong resistance from German divi-

Above: The ancient monastery on Monte Cassino, which was destroyed on 15 February 1944 when 135 B-17 Fortresses of Strategic Air Force dropped 287 tons of bombs, followed by 140 tons from B-25 Mitchells and B-26 Marauders, and fire from heavy artillery by the 5th Army. The smoke of battle in the Liri Valley beyond can be seen in the photograph.

AIR 23/8567

sions, which were helped by increased numbers of Luftwaffe aircraft. The Italians were less determined. The country had become so disillusioned with the war that on 25 July their Grand Council in Rome deposed Mussolini and placed him under arrest.

Above: 'The Balt'
by Charles J. Thompson

No 13 (Hellenic) Squadron formed part of the RAF in Egypt in May 1941, mainly with Greek pilots and other personnel who had escaped from their country after it was overrun by German forces during the previous months. The squadron operated over the eastern Mediterranean, originally with Avro Ansons, then with Blenheims, and with Martin Baltimores from October 1943. It moved to Italy in May 1944 and bombed targets in Yugoslavia, but flew to Greece in the following November after the Germans had been forced out of the country. This Baltimore V serial FW546 shows the Hellenic fin flash of light blue and white, which the squadron was allowed to use instead of the RAF's regulation red, white and blue.

By late July the defenders in Sicily had been driven to the north-east tip, where they held out skilfully until survivors crossed to the Italian mainland on 16 August. The Allies lost under 400 aircraft in this invasion but destroyed 1,850 enemy aircraft. The Axis also lost about 32,000 men killed or wounded and 162,000 captured, mostly Italians.

The stage was then set for the invasion of Italy itself. This was preceded in early August by even heavier attacks on northern cities by Bomber Command, with the objective of hastening the country's surrender. Then, on 3 September, the British 8th Army crossed the Strait of Messina and landed on the toe of Italy. The Grand Council signed an armistice on the same day, although this was not made public for five days.

At dawn on 9 September landings took place at Salerno, south-east of Naples, supported by the Northwest African Air Force. The force consisted of one American and one British Corps, forming part of the US 5th Army under General Mark W. Clark. The Germans were taken by surprise but soon counter-attacked. The outcome remained in the balance for several days but the Germans were eventually driven back by the invaders, with the aid of intense air attacks. These included heavy bombers transferred from the

Above: The lone German assault gun which held out for so long in the lobby of the Continental Hotel in Cassino.
AIR 23/8567

Below: The west coast port of Piombino, which provided a service to the island of Elba and sheltered F-boats (heavily armed naval ferry barges) under attack by B-26 Marauders of a US Bombardment Group on 20 March 1944.
AIR 23/8566

Above: Bombs dropped on 21 March 1944 by B-26 Marauders of a US Bombardment Group, exploding on a viaduct about seven miles west of Arezzo in central Italy. The viaduct, which served Florence, was closed for three weeks following this attack.
AIR 23/8566

US Ninth Air Force, which was disbanded on 13 September.

The 8th Army advanced steadily up the peninsula of Italy and on 27 September captured a large group of airfields around Foggia, from which the Allied squadrons could operate. The 5th Army also advanced and entered Naples on 1 October. It seemed that Rome would fall, but the Germans established strong defences known as the Gothic Line, from Gaeta on the west coast and across Monte Cassino to Ortona on the Adriatic. Allied squadrons dominated the battlefields and developed the rapid 'cab rank' system of attacking enemy positions, in which fighter-bombers already in the air were given orders by mobile observation posts. However, the troops became hampered by the onset of extremely wet weather which bogged them down for months.

Changes in command structure took place on 10 December 1943 when the Mediterranean Allied Air Forces were formed, with subordinate Tactical, Strategic and Coastal Air Forces. Some of the top commanders in Italy were needed back in Britain for the planning of operation 'Neptune', the forthcoming invasion of Normandy. At the beginning of 1944, General Sir Henry Maitland Wilson took over

Left: B-25 Mitchells of a US Bombardment Group over Marsciano railway bridge on 14 May 1944. This target, about seventy miles north of Rome, was frequently attacked.

AIR 23/8567

Below Left: A road bridge over the river Tiber under attack by a US Bombardment Group in late May 1944.

AIR 23/8569

supreme command in the Mediterranean from General Eisenhower, while General Montgomery was succeeded by Lieutenant-General Oliver Leese. Air Chief Marshal Tedder was replaced by General Ira C. Eaker of the USAAF, and Major-General Spaatz left to command the American strategic forces in Europe.

An attempt to break the deadlock in the fighting took place on 22 January 1944 when about 50,000 American and British troops stormed the beaches at Anzio, behind the Gothic Line, and on the approaches to Rome. In spite of overwhelming strength in the air, these were halted by determined resistance from two German divisions. Intense bombardment from the air failed to dislodge the enemy, who began to counter-attack. The Allies responded by bombarding German positions at Cassino from 15 February, but the fortress around the monastery was not finally captured until 18 May. Meanwhile, Allied squadrons opened sustained attacks on enemy communications. These shattered German resistance and the Allies were able to break through with a spring offensive which began on 11 May 1944. Rome was finally entered on 4 June, two days before the landings on the beaches of Normandy.

197

32 RAF Middle East

At the time of the landings in Sicily, RAF Middle East controlled about eighty squadrons or flights based in Egypt, Libya, Palestine, East Africa, Aden, Iraq and Persia. These included some elements of the US Ninth Air Force, although others had been transferred to the Mediterranean Air Command in the west. There was plenty of work ahead for RAF Middle East, as the enemy was active in Greece and the Aegean, while German U-boats roamed the ocean between Africa and India.

Below: On 27 June 1943, four Beaufighters of 252 Squadron from Magrun in Libya bombed a convoy in the Levkas Canal on the west coast of Greece. They hit the Italian merchant vessel *Quirinale* of 3,779 tons and left her listing and stranded.

AIR 34/237

Right: On 19 July 1943, six Beaufighters of 252 Squadron from Magrun in Libya bombed the Italian seaplane base of Prevesa on the west coast of Greece, leaving buildings and aircraft on fire. The seaplane in the foreground is a Cant Z501.

AIR 34/237

Right: This photograph is one of many in a captured Italian document which shows the damage at Campina, one of the Romanian oil refineries at Ploesti. Attacks on 1 August 1943 against several fields at Ploesti were carried out by two Groups of B-24D Liberators of the US Ninth Air Force operating from Benghazi, which had been joined by three Groups of the US Eighth Air Force from bases in England. No long-range fighters were available to escort the 178 Liberators which began taking off at 07.00 hours on a daring sortie of 1,900 miles, for those lucky enough to return. The aircraft flew across the Mediterranean to Corfu, and then crossed Albania, Yugoslavia and Bulgaria into Romania, where they were set upon by swarms of Messerschmitt Bf109s. In all, 45 Liberators were lost on the operation, while eight other crews were interned in Turkey. Almost all returning aircraft were damaged. Nevertheless, some refineries were completely destroyed and others lost production for up to eight months.

AIR 23/7777

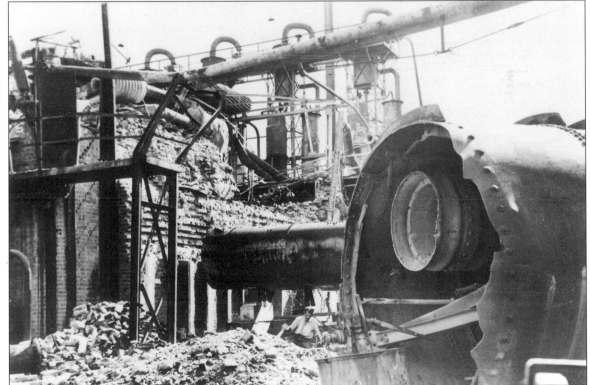

One of the most sensational operations took place on 1 August 1943 when the B-24 Liberators of the US Ninth Air Force were joined by others of the US Eighth Air Force from England to make a long-distance attack on the oil installations at Ploesti in Romania. The Ninth was disbanded on 13 September and its aircraft transferred to other units, although it was re-formed in England as part of the Allied Expeditionary Air Force.

Meanwhile, the anti-shipping squadrons of RAF Middle East made forays over the southern coasts of the Greek mainland and the western Aegean islands. However, the British had an ambitious plan further east, to be put into operation after the surrender of Italy. They intended to invade the Dodecanese Islands along the south-west coast of Turkey and use these as stepping stones to the Greek mainland, thus opening a new front against German-occupied Europe. The key to this lay in the occupation of Rhodes, which was held by the enemy. The move was anticipated by the Germans, who moved a whole division to the island. The British decided to bypass Rhodes and occupy the islands of Cos, Leros and Samos to the north. The

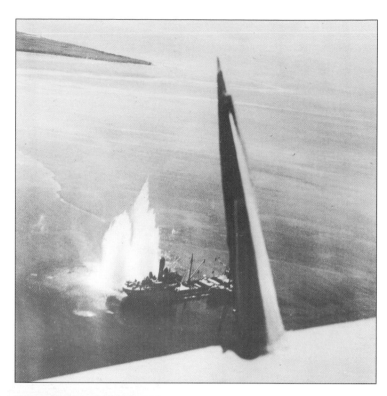

Above: On 22 August 1943, three Beaufighters of 252 Squadron from Magrun in Libya bombed shipping off Prevesa. This photograph shows a near miss on the collier *Bacchus* of 1,810 tons. The Germans renamed her *Bertha* after Italy capitulated, and she was sunk by a submarine on 3 October 1944.
AIR 34/238

Left: An attack on 3 October 1943 against the German passenger vessel *Sieglinde* of 2,500 tons was made by seven Beaufighters of 252 Squadron based at Lakatamia in Cyprus. She was carrying German troops to recapture the Dodecanese island of Cos, which had been occupied by the British. All the bombs were near misses. She was eventually put out of action in a gale at Port Laki in Leros on 5 February 1944.
AIR 34/239

Right: On 19 October 1943, two Beaufighters of 227 Squadron and two from 603 Squadron took off from Gambut in Libya with four Mitchells of the US 310th Bombardment Group, on a sweep round the north coast of Crete. They shot down this Dornier Do24 flying boat and left it disabled in the sea.

AIR 34/239

Left: A Wellington XIII of 244 Squadron, showing the aerial array used for locating submarines with air to surface-vessel radar. The Squadron was first equipped with these machines in March 1944 when based at Masirah in the Persian Gulf, and continued with these operations until the end of the war in Europe.

AIR 27/1480

Left: This Type IXD2 long-range U-boat, beached on the Horn of Africa, was photographed on 3 May 1944 from 100 feet by a Wellington of 8 Squadron. She was *U-852*, which had left Kiel on 8 January under the command of *Kapitänleutnant* Heinz Eck, and had been attacked in the Indian Ocean by a succession of Wellington XIIIs of 621 and 8 Squadrons from Khormaksar in Aden. Five men in the U-boat had been killed in the attacks but the others beached her, blew off her stern and abandoned her. They were imprisoned in Aden, but it was discovered that they had sunk the Greek SS *Peleus* of 4,695 tons on 13 March in the Atlantic. Then they had machine-gunned the survivors and thrown grenades on the rafts. Three of these seamen were not killed but picked up twenty-eight days later. Eck and some of his crew were tried after the war. He and two others were executed and two more received sentences of fifteen years. This is the only known case of a war crime committed by U-boat men.

AIR 15/277

Left: The merchant ship *Sabine* of 2,252 tons was hit by rockets fired by two Beaufighters of 252 Squadron. She burnt out and sank. This photograph shows the Beaufighter flown by the commanding officer of 252 Squadron, Wing Commander Bryce G. Meharg, going down in flames after being hit by flak. He and his navigator survived to become prisoners of war.

AIR 27/1509

Above: 'Shipbuster Beaufighters'
by Mark Postlethwaite

Americans did not favour the plan, believing it would draw forces from urgent operations elsewhere.

Operation 'Accolade' began on 13 September 1943, five days after Italy announced her surrender, with an amphibious landing on Cos. Leros was occupied the next day and Samos two days after that. The operation was supported by about 260 aircraft based in North Africa or the British-held islands of Cyprus. These included Beaufighters, Wellingtons, Baltimores, Spitfires, Hurricanes and Hudsons. The troops were received enthusiastically by the civilians and most of the Italian garrisons, but the Germans responded swiftly and effectively. The Luftwaffe in the Aegean was built up to over 350 aircraft, operating on far shorter lines that the RAF, and on 18 September began to mount devastating air attacks on the British positions, putting the airfield at Cos out of action.

On 3 October, 1,200 well-equipped German troops landed on Cos, and paratroops were also dropped. RAF

The Beaufighter force which attacked the German convoy approaching Heraklion in Crete on 1 June 1944 consisted of ten from 252 Squadron, eight from 603 Squadron, four from 16 (SAAF) Squadron and two from 227 Squadron. This first wave was followed five minutes later by twelve Marauders from 24 (SAAF) Squadron and eighteen Baltimores from 15 (SAAF) and 454 (RAAF) Squadrons, escorted by thirteen long-range Spitfires from 94 and 213 Squadrons together with four Mustangs from 213 Squadron. This was the largest anti-shipping strike force assembled by the RAF in the Mediterranean.

Left: A rocket attack on 19 June 1944 against the German torpedo boat *TA.19* of 876 tons south-west of the island of Kalymnos by eight Beaufighters of 252 Squadron from Mersa Matruh in Egypt. The warship was badly damaged and went into dock at Athens for repair.
AIR 27/1509

Below: In the early evening of 4 July 1944, two Beaufighters of 603 Squadron from Gambut in Libya attacked this Junkers Ju52 floatplane off the island of Siros in the central Aegean. The machine was hit in the starboard engine and came down into the water. It then burst into flames from end to end. Survivors were seen swimming in the sea, and one of these was later reported to have been the commander of the German forces in the Aegean.
AIR 27/2080

single-engined fighters could not reach the island but Beaufighters did their best against odds, to no avail. The British fought stubbornly but their resistance was crushed. On 12 November it was the turn of Leros, from a German invasion fleet assembled at Cos. There was a ferocious battle, with 1,100 Germans killed from an assault force of 3,000, but the defenders were forced to capitulate, while the Beaufighter squadrons trying to support them from Cyprus lost half their number. The British evacuated Samos two days later. It was realized that the whole enterprise was lost, as the RAF had been unable to achieve command of the air from its distant bases.

The anti-shipping squadrons in Egypt and Libya needed to recoup their losses after the failed campaign in the Dodecanese. New Beaufighters arrived and these were gradually equipped with rocket projectiles. Attacks were made on German shipping in the Aegean, reinforced in February 1944 with a US Bombardment Group of Mitchells under temporary loan from the Mediterranean Air Forces in the west. Ship after ship was sunk by air attack or British submarines until the German garrisons in the Aegean became seriously short of supplies. One of the most devastating blows was made against a German convoy which approached Crete on 1 June 1944. All the merchant vessels save one were sunk by Beaufighters and Marauders as it

Right: An attack on 15 October 1944 by Beaufighters of 252 Squadron from Gambut in Libya against the German headquarters in the town hall in Naxia, the capital of Naxos in the Cyclades. The garrison surrendered shortly afterwards.
AIR 27/1509

Below: Beaufighters of 252 Squadron flying over Athens as part of the VE Parade on 8 May 1945.
AIR 27/1509

approached Heraklion, or by subsequent attacks against the port by Wellingtons and Liberators.

The remaining German ships in the Aegean were picked off one by one until the garrisons in the islands were almost isolated. Meanwhile, Anglo–American troops were advancing in Italy, threatening to cut off the German forces in Greece, while the Russians also pushed through Romania. In August 1944, the Germans began to use their remaining vessels to withdraw garrisons from the islands, although some troops were left behind. RAF Middle East handed over some of its squadrons to the new Balkan Air Force in Italy.

In late September 1944, the Germans scuttled their few remaining vessels and began to evacuate Greece via Yugoslavia. British forces landed on the Greek mainland on 5 October and reached Athens five days later. The British also liberated many of the Greek islands, although about 23,000 enemy troops were left in Crete, Rhodes, Leros, Cos and Melos until the end of the war, in conditions which approached starvation.

33 The End in Italy

After the capture of Rome on 4 June 1944, the US 5th Army and the British 8th Army pressed northwards, with the retreating Germans harried by tactical fighter-bombers and medium bombers of the Mediterranean Allied Air Forces. The islands of Sardinia and Corsica had already been occupied by the Allies, and Elba fell on 17 June 1944. On 18 July, the 8th Army reached Pesaro on the coast of the Adriatic. On 4 August, advanced elements of the 5th Army entered Florence. But the resistance of the Germans stiffened and new defensive lines across the Apennine mountains of the peninsula were set up by their highly efficient commander, Field Marshal Albert Kesselring. The Allied armies still faced a hard and bloody slog.

Right: A B-25 Mitchell of the 489th Bomb Squadron of the 340th Bomb Group dropping 1,000 lb semi-armour piercing bombs on the entrance to a railway tunnel at Pistoia, north-east of Florence. There is no date on the photograph but it was probably taken in June 1944.

AIR 23/8570

Below:Twelve Baltimores of 223 and 454 (RAAF) Squadrons took off from Pescara on 8 August 1944 with an escort of Spitfires, to bomb the marshalling yards and wharf at Ravenna on the coast of north-east Italy. The bombs fell on the target and all aircraft returned.

AIR 27/1382

Right: A B-24 Liberator of VI of 34 (SAAF) Squadron, which was formed in Egypt on 14 April 1944. Early in the following July, the squadron transferred to Celone near Foggia in Italy, where it received these long-range machines and began operating at night over northern Italy, Yugoslavia, Hungary, Czechoslovakia and Austria. These operations continued until the end of the war in Europe.

AIR 27/378

Meanwhile, air power in Italy increased steadily. The US Fifteenth Air Force had been officially established on 1 November 1943 in Tunisia, under Major-General James H. Doolittle. At the end of the year, B-17 Fortresses and B-24 Liberators had been transferred to it from the US Twelfth Air Force, which was left as part of the tactical air force for the theatre. In early 1944, the Fifteenth had begun to establish itself in the complex of airfields around Foggia in south-east Italy. More heavy bombers, mainly Liberators, arrived from the USA. Meanwhile, Doolittle returned to Britain to command the US Eighth Air Force, and was replaced by Major-General Nathan F. Twining.

The End in Italy

Right: On 13 August 1944, four Beaufighter TFXs of 16 (SAAF) Squadron, based in Biferno in Italy, attacked with rockets and cannon fire the 2,300 ton *Cagliari* which was loading bauxite in the harbour of Parenzo (Porec) in Yugoslavia, and sank the vessel.

AIR 27/227

Below: A train north of Dravograd in the north of Yugoslavia near the Austrian border, under attack by fighter-bombers of the RAF's Desert Air Force in the closing days of the war in Italy.

AIR 23/7379

Above: A daylight attack on 16 March 1945 by Liberators of 34 (SAAF) Squadron against the docks at Monfalcone in the Gulf of Trieste, which resulted in heavy damage. The partly sunken vessel appears to be the merchant ship Ausonia of 9,300 tons, hit by RAF bombs on the night of 19/20 March 1944.

AIR 27/378

The US Fifteenth Air Force began its major attacks from Foggia in April 1944 and these continued with ever-increasing effect until the end of the war. Its heavy bombers operated with their fighter escorts in daylight on long-distance sorties, mainly against the enemy transport system in south-east Europe. The Liberators and Wellingtons of the RAF's No 205 Group were employed against these targets at night, although with far fewer squadrons.

In addition, the Balkan Air Force was formed in June 1944 under the command of Air Vice-Marshal W. Elliott, in south-east Italy. This had grown from a single squadron which had been supporting the partisans in Yugoslavia, until it consisted of eight squadrons and one flight. Its formation was the result of a discussion with Marshal Tito, who had been flown to Italy from a landing strip in Yugoslavia. His partisan army was containing fourteen German and six Bulgarian divisions, and the request was justified. The new air force was a strange mixture of aircraft types and nationalities, even including some Russian pilots with Yak fighters, but there can be no doubt about its effectiveness in operations from south-east Italy, sometimes to landing strips specially constructed in Yugoslavia.

On the night of 14/15 August, operation 'Dragoon' began on the south coast of France, with paratroops dropped to secure positions. Beach landings began at 08.00 hours between Le Lavandou and St Raphael by troops of the US 7th Army under Lieutenant-General A. Patch, and over 400 gliders also landed. The operation was covered by massive air attacks by the Mediterranean Allied Air Forces, and everywhere it was successful. The troops advanced rapidly and by 28 August reached Avignon. They moved north and eventually joined up with General Patton's 3rd Army, which had broken through from the Normandy

Above: Eight Marauders of 21 (SAAF) Squadron took off from Iesi on 11 March 1945 and made rendezvous with six Spitfires. They bombed the Casarsa marshalling yards in Yugoslavia from 11,500 feet, straddling the target. All returned without loss.

AIR 27/271

Left: Ten Marauders of 21 (SAAF) Squadron took off from Iesi in the afternoon of 23 March 1945 to bomb the St Veit marshalling yards in Austria. One aircraft returned early and the others formed into three boxes. Escorted by six Thunderbolts, they bombed from 13,000 feet and straddled the target. They returned safely.

AIR 27/271

Above: A Boston of the RAF's
Tactical Bomber Force over
northern Italy in 1945.
                    AIR 23/7379

Left: German transport north of the city of Vicenza under attack by fighter-bombers of the RAF's Desert Air Force. The city fell to the British 8th Army in the last week of April 1945.

AIR 23/7379

Below: An attack by fighter-bombers of the RAF's Desert Air Force on enemy transport near the city of Verona, north of the river Po and close to Lake Garda. Verona was entered by the British 8th Army on 25 April 1945.

AIR 23/7379

beachheads. They also drove east, threatening a German defensive line in the Maritime Alps between France and Italy.

Allied air attacks continued remorselessly. The Romanian oil plants were almost completely destroyed by August 1944, while sustained attacks were made on the Hungarian and Romanian railway networks. The river Danube was mined systematically by RAF Liberators and Wellingtons, while Beaufighters attacked barges and other craft at night. The volume of traffic was reduced by about sixty per cent. German positions along their defensive lines in Italy were subjected to daily attacks by tactical aircraft, and their communications in the rear were constantly disrupted.

The Allies were able to resume their offensive in the early spring of 1945. The master of defence, Field Marshal Kesselring, left on 23 March to take command of the German forces on the Western Front, and his place was taken by General O.H. von Vietinghoff. His forces in Italy were still formidable, with twenty-three German and four Italian Fascist divisions facing only seventeen divisions and ten brigades of the Allies. However, in the afternoon of 9 April these enemy forces were subjected to a colossal

Left: A railway marshalling yard at Gorizia, in north-east Italy near the border with Yugoslavia. The British 8th Army was nearing this city when the German armies in Italy surrendered unconditionally on 2 May 1945.

AIR 23/7379

Left and Below Left: This Martin Marauder letter B of 21 (SAAF) Squadron was photographed at Iesi in Italy. It was taken on strength on 5 July 1944, at a time when the squadron was converting from Baltimores, and participated in the first raid made with these new machines on 15 August 1944. The nose art shows 113 sorties by the end of the war, together with a jumping cat and the Afrikaans adjective meaning 'lucky and sly'.

AIR 27/271

bombardment by over 1,700 Allied bombers and fighter-bombers. It was one of the heaviest and most sustained air attacks of the war. The British 8th Army advanced behind it, securing all their objectives and breaking through gaps in enemy defences to fight north and reach Bologna on 21 April. The US 5th Army opened its offensive in the centre and the west on 14 April, with a similar air bombardment, and reached the river Po on 22 April. German troops were trapped everywhere, and those who managed to cross the Po left much of their equipment and transport behind. The end was inevitable and the Germans signed an instrument of surrender on 24 April, the ceasefire in Italy being ordered for 2 May.

PART THREE:
INDIA AND SOUTH-EAST ASIA

34 Japanese Victories

During the first two years of the war, Air Command Far East was starved of modern aircraft and their crews. On 16 October 1940 the various military Commands in the area urged an establishment of 556 aircraft, but this number was never attained. The surrender of France, the Battle of Britain, the entry of Italy into the war, the conflicts in Greece and North Africa and the need to supply Russia with aircraft, drained all available resources. The problem was compounded by a belief that Singapore was an impregnable fortress and that the Japanese forces were far inferior in quality to the British. There was also a dearth of accurate military intelligence, even though it was known that Japanese forces were likely to occupy Siam and were also poised to attack the Malayan archipelago by sea and air.

By December 1941, Air Command Far East could muster 362 aircraft, of which only 233 were serviceable. Many of these were outdated. The area they were supposed to cover included Malaya, British Borneo, Hong Kong, Burma, Ceylon and the Indian Ocean as far as the African coast. The supreme commander in the area was Air Chief Marshal Sir Robert Brooke-Popham, who was presented with an impossible task. His air defence in Malaya and Singapore consisted of two squadrons of obsolete Vildebeest torpedo bombers, four of Blenheim bombers, two of RAAF Hudsons, four of Brewster Buffalo fighters, and a flight of three Catalinas. In spite of unremitting efforts, insufficient airfields had been built in the Federated Malay States, and the few that existed were almost bereft of anti-aircraft defences while communications and radar warning were poor.

The Japanese assault on Malaya, which began with the landings of 8 December 1941 near Khota Baru on the east coast, proved overwhelming. A Catalina on reconnaissance was shot down. Hudsons and Vildebeests attempted to attack the seaborne forces, but with little effect, while suffering heavy losses. On the same day, the Japanese Army Air Force made its first attack on Singapore, which had inadequate air defences and almost no air raid precautions. Strong units of the same air arm attacked the RAF airfields in the north of Malaya, which were soon rendered unusable. The RAF's allies in Dutch East India, the Royal Netherlands Air Force, supplied twenty-two Glenn Martin bombers and nine Buffalos, but the odds were still against the Allies. Meanwhile, Japanese forces landed in Siam, which capitulated immediately.

The Japanese forces also proved to be masters of jungle fighting. They employed a system of rapid movement, with

Left: RAF Taiping in the Malayan state of Perak, photographed from 1,500 feet on 19 January 1935. This was one of the airfields in the north-west of the peninsula which came under air attack from the Japanese Air Force in December 1941.

AIR 27/799

Above: Vildebeest IIIs of 36 (Torpedo Bomber) Squadron lined up on 16 February 1934 at RAF Batu Pahat in the Malayan state of Johore, at a time when the squadron was based at Seletar in Singapore.

AIR 27/799

streams of lightly armed columns filtering along tracks to cut off the British and Commonwealth troops. Their soldiers were fanatical and indifferent to their own casualties. Although pockets of British and Commonwealth troops fought bravely and stubbornly with the support of Buffalos from airfields further south, their lines of communications were cut. They were forced to begin retreating down the peninsula, destroying much of their own equipment.

On 10 December, biplanes of the Japanese Naval Air Force sank the modern battleships HMS *Prince of Wales* and HMS *Repulse*, which had sailed up the east coast of Malaya without adequate air cover to oppose the landings. Thus the British lost control of the seas in this theatre of war. Hong Kong and British Borneo had few military resources and no air cover. The former fell after stiff fighting on 25 December and the latter was soon occupied by the Japanese. At the end of the year, Brooke-Popham was

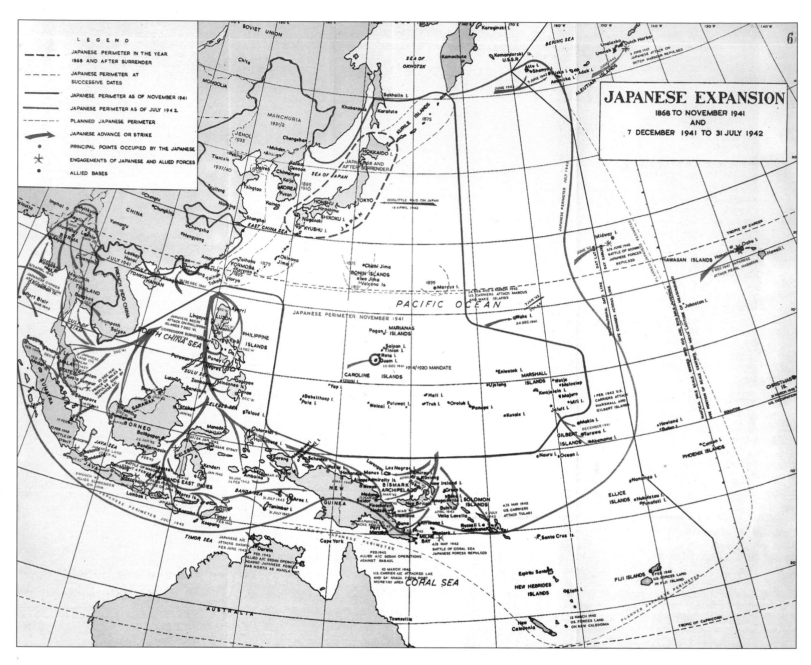

Above: The attacks by the Japanese from 7 December 1941 to 31 July 1942 scored a string of victories against American, British and Dutch forces. The map was drawn by the RAF's Air Historical Branch.

AIR 41/36

replaced by Lieutenant-General Sir Henry Roydes Pownall as overall commander, but the military situation could not be rectified.

While this fighting was in progress, a few more Hudsons and Blenheims arrived in Singapore. Fifty-one Hurricanes in crates were also unloaded and then assembled. Twenty-one pilots arrived for the latter, and these shot down eight Japanese bombers over the island on 20 January 1942. The Japanese responded by increasing their long-range fighter escorts, and several RAF fighters were lost in air combats.

Below: 'Brewster Buffalo Is of 453 (RAAF) Squadron' by Charles J. Thompson

This squadron, flown by Australian pilots, was based in Malaya when the Japanese invaded in December 1941. It fought valiantly against superior numbers and modern Japanese fighters but fell back to Singapore where it was merged with 21 (RAAF) Squadron, also equipped with Buffalo Is, on 24 December. The remnants of this single unit continued the fight from Sumatra but then were forced to withdraw to Java. The remaining personnel embarked for Australia on 22 February 1942. The squadron was disbanded on 15 March 1942 but reformed as a Spitfire squadron in Scotland during the following June.

Above: 'The Forlorn Hope' by Charles J. Thompson

Britain's highest award for gallantry to Squadron Leader Arthur S.K. Scarf is sometimes referred to as the 'unknown Victoria Cross' of the RAF. On 9 December 1941 all available aircraft at RAF Butterworth in Malaya were ordered to attack the Siamese airfield of Singora in the Kra peninsula, which had been occupied by the invading Japanese. Scarf took off in Blenheim I serial L1134 of 62 Squadron but immediately afterwards Japanese bombers swept over the airfield and destroyed all the other serviceable aircraft.

Scarf decided to make the attack alone and flew over the border, evading Japanese fighters and dropping a stick of bombs on the airfield while his gunner, Flight Sergeant Cyril Rich, fired at rows of enemy aircraft on the ground. The Blenheim was attacked repeatedly by Japanese fighters on the return journey and Scarf was hit in the arm and back, while Rich fired back. Rich and the navigator, Flight Sergeant Freddie Calder, then supported their pilot while he flew the riddled Blenheim to a forced landing at the nearer airfield of RAF Alor Star. Scarf was taken to hospital where, by coincidence, his wife Elizabeth was a nursing sister. She had the same blood group and helped in a transfusion but he died in the operating theatre. This story was lost in the confusion following the Japanese victory in Malaya and it was not until after the war that the full facts became known. A posthumous Victoria Cross was gazetted on 21 June 1946.

In this painting, the Japanese aircraft on the left of the Blenheim is a Nakajima Ki-43 Hayabusa (code-named *Oscar*) while the fighter behind it, with the fixed undercarriage, is a Nakajima Ki-27 (code-named *Nate*).

Left: The landing ground of RAF Akyab in Burma, photographed from 1,000 feet on 1 March 1935. It was enlarged and improved considerably by December 1941.

AIR 27/799

Below: A Vickers Vildebeest III of 36 (Torpedo Bomber) Squadron flying at 3,000 feet over RAF Dum-Dum, near Calcutta, on 2 March 1935. The squadron was still equipped with these obsolescent machines in December 1941 when based at Seletar in Singapore.

AIR 27/799

The Vildebeests were almost wiped out in efforts to bomb Japanese seaborne transports.

By the beginning of February, the exhausted British Commonwealth troops had retreated to Singapore, but the island could not be defended adequately against shelling or air bombardment from the mainland. It began to run out of water for the population, and the situation became untenable. The two remaining Catalinas had flown to Java. The surviving Blenheims and some Hurricanes flew across the Strait of Malacca to Sumatra, leaving only a handful of Buffalos and Hurricanes for a last-ditch defence. As many troops as possible crowded on to the few ships available for evacuation, but the majority were left behind.

Singapore surrendered on 15 February, after about 9,000 men had been killed in the campaign. Over 130,000 troops were taken into captivity, many of whom were to die under the inhuman treatment the Japanese always meted out to prisoners-of-war. It was by far the worst defeat Britain suffered in the Second World War.

This was not the end of the action in this theatre. Many of the vessels which had left Singapore were sunk by air attack. About 10,000 men reached Sumatra in the Dutch East Indies and the RAF tried to continue the fight from headquarters set up in Palembang, a port in the south-east of the huge island. Forty-eight bombers had escaped, mainly Blenheims and Hudsons, while the Hurricanes had been reinforced by thirty-five machines flown off the carrier HMS *Indomitable*. A Japanese invasion fleet already approaching Palembang was attacked by these aircraft on 15 February, and several transports were sunk. Japanese fighters flown off a carrier to nearby Banka Island were also attacked on the ground.

But, once again, the efforts were fruitless, largely because there was no organized army available to defend an island over 1,100 miles in length. Another retreat became inevitable when Japanese paratroopers were dropped. On 18 February, all serviceable aircraft were flown east to the Dutch island of Java. These had been whittled down to eigh-

Above: The landing ground of the RAF Tavoy in Burma, photographed from 1,500 feet on 25 January 1933, before erection of station buildings.
AIR 27/799

teen Hurricanes, twelve Hudsons and six Blenheims. The troops departed as best they could in a miscellany of vessels, hampered by swarms of terrified civilians.

Java was defended by Dutch, British, Australian and American troops, ill-equipped and with inadequate air cover. A Japanese invasion fleet approached the island and was attacked by the remaining aircraft on 1 March, with some success. Nevertheless, strong forces landed and began to overrun the island. The defenders fought on until 8 March, when the Dutch surrendered. A few aircraft and some troops managed to escape to Australia, but most fell into Japanese hands. Thus the campaign ended, but meanwhile the Japanese had invaded Burma and the British faced yet another acute problem.

35 Against Odds in Burma

Japanese forces began to cross into southern Burma from Siam on 14 December 1941, only six days after other divisions had invaded Malaya. They wished to occupy the country for both economic and military reasons. Firstly, the Japanese needed to obtain the country's vast supplies of oil and rice. Secondly, they intended to cut the 'Burma Road' into China, through which American supplies were passing to support the Chinese forces, which were still resisting after the Japanese had invaded their country in July 1937. Thirdly, the mountains of northern Burma formed the bulwark which shielded India, and this great sub-continent was

Below: A Japanese ferry on the Salween river. Although this photograph was taken after the surrender of the Japanese in 1945, it shows the terrain of their invasion in December 1941.

HS 7/107

Left: A poster by Roy Nockolds illustrating an attack by Blenheims IVs on Port Blair in the Andaman Islands, which was occupied by the Japanese on 23 February 1942. Enemy aircraft based on the airfield at Port Blair posed threats to both Calcutta in Bengal and Colombo in Ceylon.

INF 3/391

included in Japan's grand strategy of expansion and 'co-prosperity' which aimed to eliminate the influence of the Western Powers in southern Asia and the eastern world.

On 11 December 1941 responsibility for the defence of Burma had been passed to the commander-in-chief in India, General Sir Archibald Wavell. The 17th Indian Division held a defensive line along the Salween river, with Chinese forces on their left, but their numbers and equipment were unable to do more than provide a delaying action. Behind them lay a number of airfields which, unlike Malaya, were

well-constructed. Like Malaya, however, they lacked sufficient squadrons, modern aircraft, defences or an adequate
radar system. It had been estimated that at least 280 aircraft
were required for the defence of Burma, but only sixteen
RAF Buffalos were available, together with twenty-one P-40
Tomahawks of the American Volunteer Group which had
flown down from Kunming in China. These meagre forces
were commanded by Air Vice-Marshal D. F. Stevenson. The
Japanese Air Force had about 400 bombers and fighters
available for the invasion, supporting about 70,000 troops.

Part of the Japanese plan was to cause panic among
civilians, as with Singapore. Air raids against Rangoon began
on 23 December 1941 and within two days killed about
7,000 people, injuring many more. However, the Buffalos
and Tomahawks took a heavy toll of these bombers and
their fighter escorts. On 7 January 1942 they were reinforced
by a squadron of Blenheims, which delivered some effective
attacks against enemy airfields in Siam. About thirty
Hurricanes also arrived and for a short period these helped
establish air superiority over Rangoon.

But this situation was not to last, for the 17th Division
had been forced into a fighting retreat to Rangoon, while

Above: A view of the Chin Hills
in Burma, separating the
country from India with range
after range of mountains
covered with deep jungle.
AIR 23/4319

Below: Monsoon cloud over
Burma, photographed from a
Blenheim. Cumulonimbus
clouds, towering above the
ceiling of aircraft, broke up
those that flew through them.
AIR 27/880

Above: RAF bomber crews being briefed for a raid by a wing commander at an operational airfield in East Bengal.

AIR 27/880

under bombardment and strafing from the air. The Chinese forces had also withdrawn, up the Salween to Yunnan. Although the 7th Brigade had landed in Rangoon, an evacuation of the capital became inevitable. This was completed on 7 March, with sappers blowing up oil installations as the troops moved out.

The army units began a long trek northwards, up the central plain of Burma. They retreated slowly, mixed up with the ox-drawn carts of fleeing civilians, but smashing through Japanese roadblocks and fighting rearguard actions. Eventually, they reached the Chindwin river. Air Chief Marshal Sir Richard Peirse, the former chief of Bomber Command, had taken over command of the RAF in India and Ceylon on 2 March, but there was little he could do to support the retreat in Burma, apart from supplying air transports. Some civilians and the wounded were airlifted to safety by Dakotas, but most of the others struggled over the jungle-clad mountain ranges into India, abandoning the

Burma Road to China. The last troops arrived on 20 May, debilitated and ragged but still a fighting force. At this point, the summer monsoon descended on Burma and operations ceased.

While these actions were taking place, the RAF did its best to hinder the enemy. The Blenheims had flown to Magwe, beside the Irrawaddy in the central plain, on 21 February. The fighters hopped to other airfields, covering the retreat, and joined the Blenheims on 12 March. Eight days later, Blenheims and Hurricanes attacked their previous base of Mingaladon, near Rangoon, and destroyed many enemy aircraft. This was too much for the Japanese, who responded with a series of major attacks on Magwe, destroying all aircraft save eleven Hurricanes, three Tomahawks and six Blenheims. The surviving RAF aircraft flew on to Akyab, on the west coast, while the Americans retired to Lashio in the north-east. But from 27 March the Japanese delivered crushing blows on Akyab and effectively wiped out the remaining aircraft. The personnel made their way to India or China.

Even before Burma was fully conquered, the Japanese turned their attention to Ceylon. A strong naval force, including four aircraft carriers, approached the island on 5 April and its aircraft began to raid Colombo and the RAF airfield of Ratmalana. They sank some warships and air combats took place with defending Hurricanes, but then the Japanese fleet withdrew to refuel. Then something unexpected happened. The Japanese fleet was called back urgently to the Pacific to oppose an American fleet. On 4 June, three of its carriers were sunk by US dive-bombers in the Battle of Midway.

The tide of war had begun to turn against the Japanese. In the respite offered by the monsoon, the RAF built up its strength in India with surprising speed. By this time, aircraft outputs in Britain and the USA were attaining new peaks, while the Empire Air Training Scheme was turning out floods of new crews. Only five squadrons existed in India at the time of the Japanese invasion of Burma. They numbered twenty-six a few months after the Japanese victory, plus six fighter squadrons of the Indian Air Force. Some of the bombers began probing attacks on enemy positions. The

Below: A Blenheim of 113 Squadron from Asansol in India hit by flak and nose-diving to destruction during an attack on 10 November 1942 against the port of Akyab in Burma.

AIR 27/880

Below Right: Incendiaries dropped on 20 November 1942 by Blenheims of 113 Squadron based at Asansol in India, falling on enemy positions at Ngazaunchpet on the Irrawaddy west-south-west of Mandalay. These were very effective in setting fire to bamboo structures.

AIR 27/880

Dear friend,

I am an Allied fighter, I did not come here to do any harm to you who are my friends, I only want to do harm to the Japanese and chase them away from your country as quickly as possible. If you will lead me to the nearest Allied Military Post, my Government will give you a good reward.

Allied victories in North Africa released operational crews for the Far East. By the end of 1942 there were two RAF groups in India and one in Ceylon, comprising over 1,400 aircraft. The USAAF also built up its strength, mainly with transport aircraft. Plans were being laid which would change the course of the war in the Burma theatre.

36 A New Form of Warfare

The Japanese Air Force made few moves against India during the remainder of 1942. It was not until the night of 20 December that eight bombers made the first raid on Calcutta. Little damage was caused but some of the population panicked and streams of civilians fled the city. A series of small raids followed but by mid-January 1943 a flight of Beaufighters arrived, equipped with air interception radar. These made short work of the bombers, which lost so heavily that by 20 January the survivors never returned.

In early December 1942, the Eastern Army under Lieutenant-General N.M.S. Irwin began an advance from Bengal. This crossed the Burmese border with the object of advancing down the Arakan to seize the port of Akyab, which could provide a base to future operations into the heart of Burma. All went well for several weeks, supported by relays of RAF light bombers which flew ahead to bomb Japanese positions. The army continued down both sides of the Mayu river but on 27 December paused to bring up supplies. This gave the Japanese an opportunity to reinforce their defences and the Eastern Army found the going much tougher. There were heavy casualties on both sides and what was hoped would be a final push on 18 March 1943 was stalled. This was followed by a Japanese counter-offensive which threatened to cut off the troops. By early April, it was decided to withdraw. The army retreated and was back in

Above: Bombing-up a Blenheim IV of 113 Squadron at Chandina airfield, where the squadron was stationed from 28 February to 3 May 1943.
AIR 27/880

Below: Three Blenheims en route to bomb Japanese positions on Ramree Island, off the coast of Burma, taken from another Blenheim.
AIR 27/880

Below: The air observer in a Blenheim V of 113 Squadron working on his chart table as the aircraft formation nears its target.
AIR 27/880

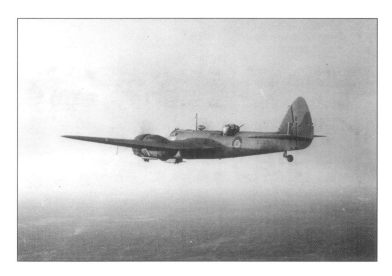

Above: A Blenheim V of 113
Squadron en route to bomb
Japanese positions in Ramree
Island, off the coast of Burma.
AIR 27/880

Above: Four bombs can be
discerned as specks in the
centre of this photograph,
dropped on 6 January 1943 by
a Blenheim of 113 Squadron
based at Jessore in India.
They are falling on Japanese
weapon pits at 'Pagoda Hill',
near Rathedaung on the Mayu
river. The squadron was acting
in support of the British and
Indian forces advancing down
the Arakan in an attempt to
take the port of Akyab, but
these were eventually repulsed
and withdrew.

AIR 27/880

Below: Photographs found on
a captured Japanese soldier
by 3/3 Gurkhas and passed to
the RAF's 113 Squadron.

AIR 27/880

India by May, having suffered about 2,500 battle casualties
and with morale shaken. Major operations then ceased with
the monsoon.

But another operation paved the way for military success
in Burma. On 7 February 1943, seven columns of troops
who adopted the name of Chindits after the mythical
Burmese lion *Chinthe* set off from Imphal in the Indian state
of Manipur and marched eastwards over the Chin Hills into
Burma. Their object was to create havoc behind enemy lines
and destroy communications. They were led by Brigadier
Orde Wingate, a soldier with a remarkable record as a guer-
rilla fighter. He had been responsible pre-war for forming a
Jewish volunteer militia against the Arabs, and during
1940–41 had led Abyssinian patriots who helped oust the
occupying Italians.

The men in these seven columns, known as the 77th
Indian Infantry Brigade, had undergone an intensive course
of jungle fighting in India. Each column was self-contained
with pack-mules and even elephants. Very unusually, they
had no lines of communication by ground with the rear.
They were to be supplied entirely from the air, by two RAF
squadrons of Dakotas guided by W/T signals from the
Chindits who also marked dropping zones.

This first Chindit operation was not successful in every
respect. One of the columns was ambushed and another
broken up before it reached its objectives. As the others
advanced further, the supply drops by the RAF became less
certain and sometimes missed the correct zones. Heat and

A New Form of Warfare

humidity resulted in sickness, and there was a shortage of water. The men were pushed to the limit of endurance, but they blew up four bridges and cut railway lines in many places. Above all, they created immense confusion among the Japanese, who buzzed around like wasps. About a third of the Chindits did not return. Wingate dispersed the columns into smaller groups and most of these crossed the Chindwin river to make their way back into India. They

Left: 'Douglas C-47 Dakota over the Hump' by Charles J. Thompson

After the Japanese cut the Burma Road to China, the USAAF pioneered an air route from Bengal to Kunming during the summer of 1942. Curtiss C-46 Commandos transported vital supplies to the Chinese armies under General Chiang Kai-shek, returning with troops to fight in Burma. The RAF's 31 Squadron, equipped with Dakotas, joined in this 'Hump Run' in 1943. The route lay over the towering Patkai mountains and through turbulent weather, with no possibility of an intermediate landing. One of 31 Squadron's Dakotas is depicted here, when 'the dawn comes up like thunder'.

Below: On 27 February 1943, B-24 Liberators of the USAAF bombed the Japanese merchant ship *Asakasan Maru* of 8,709 tons off Moulmein in southern Burma. The crew took to the lifeboats and the vessel sank.

AIR 34/236

Below: This oil storage tank at the Seaing Tank Farm, south of Yenangyaung, with a capacity of a million gallons, was the only one of five not completely destroyed by the British when they retreated from Rangoon in March 1942. It had been damaged but the Japanese repaired and camouflaged it. On 7 July 1943, it was attacked and set on fire by RAF Beaufighters.

AIR 34/238

arrived in June, with the onset of the summer monsoon. One small group headed for China, to be welcomed as heroes. Every man had marched 750 miles and some as much as 1,000.

This expedition set the pattern for the future. It became evident that a whole army could be supplied from the air if

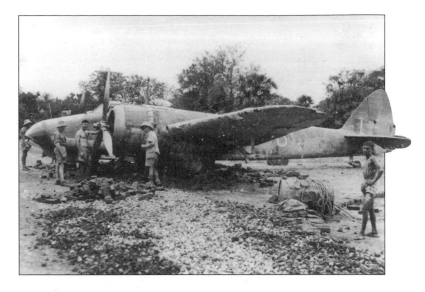

Below: On 15 December 1943, two Beaufighter VIs of 177 Squadron took off from Feni in East Bengal to strafe the railway system near Magwe on the Irrawaddy. They attacked buildings along the track and then hit an engine north of Kokkogon which burst into flames. Fire spread rapidly along the wagons, producing dense black smoke which indicated that they were carrying oil drums.
AIR 34/239

Above: No 113 Squadron was the first to occupy RAF Comilla in south-east Bengal, near the Burmese border, arriving on 4 May 1943. By then, the squadron was equipped with Blenheim Vs. The summer monsoon broke soon afterwards and aircraft became bogged down in their dispersals. The bombs were removed from this Blenheim V shortly before the undercarriage sank in the mud.
AIR 27/880

Below: Seven Blenheim Vs of 113 Squadron took off from Comilla in India in the afternoon of 20 May 1943 to bomb Pauktaw in Burma. One aircraft crashed on take-off but each of the others dropped four 500 lb bombs from 7,000 feet. The bombs in this photograph missed the target.
AIR 27/880

Above: A Spitfire PR XI, serial PA935, on the strength of 681 Squadron, which was equipped with this mark of machine from September 1943.
Photo-reconnaissance Spitfires played an indispensable part in the campaign in Burma, photographing enemy positions and vast tracts of inadequately mapped territory.

AIR 23/4291

Below: Four or more river craft in the Minlayathaya area, about fifteen miles south-south-east of Magwe on the river Irrawaddy, were set on fire by Beaufighters during an attack on 16 December 1943. The instantaneous flames and dense smoke showed that they were carrying petrol or oil.

AIR 34/239

facilities could be provided. By this time, the RAF in India numbered fifty-three squadrons and was set for further expansion. This took place partly with an increase in Dakota squadrons, to be added to those of the USAAF already in India. Fortunately, streams of these machines were coming off the production lines. They were highly reliable, easy to fly and could operate in tropical conditions.

Another enterprise stressed the importance of transport aircraft in this theatre of war. With the cutting of the Burma Road, some other method of supplying the Chinese armies under General Chiang Kai-shek had to be found. Some of these troops were fighting the Japanese on the northern frontier of Burma, under the leadership of General J.W. 'Vinegar Joe' Stilwell, an unconventional American with a caustic manner. Although aged sixty-four years, he was capable of marching thirty miles a day with his 'long range penetration' groups. The method of supply had been pioneered by another American, Lieutenant-Colonel William D. Old of the USAAF, who in April 1942 made an experimental flight from Bengal over the formidable Paktai mountains into China. From this beginning, a regular supply was flown by US transport aircraft over this dangerous route, largely unmapped and beset by cumulo-nimbus clouds. It became known as the 'Hump Run' and remained almost entirely an American operation, although RAF Dakotas joined in from December 1943.

37 The Rise of the Phoenix

South East Asia Command was formed at midnight on 15/16 November 1943, in accordance with a decision made on 25 August by British and American Chiefs of Staff at a conference held in Quebec. Admiral the Lord Louis Mountbatten was appointed the supreme commander. He adopted the phoenix, the legendary bird which rises from the ashes, as the mascot of his command. The British 14th Army had already been created on 15 October 1943 under Lieutenant-General William J. Slim, and formed part of the new command. The British troops fighting in this theatre had been dubbed by the press 'The Forgotten Army', but the public was to read a great deal about them from this time.

Within this new organization, Air Command, South East Asia was also formed on 16/17 November 1943 under Air

Left: 'Aircraft attacking troop convoy' by war artist Roy Nockolds

The Hawker Hurricane IIC fighter-bomber, fitted with four 20 mm cannons and carrying two bombs, first went into action in September 1941. This painting represents a machine on the strength of 42 Squadron, which was equipped with 'Hurribombers' in the Burma theatre from October 1943 until almost the end of the war with Japan.
INF 3/1822

Above: Hurricane pilots run through the mud to reach their aircraft in response to an urgent call for an air strike.
AIR 23/1956

Chief Marshal Sir Richard Peirse. His deputy was an American, Major-General George Stratemeyer. Thus the RAF and USAAF squadrons were combined in a single operational whole. This included the US Tenth Air Force, already operating in the theatre. Within the command were a Strategic Air Force under an American, Brigadier-General Howard C. Davidson, a Tactical Air Force commanded by Air Marshal Sir John Baldwin, and a Troop Carrier Force under Brigadier-General William D. Old, the American who had pioneered the 'Hump Run'. The photo-reconnaissance units came initially under Wing Commander S.G. 'Bill' Wise. Opposing this burgeoning command, which numbered forty-eight RAF and seventeen USAAF squadrons, the Japanese could muster about 740 aircraft in the whole of South-East Asia, of which only 370 were based in Burma.

The 14th Army began the last day of 1943 with another assault in the Arakan. British, Indian and West African

Below: A heavy gun being loaded on a Dakota of 194 Squadron, to be flown to the 14th Army in the Imphal valley.
AIR 23/1956

Above: These stationary box wagons, flat wagons and passenger coaches north of Thazi on the line between Mandalay and Rangoon came under cannon fire on 21 November 1943 from Beaufighter VIs of 27 Squadron based at Agartala in Bengal. The train had been dispersed into six sections, with the engine uncoupled and moved to an adjoining line, probably to refuel with wood and water. Some wagons had their doors open and sides down, indicating that troops has disembarked. Others had their doors closed, suggesting that they carried stores and equipment. The flat wagons carried motor transport or armoured fighting vehicles, covered with tarpaulins. It was estimated that the train carried a battalion of about 740 men.
AIR 34/240

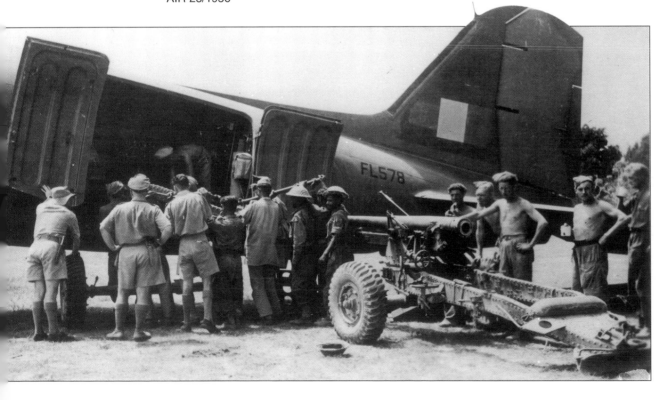

Above: A Dakota dropping canisters of supplies to the British 14th Army in Burma.
AIR 23/4291

Below: The Mosquito II fighter arrived in the Burma theatre in April 1943. It was followed by the Mosquito VI fighter-bomber in December 1943, which replaced the obsolete Blenheim V. These Mosquito VIs operated over the Arakan and Mandalay fronts, armed with four 20 mm cannons in the nose and four .303 inch machine-guns in the wings. They could also carry two 500 lb bombs or rocket projectiles.
AIR 23/4291

troops advanced towards the Mayu Peninsula, under the command of Lieutenant-General Sir Philip Christison. On this occasion the Allies had established air supremacy over the Japanese. When the troops were surrounded in early February 1944 at Sinzweya, in what became known as the 'Admin Box', they were supplied from the air. At the same time, strategic and tactical bombers destroyed enemy lines of communication and shipping. The besieged troops were engaged in a lengthy and bloody battle but able to hold their ground. The Japanese lost so many men that by the beginning of April 1944 they were forced to withdraw.

In the course of this campaign, the Chindits under Major-General Orde Wingate mounted another operation, code-named 'Thursday'. The majority did not march over the Chin Hills. On 5 March 1944, a massive air lift began from Lalaghat in north-east India, when US Dakotas towing gliders took off with the advanced sections of about 9,000 armed troops, 1,150 pack-animals, guns, stores and even bulldozers, over the mountain ranges. Their destinations were clearings in the jungle about forty miles south-west of Myitkyina, the main Japanese base in north-east Burma. These glider-borne troops hacked out airstrips for Dakotas.

Within six days, the majority of the men and their equipment had been landed, the equivalent of two divisions. Sentinel L-5s swarmed in, to bring out the wounded. This operation coincided with an advance from the north by Stilwell's Chinese-American long-range penetration groups. On their right flank, 2,000 more men of the Chindits were already marching over the Naga Hills to meet up with their

Left: After servicing aircraft during the day, ground crews of a Spitfire squadron were called upon to take up defensive positions at sunset in trenches around their airfield in the Imphal plain, in Manipur Territory of north-east India. The squadron dance band toured their positions to give them a little entertainment before dark. Spitfire VCs first arrived in the Burma theatre in September 1943 and the Battle of Imphal opened with Japanese thrusts on 8 March 1944.

AIR 23/1956

Left: Fitting rockets to a Hurricane IV. This version of the famous fighter was built with a 'universal armament wing' which could carry two 40 mm guns or eight rockets or two 250 lb bombs or long-range tanks. In the Burma theatre, 42 Squadron was equipped with Hurricane IVs from November 1944 and 20 Squadron from December 1944.

AIR 23/4291

airborne comrades. The intention of all these forces was to disrupt Japanese communications in the north of Burma and then eliminate the enemy forces. But Major-General Orde Wingate did not see the full success of the operations he had masterminded, for he was killed on 24 March, in a US Dakota which crashed in the Naga Hills during a storm.

These two Allied operations disrupted offensives planned by the Japanese, who were intent on advancing into India. The fighting in the Arakan had thwarted one of these plans, but an assault began in the north on 7 March when Japanese patrols came up against British advanced positions east of Imphal, on a plain in the Manipur mountains, and Kohima further north in Nagaland. These initial encounters were followed with major thrusts by three Japanese divisions, with another brought up soon afterwards. Eventually, over 100,000 crack troops of the Japanese army were engaged in the battles.

By early April, both Imphal and Kohima were under siege, and the greatest battles of the war in Burma took place. Spitfires and Hurricanes strafed the Japanese troops and destroyed enemy fighters, tactical bombers hammered at

Above: This undated publicity photograph is captioned 'RAF Spitfire pilots operating from an airstrip in Burma close behind the 14th Army. Left to right: Flight Sergeant K. Park; Flying Officer R. Dalrymple; Squadron Leader I.R. Krohn; Wing Commander P.H. Lee DFC'. Records show that Park, Dalrymple and Krohn served with 155 Squadron in July 1944, when the squadron was based in north-east India and equipped with Spitfire VIIIs. It moved to Tabingaung near Swebo in Burma on 12 January 1945 and was stationed near Rangoon when the war ended.

AIR 23/4291

Below: Vultee-Stinson L-5 aircraft were used widely in the Burma theatre by the US Army and the British 14th Army for artillery spotting and liaison. Named the Sentinel by the RAF, several formed a flight with 194 Squadron from January 1945 onwards; they were employed mainly on casualty evacuation from small jungle clearings.

AIR 23/4291

Left: 'Attack on Moulmein'
by Roy Nockolds

Wellingtons bombing a
Japanese airfield at Moulmein
in southern Burma.

INF 3/392

lines of communication, and transport aircraft were withdrawn temporarily from the 'Hump Run' to drop supplies to the defenders, protected by fighters. Much of the fighting on the ground was at close quarters, with some villages changing hands several times. Eventually, the Japanese broke.

Reinforced in numbers and with massive artillery backing, the 14th Army advanced and rooted out the enemy. By late June, about 50,000 of the best Japanese troops were killed and almost 100 guns destroyed. The remainder were in retreat.

38 Advances into Burma

While the battles of Imphal, Kohima and the Arakan were taking their bloody courses, American–Chinese forces under General Stilwell pressed the enemy in north-east Burma. The summer monsoon of 1944 broke in June, with 175 inches of rain in northern Burma, but the Allies continued to make progress in spite of restrictions in air support. The Japanese fought on all three fronts with their usual ferocity and fanaticism but everywhere were forced back. Stilwell was recalled to the USA in October, to take command of the training of all American land forces, and his place in Burma was taken by Lieutenant-General D.L. Sultan. Mountbatten was determined to press home his advantages on every front. By November, the Japanese had been cleared out of the northern mountains and pushed back to the central plain of Burma. For the Allies, the objectives of Mandalay and then Rangoon lay ahead.

Air Command, South East Asia was strengthened further in this period. Liberators arrived to replace Wellingtons in RAF strategic squadrons, P-47 Thunderbolts took over the fighter-bomber role from some of the Hurricanes, and more Mosquitos arrived. In addition to all the squadrons directly engaged in the war over Burma, others were based in Ceylon. These operated over the Indian Ocean, from Madagascar to the Cocos Islands and sometimes as far as Sumatra, sweeping the seas for German U-boats and Japanese submarines or helping to rescue Allied survivors in lifeboats. They made use of bases in the Seychelles, the

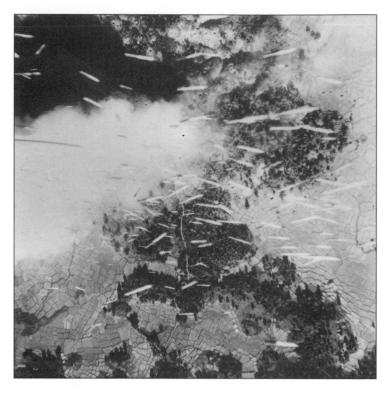

Above: On 23 December 1944, twelve RAF Liberators of 215 Squadron from Digri in India bombed dock installations at Taungup, on the west coast south of Ramree Island. The weather was good and bursts were seen on the target, with smoke rising to 3,000 feet. All aircraft returned safely. This photograph shows incendiaries falling from 6,600 feet.

AIR 23/4305

Right:: Twenty-two B-25 Mitchells of the USAAF, Third Tactical Air Force, bombed three railway bridges in the area of Nattalin, south of Prome on the Irrawaddy, on 24 December 1944. No direct hits were claimed but the tracks were damaged.
AIR 23/4305

Maldive Islands and Diego Garcia. As the campaign continued, they laid mines in enemy waters and sank some vessels.

The worst of the monsoon in Burma came to an end in late October 1944, enabling the strategic and tactical squadrons to resume intensive air attacks. By this time, the Japanese Air Force in Burma had been reduced to less than 125 aircraft. The Allies had not achieved complete air supremacy in all areas, but they were certainly greatly superior. They bombed bridges, strafed trains, cut Japanese supply routes, destroyed fuel and other supply dumps, sank enemy river craft and sea-going vessels, and hammered continuously at enemy forces on the battlefields. The strategic bombers ranged further afield, to southern Burma, the Kra Isthmus and Siam. Photo-reconnaissance aircraft brought back vital information on enemy positions and enabled vast tracts of little-known territory to be mapped from photographic mosaics. Transport aircraft continued their colossal undertaking of maintaining air supplies to the Allied armies

Above: On 21 January 1945, forty-seven B-25 Mitchells of the Tactical Air Force bombed bridges in the areas of Sqa, Ela and Pyinmana, along the railway from Rangoon to Mandalay. This photograph shows a direct hit on a bypass railway bridge at Swa, the main bridge having been destroyed previously. The main railway bridge at Pyinmana and a bypass bridge at Ela were also destroyed, on a particularly successful day for the USAAF

AIR 23/4305

Right: Liberator VIs of 356 Squadron, based at Salbani in India, at 3,300 feet over Ramree Island south of Akyab in Burma, on 21 January 1945, during a raid on Japanese positions. This was the day the island was captured by British amphibious forces, with the deaths of all but twenty of its Japanese garrison of a thousand men.

AIR 23/4305

in the field, over ever-increasing distances. When the Japanese armies in China made an unexpected advance towards Kunming, they transported 25,000 Chinese troops from Sultan's force, with their equipment, across the 'Hump' to meet the threat in their home country.

Air Chief Marshal Sir Richard Peirse came to the end of his period of command on 26 November 1944. It had been intended that his place would be taken by Air Chief Marshal Sir Trafford Leigh-Mallory, who had commanded the Allied Expeditionary Air Force in Europe, but he was killed in a flying accident while en route to India. Air Marshal Sir Guy Garrod took over temporarily, until Air Marshal Sir Keith Park arrived on 23 February 1945.

On 2 January 1945, it could be seen from the air that the Japanese had evacuated Akyab Island. Thus the troops on the Arakan front were able to land and the RAF could use the airfield as a base. An amphibious assault on the mainland followed, with strong protection from tactical and strategic bombardment. There was heavy fighting, with about 2,000 Japanese killed. The enemy also lost about 1,000 men when Ramree Island to the south was invaded on 21 January. This island provided flat ground for airfields.

On the northern front, the 12th Army advanced as far as the Irrawaddy while General Sultan's forces, depleted in

Above: Twenty-four Liberators of the USAAF, Strategic Air Force, bombed railway bridges in the area of Pegu to Martaban on 29 January 1945. This was the northern part of the infamous Siam to Burma railway. Escorted by twenty-four Thunderbolts and twenty-one Lightnings, they dropped sixty-nine tons of bombs, destroying four bridges and damaging two more.
AIR 23/4305

Right: 'Catalina VI of 191 Squadron over Ceylon' by Charles J. Thompson

The Indian Ocean became a hunting ground for German U-boats and Japanese submarines. One of the RAF's counter-measures was the employment of reconnaissance aircraft armed with depth charges. In May 1943, 191 Squadron was formed at Korangi Creek near Karachi for this purpose, equipped with Consolidated Catalinas. It then operated from various bases in India and Ceylon. Catalina VI serial JX293 of 191 Squadron is depicted here, flying from Koggola in Ceylon in 1944.

Right: A major attack by forty-nine RAF and twenty-five USAAF Liberators of the Strategic Air Force was mounted on 3 February 1945 against the Siamese port of Jumbhorn (Chumphon) on the east coast of the Kra Peninsula. There were direct hits on a railway bridge and a vessel in the harbour, while five trains, a railway track and numerous buildings were damaged. This photograph was taken from a Liberator of 215 Squadron based at Dhubalia near Calcutta.

AIR 23/4305

Left: A single Beaufighter X of 211 Squadron, flown by Flight Lieutenant P.N. Smith, took off from Chiringa in south-east Bengal in the afternoon of 10 February 1945 to strafe lines of communication between Prome and Taikkyi in southern Burma. Among the targets attacked was a train with twelve wagons, as shown here.

AIR 23/4307

243

Left: Twenty-one Liberators of the USAAF, part of the Strategic Air Force, bombed three enemy-held villages south-west of Mandalay on 16 February 1945. This photograph was taken over Myingan.

AIR 23/4305

Below: One of four rockets fired in the afternoon of 24 March 1945, by Flight Sergeant G.S. Hook in Beaufighter X serial NV591 of 177 Squadron from Chiringa, scored a hit on the bypass bridge at Myogwin in the Bassein Delta.

AIR 27/1118

Right: A Mosquito VI about to take off from a forward airfield in 1945 against Japanese positions. The wooden construction of the Mosquito resulted in some serviceability problems in the Burma theatre, especially in the extreme climate of the summer monsoon.

AIR 23/4291

Below: In the afternoon of 31 March 1945, nine Mosquito VIs of 45 Squadron from Joari in south-east Bengal attacked a Japanese headquarters at Myotha, south-west of Mandalay. Each aircraft dropped four 500 lb bombs. Twenty-three strafing runs were made, resulting in complete devastation. This was prior to the main attack by the 14th Army in central Burma.

AIR 23/4292

numbers, fought their way from the north-east. They had left the jungle-clad mountains behind them and needed to adapt to warfare in open country. Both armies converged on Mandalay, fighting bitter battles. The tactical fighters and fighter-bombers advanced with the ground troops, operating from hastily-built airstrips and destroying enemy artillery.

The Japanese fought almost to the last man in a series of pitched battles, but could not withstand the onslaughts. A Chinese Army from Yunnan also advanced and entered Lashio on 6 March, suffering heavy casualties but opening the vital link for the Burma Road. The 14th Army cut round to the south of Mandalay and occupied Meiktila on 4 March. Mandalay itself fell to the 14th Army on 20 March, after fighter-bombers had blasted holes in its defences. On the western coast, the troops on Ramree Island moved to the mainland in April and began advancing down the coast.

By this time, there were 356,000 Allied troops in Burma, supplied almost entirely from the air. A pause for regrouping was required before they pushed on to the capital of Rangoon. They knew it was advisable to achieve this success before the monsoon, which usually broke at some time in May.

39 The Defeat of Japan

The British were anxious to reach Rangoon for two reasons. The first was the onset of the 1945 monsoon, which usually broke in May in this area. The other concerned the American forces, including their air force, for these were about to be transferred to the China theatre.

The 14th Army had advanced 800 miles from the Battles of Kohima and Imphal, breaking the back of the Japanese Army in the process, but a final concerted effort needed to be made. An advance down the plain of the Irrawaddy was required, and an armoured corps swept south for 250 miles as far as Pegu. It reached this town on 1 May 1945, bypassing Japanese contingents in the hills on either side of its long advance. Rangoon lay about forty miles to the south-south-west.

But a simultaneous attack from a different direction was also planned, by seaborne forces which had set off from Akyab in six convoys from 27 to 30 April. On 1 May, parachute troops were dropped at Elephant Point near the mouth of the Irrawaddy, to clear away any opposition. The first convoy sailed up the river and reached the capital on 3 May, in advance of the force from Pegu, only to find that the enemy had fled. The monsoon broke early, on the following day, and the deluge was particularly heavy and prolonged.

Above: The Japanese base of Bilin in the south of Burma attacked on 8 April 1945 by Liberator VIs of 215 Squadron from Dhubalia in India, each aircraft dropping four 1,000 lb and six 500 lb general-purpose bombs.

AIR 23/4307

Right: Flying Officers A.H. Rieck and N.T. Allen patrolled southern Burma during the late afternoon on 9 April 1945, in their Beaufighter X serial NV591 of 177 Squadron from Chiringa. Their mission was to support clandestine organizations known as 'Jedburghs' which operated behind Japanese lines. They were over the Bassein Delta on their way back when they spotted this Mitsubishi Ki-21 bomber (code-named 'Sally' by the Allies) on the ground, apparently intact. It was silver, with red roundels. Rieck made three attacks, scoring hits on the wings and fuselage, shooting away most of the rudder and producing smoke from the cockpit. It was not claimed as a kill since it had probably been there for several weeks.

AIR 27/1118

Left: Gurkha paratroopers entering an RAF Dakota at Akyab on 1 May 1945 in advance of the seaborne landings of the Royal Navy intended to seize Rangoon.
AIR 23/2131

Below: Gurkha paratroopers descending on 1 May 1945 near Elephant Point in the south of Burma, with a Dakota of the USAAF in the foreground. On the day after, the 26th Indian Division was landed by the Royal Navy, ready to sail up the river behind minesweepers to Rangoon.
AIR 23/2131

The Defeat of Japan

By 1 June, all forty-seven squadrons of the USAAF in the Burma theatre had left for China. Many of the divisions of the 14th Army had been withdrawn to India by this date, to prepare for a combined operation against Malaya. Those who remained were formed into the Burma Army, soon to be named the 12th Army. Only one major battle needed to be fought by this new army. About 21,000 Japanese had been scattered and cut off by the advances down the Arakan and the central plain. A larger force, about 30,000 men of the 28th Army, had gathered in the Pegu Yomas, a huge range of hills to the north of Rangoon. These Japanese intended to break out across the Sittang river near Toungoo and fight their way south-east to the Burmese district of Tenasserim in the Kra Peninsula, to join about 24,000 of their comrades.

Below: RAF Liberators of Eastern Air Command bombing a railway bridge at Chumphon in the Kra Peninsula of Siam on 22 May 1945. The photograph shows a steel girder span lying in the river bed while a bomb explodes on the end of the bridge. This railway ran from Singapore to Siam, and the attack was part of a plan to destroy lines of communication for the Japanese troops retreating from south-east Burma.

AIR 23/4307

Above: Rangoon photographed from 500 feet on 3 May 1945 from a Liberator VI of 159 Squadron flown from Digri in India by Pilot Officer R. Lee. The purpose of the flight was to drop food and medical supplies to Allied prisoners-of-war in a jail nearby. The Japanese had already evacuated the capital and it was entered by the British 26th division on the day of this flight.

AIR 23/4291

Below: Master Sergeant Jack L. Recht of South-East Asia Command, reading about the end of the war in Europe. It was believed at the time that the war against Japan would last for several more years. His home was in West Eddy Street, Chicago.

AIR 23/3598

Right: Eight Liberator VIs of 356 Squadron took off from Salbani in India in the early morning of 1 June 1945 to attack a railway station at Rajburi, near Martaban in the south-east of Burma. Each dropped five 1,000 lb bombs from 500 feet and all returned safely.

AIR 23/4292

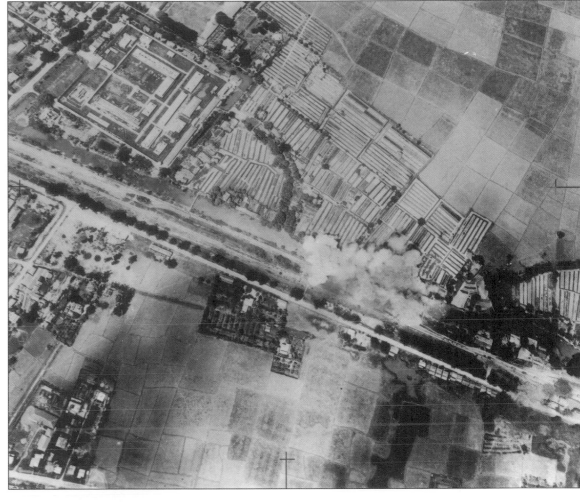

Below: On 5 June 1945, seven Liberator VIs of 355 Squadron took off from Salbani in India on a 2,400 mile sortie to attack railway yards at Surasdilani in Siam, on the south-east side of the Kra Peninsula. This was an important staging post for the Japanese on the Singapore-Bangkok railway. They encountered the worst of the monsoon over the Bay of Bengal, and four were forced to turn back. The remaining three managed to find their way round towering cumulo-nimbus clouds and through torrential rain to the target, where the weather was clear. Each dropped six 500 lb bombs on railway and jetty installations, leaving at least eight fires burning from storage of inflammable material.

AIR 23/4292

This move began in July, but a terrible fate awaited the men, for their plans were known to the British. The RAF mounted fighter-bomber attacks in the clearer days, while strategic bombers raided communications in the south of Burma and Siam. The 12th Army had positioned forces along their paths and subjected the Japanese to intense shelling and gunfire. Many others were killed by guerrillas. Clandestine teams of the SOE, known as Force 136, had been dropped behind Japanese lines from the end of 1944 to organize such groups. Other Burmese who had welcomed the arrival of the Japanese in 1942 and formed a Burma Defence Army of about 8,000 strong had changed sides on 25 March 1945. The number of Japanese killed by the armed forces and guerrillas in this breakout was known to have been 12,000, but many more died undiscovered in the jungle. It was more of a massacre than a battle. Only about a third of those who left the Pegu Yomas eventually reached Tenessarim.

Left: 'Supply Drop'
by Charles J. Thompson

Consolidated Liberator VIs of 357 (Special Duties) Squadron, based in India from February 1944, were engaged on supply dropping to troops and special forces in Burma until the end of the war. Other duties included flying over the 'Hump' to Kunming and long-range supply missions to special forces in Malaya and Sumatra. The squadron was also equipped with Hudsons until January 1945, when they were replaced by Dakotas and Lysander IIIAs.

Right: Eight Liberator VIs of 355 Squadron took off from Salbani in India on 15 June 1945 on a long haul to attack the Japanese tanker *Toho Maru* of 10,238 tons near the island of Koh Samui off the east coast of the Malayan peninsula. Six turned back in the monsoon weather but the other two reached the target. Each dropped eight 500 lb medium-capacity bombs, and one of these hit the stern of the tanker. She was set on fire and sank.

AIR 23/4307

Left: A truck belonging to the Japanese 28th Army on the Mawchi road, east of Toungoo, after being destroyed by grenades. Groups of SOE men known as 'Jedburghs' from Force 136 were parachuted in teams of three south of the Toungoo–Mawchi road during April 1945. Together with Karen guerrillas, they spread out in order to help prevent the Japanese 28th Army from breaking out of the Pegu Yomas and joining other forces in the far south of Burma. The men in this photograph were part of Group OTTER.
HS 7/107

Above: A Lysander IIIA of C Flight, 357 (Special Duties) Squadron, taking off from Bolo-Auk after bringing supplies for the Jedburghs of Group MONGOOSE WHITE. C Flight was detached to Mingaladon near Rangoon on 26 May 1945, and operated from there. This special duty Lysander is fitted with a 150 gallon long-range tank under the fuselage, increasing its range from 600 miles to about 1,250 miles. The runway is of bamboo matting, in a jungle clearing. This strip was also used as a dropping zone for Dakotas.
HS 7/107

Meanwhile, plans for the invasion of Malaya forged ahead, under operation 'Zipper'. This would be the largest all-British combined operation of the war, with seven infantry divisions and an armoured brigade to be landed on 9 September near Port Swettenham, on the west coast 200 miles north of Singapore. A fleet of battleships, cruisers and destroyers would be involved, with Fleet Air Arm aircraft flown from ten auxiliary carriers. Over 500 RAF aircraft would be provided to support the operation, landing on airfields as soon as they were captured.

Then, to the astonishment of almost all in the fighting services, an atom bomb was dropped on Japan on 6 August and on Nagasaki three days later. Japan surrendered unconditionally on 14 August. The landings went ahead on the date planned, with over 100,000 men going ashore as an occupying force instead of an assault. Other divisions went direct to Penang and Singapore by sea. On 12 September the Japanese commander in Singapore, General Itagaki, formally

Right: A Lysander IIIA of 357 (Special Duties) Squadron on a landing strip at Bolo-Auk in south-east Burma after bringing supplies to Jedburghs of SOE's Group MONGOOSE WHITE, dropped behind Japanese lines. The man smoking a pipe is a Captain of the 12th Army Photographic Unit sent to make a photographic record of the levy force. The others are Karen Levies.

HS 7/107

Right: Lieutenant Inchi, a member of a three-man team from the staff of the Japanese 28th Army under General Sakurai, with Major F. Milner of Force 136 at Bolo-Auk in the Salween District after the Japanese surrender. Milner was dropped into the area on 15 March 1945 as leader of Group MONGOOSE WHITE. The other members of the Japanese team were a Major and a Sergeant. They were trying to stop large parties of their countrymen north of the river Shwegyin who were still fighting and trying to escape southward. The last shots in this area were fired on 21 September 1945, well after the surrender of Japan.

HS 7/107

Left: A general view of Hiroshima showing the effect of the atom bomb dropped at 08.15 hours on 6 August 1945. The roof of the concrete building in the foreground has been dished and contains a pool of water, while its nearer parapet has been blown away. The bomb killed 78,150 people and wounded 51,048.
CAB 80/99

Right: A general view of Nagasaki, looking north-east, after the atom bomb exploded at 11.30 hours on 9 August 1945. Japan accepted the Allied demand for unconditional surrender five days later. This bomb missed the centre of the target area but killed 23,753 people and wounded 43,000. The firestorm in Tokyo caused by conventional bombing on the night of 9/10 March 1945 had resulted in even greater casualties: about 84,000 killed and over 40,000 wounded.
AIR 23/4758

signed an instrument of surrender of 650,000 men in South-East Asia.

The surrender of Germany had released many RAF crews for this theatre. These anticipated a long war ahead, with much of South-East Asia to be liberated and Japan to be invaded. The casualties on both sides would be colossal. One of those en route was the author of this book, pre-pared for another tour of operations. The unexpected sur-render of Japan resulted in numerous flights from RAF Dum-Dum in India to Burma, Siam, French Indo-China, Hong Kong, Malaya and Singapore. Then, after more than five years of active service from the age of eighteen, it was time to consider returning to civilian life in a country exhausted and impoverished by the war.

Aircraft Index

Page references in italic refer to picture captions

Airspeed Horsa *111*, 113, *113*, 114, 115, 141, *141*, *142*

Arado Ar96 *46*

Armstrong Whitworth Albemarle 141, *141*, 192

Armstrong Whitworth Whitley 15, 22, 31, 50, 51, 52, *52*, *53*, 57, *75*, 82, 85, *103*, 166

Avro Anson 16, *196*

Avro Lancaster *2–3*, *57*, *59*, 61, *61*, *80*, 82, *83*, 92, *92*, *93*, *94*, *96*, *98*, *101*, *102*, *107*, 112, 113, *131*, *133*, 138, *140*, *149*, 151, *153*, *156*, *158*, *161*, *162*, *184*

Avro Manchester *58*, 82, *103*

Bloch 174 *186*

Boeing B-17 Fortress 74, *75*, 85, *100*, 101, 112, *152*, *156*, 177, *194*, 207

Boulton Paul Defiant *8–9*, *10–11*, 22, 24, *25*

Brewster Buffalo *33*, 216, *219*, 220, 224

Bristol Beaufighter *25*, 31, 33, 49, 65, *86*, 87, *87*, 88, *88*, *89*, *90*, 91, *91*, *147*, *148*, 149, *149*, *150*, *173*, *175*, 177, *182*, *188*, *198*, *199*, 200, *201*, 202, 203, *203*, 204, *204*, *205*, *208*, 212, 228, *231*, *232*, 233, *235*, *243*, *244*, 246

Bristol Beaufort 31, *31*, 37, 42, 43, 86, 87, *173*, *175*, 177, 181

Bristol Blenheim V 'Bisley' 181, *185*, *228*, *229*, *232*

Bristol Blenheim 13, *14*, *19*, 21, *21*, 24, *30*, *32*, 33, *34*, *35*, *36*, *37*, *38*, *39*, *43*, 47, 48, *49*, 57, *166*, *168*, 169, *169*, *171*, *196*, 216, *219*, 220, 221, *223*, *224*, 226, *226*, *228*, *230*

Bristol Bombay *182*

Cant Z501 199

Consolidated Catalina 31, *79*, 216, 220, *242*

Consolidated Liberator B-24 74, *75*, *78*, 79, *79*, 149, 177, *179*, *199*, 200, 207, *207*, 209, *209*, 212, *214–215*, *231*, *240*, *241*, *242*, *243*, *244*, 246, *248*, *249*, *250*

Curtiss C-46 Commando *231*

Curtiss P-40 Kittyhawk *171*, *191*

Curtiss P-40 Tomahawk *171*, 224, 226

Curtiss P-40 Warhawk *192*

De Havilland Mosquito 17, 65, *80*, *82*, 85, *85*, 86, 91, 97, *102*, *103*, *106*, *107*, *108*, 109, *109*, 116, 117, 131, *132*, *139*, 146, *146*, 149, *149*, *150*, *151*, *155*, *158*, *163*, *236*, 240, *245*

Dornier Do17 *28*

Dornier Do18 *13*, 16

Dornier Do24 *201*

Douglas DB-7 Boston *6–7*, 57, *60*, *81*, *84*, *104*, *105*, *108*, 109, *117*, *123*, *128*, *129*, *133*, *135*, *153*, *155*, *177*, *187*, *211*

Douglas Dakota *111*, *125*, *142*, 143, *143*, 163, 192, 225, 229, *231*, 233, *235*, 236, *236*, 238, *247*, *250*

Douglas B-20 Havoc 123, 126

Douglas C-47 Skytrain 123

Douglas C-53 Skytrooper 123

Fairey Battle 12, *14*, *15*, *16*, *17*, 21, *21*

Fairey Swordfish 45, *192*

Focke-Wulf Condor 77

Focke-Wulf FW58 *46*, *58*

Focke-Wulf FW190 62, *65*, 66, *67*, *81*, *82*, *86*, *105*, *107*, *151*, *185*

General Aircraft Hamilcar *142*

Gloster Gladiator 13, 19, 24, 167, *167*, 169, *171*

Handley Page Halifax *41*, 44, 82, *99*, 102, 112, *112*, 113, 115, *129*, *133*, *136*, *137*, *139*, 141, *148*, 149, *160*, *173*, *176*, *180*, *184*, 192

Handley Page Hampden 15, 22, *29*, *32*, *43*, 46, 57, *58*, 82, 85, 87, 91

Hawker Hardy *171*

Hawker Hurricane *1*, 13, 16, *16*, 19, 21, *21*, 22, 24, *25*, 28, *29*, 30, 33, *34*, *38*, 62, *62*, 65, *67*, 71, 166, 167, *169*, *172*, *188*, 203, 218, 220, 221, 224, 226, *234*, *237*, 238

Hawker Tempest 116, *135*, *155*

Hawker Typhoon 71, *84*, *88*, *104*, *105*, 116, *116*, *119*, *121*, 131, 144, 154, *155*

Heinkel He111 12, *19*, *58*, 137, *168*, *175*

Heinkel He219 85

Junkers Ju52 *20*, *58*, *186*, *203*

Junkers Ju87 Stuka 20, 24, *62*

Junkers Ju88 *25*, *58*, *67*, *99*

Lockheed Hudson *13*, 16, *20*, *22*, 31, 37, 74, *74*, *75*, 79, 86, *172*, *192*, 203, 216, 221

Lockheed Lightning 122, 126, *130*, *136*, *242*

Lockheed Ventura *84*

Picture Captions

Martin Baltimore *164–165*, *191*, *196*, 203, *204*, 207

Martin B-26 Marauder *105*, 109, *122*, 123, *123*, *124*, *127*, *191*, *194*, *195*, 204, *204*, *210*, 213

Messerschmitt Bf109 22, *28*, *39*, *46*, 47, 48, *58*, 62, *81*, *89*, *180*, *185*, *199*

Messerschmitt Bf110 22, *25*, *56*, *180*

Messerschmitt Me323 85, *191*

Mitsubishi Ki-21 'Sally' *246*

Nakajima Ki-27 'Mate' *219*

Nakajima Ki-43 Hayabusa 'Oscar' *219*

North American B-25 Mitchell *108*, 109, 116, 117, 126, *133*, *153*, *155*, *194*, *197*, *201*, 204, *206*, *240*, *241*

North American P-51 Mustang 66, 67, 71, *88*, *91*, *104*, 116, 118, *118*, 122, *122*, *123*, *127*, *150*, *153*, *155*, 158, *204*

Republic P-47 Thunderbolt 122, *123*, *124*, 126, *127*, *130*, *210*, 240, *242*

Savoia-Marchetti 82 *186*

Short Stirling 31, *57*, *58*, 82, *82*, *84*, 102, *103*, 112, *112*, 141, *184*

Short Sunderland 16, 31, 74, *79*, *146*, 149, *151*

Stinson L-5 Sentinel 236, *238*

Supermarine Spitfire 16, 17, 22, 24, *25*, 27, 28, *28*, *29*, 30, *30*, *33*, *34*, *38*, *39*, 42, 50, *50*, *60*, *63*, 64, *64*, 65, *65*, 66, *66*, *67*, 71, *81*, *84*, 86, *86*, 88, *88*, *89*, *105*, *107*, 116, *116*, *117*, *118*, *123*, *147*, 149, *152*, *153*, 154, *154*, 175, *175*, 177, *187*, *193*, 203, *204*, *219*, *233*, *237*, 238

Vickers Valentia *168*

Vickers Vildebeest 216, *217*, 218, 220

Vickers Vincent *167*, *171*

Vickers Wellington 13, *20*, 22, *22*, *27*, *40*, 43, *43*, *56*, 57, *58*, 74, 75, 82, 85, *103*, 149, *170*, *173*, 177, *177*, 181, *184*, *192*, *201*, *202*, 203, 209, 212, *239*, 240

Vickers Wellesley *167*, *171*

Waco Hadrian *144*

Westland Lysander *12*, 13, *13*, 21, 34, *250*, *251*, *252*

Jacket front (main picture):
see page 27

Jacket front (inset, top):
A Martin B-26 Marauder of the Desert Air Force based in Italy making an attack on 25 March 1945.

AIR 23/7379

Jacket front (inset, bottom):
see page 37

Jacket back (top left):
see page 166

Jacket back (bottom left):
see page 119

Jacket back (right):
see page 78

Half Title (page 1):
Hurricane Is over the Western Desert. The first to be equipped with these machines in the Middle East was 274 Squadron, on 19 August 1940 when re-formed at Amriya in Egypt.

INF 1/244

Title (pages 2-3):
Incendiary clusters falling on Hanover during the raid of 25 March 1945. They were dropped from a Lancaster of 100 Squadron based at Grimsby in Lincolnshire.

AIR 14/3696

Foreword (pages 6-7):
Boston IIIs taking off from a desert landing-ground. In November 1941, 24 (SAAF) Squadron received these bombers when based at LG112.

AIR 41/50

Introduction (pages 8-9):
The Boulton Paul Defiant had a chequered career in the RAF. It entered squadron service with 264 Squadron in December 1939, as a two-seater fighter with a four-gun turret but no forward armament. Defiants shot down numerous enemy aircraft while operating from England during the Battle of France, when they were mistaken for Hurricanes, but the Luftwaffe pilots soon learnt of the defects and attacked from head-on or under the belly. The squadrons lost heavily in the Battle of Britain and in August they were transferred to the role of night-fighters. They enjoyed some success, especially when fitted with airborne interception radar, but Beaufighters began to replace them towards the end of 1940. This Defiant was on the strength of 264 Squadron.

INF 1/244

Section opener, Part One (pages 10-11):
A publicity photograph of Battle of Britain airmen. From the combination of pilots and air gunners, they appear to be from a Defiant squadron.

INF 1/244

Section opener, Part Two (pages 164-165):
The Martin Baltimore light bomber, which was employed by the RAF only in the Mediterranean theatre. It first entered service in January 1942.

AIR 41/50

Section opener, Part Three (pages 214-215):
Showers of 100 lb fragmentation bombs were dropped on 8 June 1945 by eight Liberator VIs of 159 Squadron from Digri in India over a Japanese troop concentration and stores dump at Bilin in the south of Burma.

AIR 23/4292

Front endpapers:
A Fairey Battle flying over Sarreguemines, in the Moselle district of France near Saarbrücken, on 29 September 1939. The letters ON on the fuselage indicate that it was on the strength of 63 Squadron at Benson in Oxfordshire. This was a training squadron for aircrew on Battles, working in combination with 52 Squadron at Abingdon in Berkshire.

AIR 34/238

Back endpapers:
A Mustang III of the 2nd Tactical Air Force on patrol over France on 2 November 1943. This later version of the aircraft was fitted with a Merlin-Packard engine and armed with four 20 mm cannons. It could also carry bombs or rocket projectiles.

AIR 37/1231